CRUCIFIXION TO CREATION

ROOTS OF THE TRADITIONAL MASS TRACED BACK TO PARADISE

FR JAMES MAWDSLEY

NEW OLD

Published by New Old
© 2023 Fr James Mawdsley
ISBN 978-1-7395816-2-6

Who hath wrought and done these things,
calling the generations from the beginning?
I the Lord, I am the first and the last.

— Is 41:4

FOR MY ELDER BROTHER

Contents

I: CRUCIFIXION
TO CREATION

H ave you ever wondered what it will be like to enter
eternity? Is there anywhere in the world, a place or an
event, where the fullness of being expresses itself so that
we can begin to behold it already? Can we taste boundless life
here on earth? Yes.[1] But we must search hard amid seas of change
for an unchanging pattern, to learn to see now what always is and
to discern which new things endure forever. Concretely, if we
enter the traditional Mass, we find it leads to Heaven.

The old Mass is obviously older than 1955; the Tridentine Rite
goes back much further than the Council of Trent; the Gregorian
Mass existed before Pope St Gregory. For two thousand years the
same Mass of Ages has faithfully commemorated the Sacrifice of

---

[1] *"That which was from the beginning, which we have heard, which we have seen
with our eyes, which we have looked upon, and our hands have handled... we do
bear witness, and declare unto you the life eternal... that you also may have
fellowship with us..."* (1 Jn 1:1-3).

1

Jesus Christ on Calvary. Yet this Holy Sacrifice was anticipated long beforehand, even back to the events in the Garden of Eden. The DNA of Holy Mass is eternal, from beyond the beginning of time. Tracing the roots of the Mass, our meditations move from the *Crucifixion to Creation*.

The night before He died, Jesus offered the first Holy Mass, commemorating His Crucifixion before it actually happened. For a thousand years prior to the Last Supper, the meaning of the Crucifixion was given in code by the ceremonies of Jerusalem's Temple. Earlier still, Christ's same Sacrifice was prefigured by the arrangement and rites of the tabernacle in the desert, built by Moses following a pattern given him by God. In both tabernacle and Temple there stood, precisely as God commanded, the table for the bread of presence, the seven-branched candlestick and the altar of incense. Each concerns Christ, for He is the Bread of Life, the Light of the World, the Resurrection. The same signs — bread, light, incense — feature in Holy Mass with the same meaning: Jesus, Saviour.

Centuries before Moses, the willingness of Abraham to sacrifice Isaac on Mount Moriah won blessings for all nations. In a manner which could not be understood until some two thousand years later, these men proclaimed the unwavering intention of God the Father to give His only-begotten Son, Jesus, to redeem the world. The same divine intention is written into Abel's holy sacrifice, and allegorically by Adam's yearning for the Tree of Life. The very location of Eden and the nature of fruit-bearing trees, described in Genesis 1-2, beside their literal meaning, frame parables of the Crucifixion to come.

By tracing how essential elements of the traditional liturgy run like roots through the entire Old Testament (OT), we see Christ's Sacrifice, which stands at the centre of time, reaches the beginning. Therefore His Sacrifice will remain beyond today unto the end. Nobody can destroy the traditional Mass.

How can we be so confident? St Thomas Aquinas teaches that Absolute Wisdom, God, in consideration of the last end of the universe, writes this purpose into the very beginning. God, as the definitive *"wise architect"*, already had the final plan in mind before the foundation was first laid. Hence the Angelic Doctor teaches, with the most rational of the Greeks, that "the final end of the universe... is also the beginning of the universe".[2] If we discern what this end is, this beginning, we can be sure that what has existed for all time cannot be moved.

Not everyone can arrive at this conclusion by philosophy, but we can all appreciate it in the Psalms: *"Qui fundasti terram super stabilitatem suam: non inclinabitur in sæculum sæculi"* — *"Who hast founded the earth upon its own bases: it shall not be moved for ever and ever"* (Ps 103:5). The stability of the earth, or the universe, speaks of the immutability of God's purpose. His unchanging purpose, maintained through all generations, is comprehensively transmitted by the traditional Mass, the backbone of creation which holds the entirety together.

THE WAY TO HEAVEN

Why does this matter? Because without the traditional Mass we have hell on earth. With it a way is found to Heaven. This present life is a foretaste of our own eternity: Heaven or hell. The choices we make as individuals aggregate to give life or death to whole societies. Our sacrifices help save many.

In a world where change accelerates, where advances in communication, travel and artificial intelligence enable ever more dramatic innovations, it is important for man to find rest in the eternal. Confusion rages around us: killing humans in the womb is claimed as a right; the sterilisation of children by transgender surgery is supported by governments; for personal profit financiers provoke ever more destructive wars; the appointed guardians of sacred tradition seek to uproot it (for example, with *Traditionis custodes*). In such a world, contemplating Calvary

---

[2] St Thomas, *SCG*, I, 1 *"As a wise architect, I have laid the foundation* (1 Cor 3:10) ... the name of being wise simply is reserved to Him alone whose consideration is about the final end of the universe, which end is also the beginning of the universe: wherefore, according to Aristotle, it belongs to the wise man to consider the *highest causes* (*Metaphysics* I, 2-3)."

gives clarity to see what always was will always be. What God laid into the foundation of creation — the Cross, Sacrifice, Love — cannot be removed without creation itself collapsing. Before that happens, Jesus will return to judge the living and the dead.

To give substance to our hope, the first section of this book inspects four *Eternal Elements of the Mass*. These have been prepared since the outset: the Lamb, the Cross, the Altar and Light. All carry meaning connected with Calvary and each fills time more constantly than we might have realised. Contemplating them stretches our perspective so our minds are made readier to take in eternity. And where will you meditate better on the sublime meaning of a lamb than at Mass? Where else can you come so close to Cross and altar? Where but there have you light to understand everything?

The various elements of Holy Mass work together in a perfectly ordered whole. *The Immutable Pattern of the Mass*, our second section, unearths a phenomenal continuity from Eden to Golgotha. The most important events before Christ — including the creation of man, the *Akeidah*, the rites of Yom Kippur — happened with a tight geographical focus and a meaningful development of detail which demonstrate that the Passion of Christ stands at the heart of history. His Passion fulfils these prior events and indeed reaches every time and place, which mystery is made manifest by Holy Mass spreading to every nation on earth. The form of the Mass, which is the Cross connecting Heaven and earth, was anticipated in Solomon's Temple, in Moses' tabernacle, on Mount Moriah, in the Garden of Eden and even the first letters of the Bible. God communicates to us through chosen men, through history, geography, creation and through His most eloquent Word. His intention is that all who reciprocate by choosing Him can reach the summit of the mountain of God: eternal life with the Blessed Trinity. Contemplation of our Three-in-One destination fixes our eyes on the goal of life.

There is an aspect of this ancient continuity so marvellous that seeing it may help to heal the deepest division in human history.

Orthodox Jews attribute a cosmic and profoundly personal significance to *the place* of the Temple:

> the entire universe, the entirety of creation, is located in the place of the Holy Temple [in Jerusalem]. For it is in the place of the Holy Temple, Mount Moriah, as G-d disclosed to *Avraham*, that the Garden of Eden exists, and it was here that *Adam* was created, shaped from the dust of the four corners of the earth, gathered up by G-d to this one spot where the Temple altar stands, an altar of earth, the very earth of mankind, upon which we bring our gifts of thanks and gratitude to HaShem and atone for our failings and are embraced by HaShem. Making pilgrimage to the Holy Temple is nothing less than a homecoming for man.[3]

What the rabbi writes is fundamentally true. But he does not go far enough, for it is infinitely truer in Christ. The quoted passage, with its colossal claims about the Temple rites, is ultimately about Calvary and Holy Mass. This is our homecoming not merely back to Eden, but, as the Requiem Mass expresses it, "to be borne to our home in Paradise [*paradisi*]", meaning Heaven. The cipher to unlock the rabbi's quotation is given by Jesus, Who identified Himself as the true Temple (Jn 2:21; Apoc 21:22). The last line of the passage then reads: "journeying to Jesus is nothing less than a homecoming for man". In Christ all things are re-established (Eph 1:9-10).

Thankfully, our work is surprisingly uncomplicated. To know Jesus Christ crucified is to have apprehended the unchanging pattern of reality. Bringing everything together in Him is the theme of the third major section of this book, *The One Perfect Actor of the Mass*. All need redemption. None can attain it without becoming members of the Body of Christ. He poured out an immeasurable price for this: His Precious Blood, which is the life of the universe. Sole Mediator between Heaven and Earth, Christ's singular priesthood is immense. He calls millions of men

---

[3] The Temple Institute (hereafter TI), subscriber email, 26/8/2022.

to be His ministers, to receive Holy Orders, thereby establishing the greatest patriarchy on the planet. Their celibacy, like His, is infinitely fruitful, and hence hated by the devil. These priests are sent to continue Jesus' greatest work: sacrifice. God had in mind even their vestments when in the wilderness He clothed Aaron, the High Priest, and earlier in Eden vested Adam, our father. Until today the vestments used in Holy Mass transmit saving truths.

Everything so far leads to *The Greatest Wonder of the Mass.* This is the most stupendous happening on earth today, an event which contains the meaning of everything, yet it is hidden from all human eyes. It occurs more often than human conception but is believed by a minority only and is comprehended completely by none. I am referring to transubstantiation. Without it, the most important human activity, the traditional Mass, would be empty. By transubstantiation things once of the soil — bread, wine and even man — are made divine. The lowest joins the highest. Earth is quickened by Heaven.

That God gives Himself to us in Holy Communion raises the demented fury of satan. The devil's most audacious attack on man's participation in Mass is detailed in *Part II: Tearing out Ancient Roots.* This part of the book might seem excessive. But in the light of everything preceding, the new Mass (*novus ordo*) is an indefensible turning away from eternal goods, a worldly aversion to the things of God, a diabolical assault on salvation. If some are shocked to read that hierarchs like Judas serve satan still, were we not warned of this from the beginning? Genesis recounts that God permitted the serpent to slide into Eden, its purpose to deceive Eve so she would corrupt Adam. Yet paradise is a picture of the liturgy. So the fallen world has tempted and brought down bishops: men who, like Adam, are supposed to represent Christ. Following after the world, clerics have dishonoured the Holy Eucharist, and thereby our earthly paradise, the liturgy, is become full of thorns like the first paradise.

The Good News is this rebellion will fail. Servants of hell rip up traditions, but God *"Who dwells in Heaven laughs at them"* (Ps 2:4; 36:13; 58:9). So can we. The Mass of Ages, being an expression of eternity, is indestructible. The liturgy calls us with a supernatural force stronger than anything the world or Curia can obstruct. This power is grace, participation in divine life, on copious offer through the immortal channel of Tradition.

In thanksgiving, this book concludes with *Part III: Homecoming to Paradise*. God has planted immemorial Tradition to draw souls to Himself. He cannot fail. Our efforts to restore the liturgy are in fact our response to God restoring us: *"Thou shalt send forth thy spirit, and they shall be created: and thou shalt renew the face of the earth"* (Ps 103:30).

INTERWEAVING ROOTS

Throughout this book connections are made between nature, the OT, the NT, Jesus Christ, His Mother Mary, the Church and Holy Mass. If the reader is not accustomed to juxtaposing these varied sources, then it might be difficult to remain orientated. It helps if we recognise that God is communicating the same story in multiple ways, through all these layers of reality, which are gloriously congruent. Moving quickly through many ideas is an attempt to assess reality from the perspective, as it were, of eternity, by seeing what connects the various layers together.

St Boethius (✝524) defined eternity as "the whole, simultaneous and perfect possession of illimitable life".[4] Everything is present, nothing missing of the future, nothing lost of the past. If there is no change in eternity, this is not because *nothing* is happening, but because *everything* is happening. Nothing more can happen. In time, goods are laid out separately so that we may be directed by the differences. Together they teach us a pattern. Rightly arranged they point to something higher than earth can contain. The pattern is personal. The creatures which point it out best are saints, because they love. The ultimate act of love is to lay down one's life. Self-sacrifice is divine. To know this — or to fully know Who does this — is to know everything

---

[4] St Boethius, *The Consolation of Philosophy*, V *"Æternitas est interminabilis vitæ tota simul et perfecta possessio."*

all at once. It is to know Christ, to know God, to enter eternity. Jesus taught us *"Now this is eternal life: That they may know Thee, the only true God, and Jesus Christ, Whom Thou hast sent"* (Jn 17:3). Paradoxically, self-sacrifice is not death but invincible life. We learn this best at Mass or in martyrdom (or however close we get to them, Mass being recommended, as we cannot schedule martyrdom).

For simplicity, each chapter of this book can be read as a meditation on its own, independently of the others. Still, they interweave a lot in order to offer a holographic view of reality. For orientation, besides the main contents page above, intermediate tables of contents have also been inserted to offer timely overviews of what lies ahead.

The first section shows the great length of the liturgy's roots, stretching our thoughts from the Crucifixion back to the beginning. *The Immutable Pattern* shows they form a system, being connected in a harmonious whole. Lest the intricacy of ideas become overwhelming, *One Perfect Actor* simplifies it all by lauding the chief agent of the whole: like a tree transmitting one life, Jesus Christ. If in all this we can conceive the roots, trunk and branches, then the fourth section, on transubstantiation, shows their fruit. Contemplating the Holy Eucharist helps us understand this unique organism which fills history: *"For by the fruit the tree is known"* (Mt 12:33).

Such a magnificent tree cannot be uprooted, however radically or subtly the enemy fights. The traditional liturgy exists to serve our entering eternity, our homecoming to Paradise: not the earthly one that was Eden, but our ultimate home promised by it, infinitely better than the world once known by Adam and Eve. Our final aim is to return to Him from Whom everything takes its beginning, God in Heaven (Jn 16:28). He is our true Paradise.

α) Eternal Elements
of the Mass

*I will open my mouth in parables. I will speak
about concepts that are from the beginning.*

— Ps 77:2

What is the life of man on earth? It is a journey, a labour, a warfare. More fundamental than these, for a human to live truly, self-sacrifice is essential. Otherwise the journey goes nowhere, the labour is in vain, the warfare is lost. This fact is presented to us from the beginning by the lamb, and the altar, and the cross, and the light. These four are essential to Holy Mass, they are present throughout all history, their roots penetrate into the very foundation of the world.

Light was the first thing God created. It signifies understanding. What should we understand? Before God created light, He showed the Cross connects earth to Heaven, time to eternity. The Cross is Christ's altar, and becomes our altar when we receive it, understand it. Then we may be able to make sacrifices as pleasing as Adam's son Abel. We are taught how by the lamb, for when it comes to self-sacrifice, the proper approach is silence. The reward for doing so is immense.

God sees our sacrifices always, as He sees every Mass. He loves them. He remembers them forever, which for us is the matter of our eternal life. Adoring at Mass requires self-sacrifice.

The Lamb

Cleanse me, O Lord, and purify my heart, that, washed in the Blood of the Lamb, I may attain unto everlasting joys.

— Vesting prayer when putting on the alb

In his book *The Lamb's Supper: The Mass as Heaven on Earth*, Scott Hahn masterfully explains how Holy Mass connects with the eternal worship offered to God in Heaven, as revealed by the last book of the Bible, *The Apocalypse*. Being profoundly bound with eternity, the Mass is portrayed not only in the last pages of the Bible, but throughout, including the first book, *Genesis*. The Lamb so vital after the end of time, Who died and rose at the centre of time, is in fact crucial from the beginning.

When St John the Baptist *"saw Jesus coming to him"*, he spoke spontaneously of an everlasting reality: *"Behold, the Lamb of God, behold Him..."* (Jn 1:29). One man, who heard the Baptist and beheld intently, had a vision of the Lamb reigning in Heaven: *"in the midst of the throne... a Lamb standing as it were slain"* (Apoc 5:6). *"Slain"* means killed while *"standing"* means Risen. The crucified Lamb rules for eternity. The end of history will arrive specifically because *"the marriage of the Lamb is come, and His wife hath prepared herself..."* (Apoc 19:7). Christ's Bride, *"the wife of the Lamb"* (Apoc 21:9), is the Church. As the full fruit of history, the Communion of the Lamb with His beloved is generated through the centuries at Holy Mass.

Seeing this Lamb standing at the centre of history and after the end of history, below we seek out the sacrificial lamb prior to Calvary. We find that its role, central to divine worship long before Mass was instituted, was planned before *"the beginning"*.

The Temple

For one thousand years prior to St John beholding Jesus, various animals were offered in Jerusalem's Temple: sheep, goats, doves,

> yet the daily sacrifice... was a lamb... signifying the offering up of the true lamb, that is Christ, was the culminating sacrifice of all. Hence it is said: *'Behold the Lamb of God, behold Him Who taketh away the sin of the world.'* (Jn 1:29)[5]

This daily offering of lambs in the courts of the Temple was so important that whenever it was interrupted by some catastrophe it would later be renewed on a massive scale. The Bible wants us to be struck by the numbers. Five hundred years before Christ, when Ezra oversaw the rebuilding of the Temple, 400 lambs were slaughtered for its rededication (Ezra 6:17). A century before this, after Josiah purified the Temple of idolatry, 37,600 lambs (and kids) were sacrificed for the restored Passover (2 Chron 35:7-9).[6] Earlier, about 715 BC under King Hezekiah, some 3,000 sheep and 200 lambs were sacrificed for the rededication of the Temple (2 Chron 29:32-33) and soon after a further 17,000 sheep killed for the restored Passover (2 Chron 30:24). It was a tremendous labour for at first *"the priests were few, and were not enough to flay the holocausts"* (2 Chron 29:34). But the Levites applied

---

[5] St Thomas, *S.Th.* III Q.22 a.3 ad.3.

[6] First, King Josiah *"broke down the houses of the male cult prostitutes which were in the house of the Lord"* and the idolatrous *"altars"* (2 Kngs 23:7,12 RSVCE).

themselves and restoration succeeded: *"Hezekiah and all the people rejoiced because of what God had done for the people; for the thing came about suddenly"* (2 Chron 29:36 RSVCE).

In any case, all these magnificent recoveries pale in comparison with the first inauguration of the Temple when

> *King Solomon offered as a sacrifice twenty-two thousand oxen and a hundred and twenty thousand sheep. So the king and all the people dedicated the house of God.* (2 Chron 7:5 RSVCE)

Who kills 120,000 sheep?! Why?

For its thousand-year lifetime, the main activity of the Temple was sacrifice. All those hundreds of thousands of lambs and rams and sheep and goats and oxen and bulls and doves — all that blood — prefigured what was to come: the Most Precious Blood of Christ. The ram's steady gaze shows Jesus' imperturbability. The strength of bulls signifies our Redeemer, Who defeated death. The workload of oxen indicates He laboured under the burden of the world. The simplicity of doves signals His poverty. The many scapegoats — taken out of the city — showcase Him Who was unjustly accused and abandoned. The innocence of year-old lambs, the purity of immaculate victims, points to sinless Jesus. They opened not their mouths; nor He.

Understanding this, St Philip interpreted Isaiah's Suffering Servant prophecies as thoroughly Christocentric, a lamb's silence bespeaking Jesus' humility before His unjust judges:

> *He was led as a sheep to the slaughter; and like a lamb without voice before his shearer, so openeth he not his mouth. In humility his judgment was taken away. His generation who shall declare...?* (Acts 8:32-33; cf. Is 53:7-8)

Moved by the Holy Spirit, St Philip, *"opening his mouth, and beginning at this scripture"* evangelised (εὐηγγελίσατο) the eunuch about Jesus (Acts 8:35). The Gospel is there.[7] He declared Jesus' mysterious *"generation"* — at Christmas from the Virgin's

---

[7] Origen, *Supra Johannem*, I, 15: "How can he begin with the prophet and preach Jesus, if Isaiah were not a part of the beginning of the Gospel?"

womb, at Easter from the garden tomb, through eternity from the
the divine *"womb"*[8] — so convincingly that the eunuch
exclaimed: *"I believe that Jesus Christ is the Son of God."*

What great dignity each lamb has, that silently it serves to
indicate our meek Redeemer. How helpless lambs seem, yet how
unconquerable the Self-surrender of God's Lamb (Apoc 17:14)!
His silence on earth is God's thunder from Heaven (Sir 46:19-21).

Moses' Lambs

Lambs foreshadowing Christ did not begin with Solomon's
Temple. Four centuries earlier God instructed Moses on Sinai:
*"This is what thou shalt sacrifice upon the altar: Two lambs of a
year old every day continually"* (Ex 29:38).

This daily offering was instituted as a continuous memorial to
the Exodus, to the escape from slavery in Egypt which had been
won through the blood of the Paschal lamb. Almost every detail
of the passage that follows can be aptly applied to Jesus Christ:

> *Speak to the entire assembly of the sons of Israel... let
> everyone take a lamb, by their families and houses... It shall
> be a lamb without blemish, a one-year-old male... And the
> entire multitude of the sons of Israel shall immolate it toward
> evening. And they shall take from its blood, and place it on
> both the door posts and the upper threshold of the houses, in
> which they will consume it... It is the Passover (that is, the
> Crossing) of the Lord... And I will see the blood, and I will
> pass over you... Then you shall have this day as a memorial,
> and you shall celebrate it as a solemnity to the Lord, in your
> generations, as an everlasting devotion.* (Ex 12:3-14 SB)

This was the defining moment in Hebrew history where God
granted them freedom through the lamb which they killed and
consumed. It is blindness not to see Christ here. The memorial is
an *"everlasting devotion"* in the *"families and houses"* of the
Church, that is her parishes and cathedrals.

---

[8] The *"only begotten Son [is] in the bosom of the Father"* (Jn 1:18) through an
eternal generation: *"from the womb before the day star I begot thee"* (Ps 109:3).

To fulfil the types comprehensively, Jesus chose the manner and timing of His sacrificial death, that it occur while the paschal lambs were being slaughtered (Jn 19:14), for He *is* the Passover lamb (1 Cor 5:7). Even the figurative lambs were, in a manner, crucified:

> that lamb which was commanded to be wholly roasted was a symbol of the suffering of the cross which Christ would undergo. For the lamb [was] dressed up in the form of the cross. For one spit is transfixed right through from the lower parts up to the head, and one across the back, to which are attached the legs of the lamb.[9]

Zooming out for an overview, the escape from Egypt was preceded by days of unnatural darkness, anticipating the sun being obscured on Good Friday as Jesus descended into death. So it will be at the end of time, a formidable waxing of evil just before God marvellously restores all things. In all three cases the darkness was followed by a day of redemption in order that God could be worshipped truly: first, after escaping Pharaoh, worshipping in the Sinai desert; then after Calvary, adoring in Holy Mass; finally after all history, praising at His throne in Heaven. Hence the Book of Apocalypse reveals that God's awesome victory over the Egyptians, celebrated in the Canticle of Moses, concerns the same ultimate triumph as does the Canticle of the Lamb, for the two are sung in heavenly harmony:

> *those who had overcome the beast and his image and the number of his name, were... singing the canticle of Moses, the servant of God, and the canticle of the Lamb.* (Apoc 5:2-3)

Both Exodus and End Times hold Christ the Lamb as their hero.

Abraham's Ram

Centuries before meek Moses, the sacrificial lamb was anticipated by its royal father, the ram. On Mount Moriah, Abraham was ready to give his beloved son, Isaac, as a sacrifice

---

[9] St Justin Martyr, *Dialogue with Trypho*, 40.

to God. Abraham prefigured God the Father giving His Son on Calvary. As the Divinity of Jesus was not injured in the slightest on the Cross, though His Sacred Humanity was immolated there, so Isaac, representing the Divinity of Christ, walked away from Mount Moriah unscathed while a ram, representing Jesus' Humanity, was killed and offered up.

> *Abraham lifted up his eyes, and saw behind his back a ram amongst the briers sticking fast by the horns, which he took and offered for a holocaust instead of his son.* (Gen 22:13)

How did Abraham see *"behind his back"*? We are told, by lifting *"up his eyes"*. This phrase connotes liturgical action, indicating that in Mass we see backwards in time to Christ the victim.

The *"horns"* of the ram come from the same word as for the horns on the corners of Hebrew altars — קֶרֶן (Ex 27:2; 30:2). This symbol of power over the four corners of the world connects each altar with the ram. The ram's regal head being stuck in the briers signifies Jesus crowned King with thorns, battling headfirst against sin.

God arranged a ram be found here, rather than a lamb, as the *Akeidah* is more about Abraham's faith than Isaac's meekness, more about the father than the son. This angle causes us to praise also the goodness of God the Father for Calvary, not the Son alone.

Abel's Firstling Lamb

Much earlier than Abraham's day, the first lamb to be offered to God was Abel's. This lamb foreshadowed Abel's own imminent death at the hands of his brother Cain, even as Abel foreshadowed Jesus' coming death at the hands of His brethren.

There are layers of typology here. Innocent Abel was both *"shepherd"* and sacrificial lamb (Gen 4:2,8; Mt 23:35). He gave to God *"of the firstlings of his flock"* (Gen 4:4) and was himself taken as the firstling of God's flock. Jesus too is both *"Good Shepherd"* (Jn 10:11,14) and victim, only whereas Abel's life was taken from Him, Jesus freely laid down His own (Jn 10:17-18).

By this offering Jesus is simultaneously "priest and victim" as Abel is shepherd and firstling.[10] Jesus fulfils all positive possibilities because God is above and below everything, outside and inside, transcendent and immanent.

The *"blood of Abel"* is mixed with Jesus' Blood (Mt 23:34-36; Heb 12:24). So is *"the blood of all the prophets which was shed from the foundation of the world"* (Lk 11:50). This gives deeper content to the command for a *"perpetual holocaust"*:

> *These are the sacrifices which you must offer: Two immaculate one-year-old lambs each day as a perpetual holocaust. You shall offer one in morning, and the other in the evening.* (Num 28:3-4)

The beginning and end of each day is sacrifice, as is all history.

Before Abel's day dawned, sheep were presented to Adam to be named (Gen 2:19-20), even as Jesus *"calls His own sheep by name"* (Jn 10:3; cf. Is 43:1; 49:1; 62:2; Apoc 3:5,12). God created lambs to sustain us as our food while also being revealing of Himself. Intentionally lambs are symbolic of innocence (their gambolling), of purity (their snow-white locks), of silence (more comfortable with jaws closed than open, their lips sealing the mouth).[11] With these creatures, God was signalling His Son yet to come. But the Lamb has roots going back still further.

Before the World's Foundation

From eternity it was planned that we be redeemed

> *with the Precious Blood of Christ, an immaculate and undefiled lamb, foreknown, certainly, before the foundation of the world, and made manifest in these latter times for your sake.* (1 Pet 1:18-20 SB)

---

[10] St Augustine, *De civitate dei*, X, 20. St Thomas, *S.Th.* III Q.22 a.2 and *Selected Writings, Sermon on Corpus Christi* "[Jesus is in the Holy Eucharist] both shepherd and green pasture, priest and victim, meat and drink of the elect."

[11] For affecting examples of the silence of the lamb depicted in sacred art, see the Ghent altarpiece (c.1430); Zurbarán's *Agnus Dei* (c.1635); Murillo's *St John the Baptist with Lamb* (c.1660).

Here the first pope tells us of the Lamb foreknown *"before the foundation of the world"*. St Peter's co-apostle, St John, also avers to this ever-present reality. He warns that those who adore the beast are those *"whose names are not written in the book of life of the Lamb, which was slain from the beginning of the world"* (Apoc 13:8).

What book is this? As the conclusion is contained in the premises, as the Alpha and Omega are One, so the final populations of Heaven and hell have always been known by God. Without denying our free will, He knew how each soul would respond to the eternal Lamb. Therefore the *"Book of Life"* is the Lamb's book (Apoc 5:3-8). Only He Who was before the beginning understands what will come in the end, or *"Where were you, when I set the foundations of the earth? Tell me, if you have understanding"* (Job 38:4). Hence the Baptist's declaration:

> *Behold, the Lamb of God. Behold, Him Who takes away the sin of the world. This is the one about Whom I said, 'After me arrives a man, who has been placed ahead of me, because He existed before me.'* (Jn 1:29-30 SB; cf. Jn 1:15)

Jesus' cousin St John was conceived and born six months before Him, but Jesus existed before him, the eternal Son of God. St John believed in the greatness of the Lamb of God, made manifest among us to take away the sins of the world. Our names, too, are written in the Book of Life if we adore the Lamb. We are invited to do so today at Holy Mass.

The Lamb at the Holy Sacrifice of the Mass

When the *Gloria* is sung at Mass, we may think of the Lamb of God eternally in Heaven. We hear: *"Domine Deus, Agnus Dei, Filius Patris"* — "O Lord God, Lamb of God, Son of the Father".

The Lamb helping us here on earth may be recalled just before and after the consecration, especially when mention is made of His martyrs Pope St Clement and St Agnes. The first, a shepherd of the universal church, had a vision of a Lamb by which he and his companions found water while labouring in quarries in exile.

Without it they would have died of thirst.[12] In sacred art, St Agnes is most often depicted with a lamb (Latin: *agnus*). St Ambrose tells us that Agnes' name comes from the Greek word for purity (Ἀγνή).[13]

More obvious than these, after the *Pater noster* the priest repeats: *"Agnus Dei, qui tollis peccata mundi: miserere nobis"* — "Lamb of God, who takest away the sins of the world, have mercy on us".[14] The first recitation is an opportunity for those present to recall the Lamb foreordained and prefigured throughout the Old Testament, for example in Abel's sacrifice, Moses' Passover and Solomon's Temple. At the second recitation one may recall Jesus at the beginning of His public ministry being gazed upon by St John the Baptist as the Lamb of God and at the end of His public ministry being gazed upon by St John the Evangelist as the Lamb led to slaughter. The third recitation ends with *"dona nobis pacem"* — "grant us peace". Here we may hope for Heavenly rest, contemplating the Lamb in Heaven, slain and standing, throning forever. The Lamb on our altars is the same as in Heaven. The business of Heaven and the Mass are the same: the worship of God.

If at Mass anyone were distracted during these references to the Lamb, soon there is another which can scarcely be missed. Shortly after the Baptist first said *"Ecce agnus Dei"* (Jn 1:29), he repeated it with the result that some of his own followers went and followed Jesus:

> *Catching sight of Jesus walking, he said, 'Behold, the Lamb of God.' And two disciples were listening to him speaking. And they followed Jesus.* (Jn 1:36-37)

Similarly in Holy Mass, immediately before the Communion of the faithful, the priest turns to them and announces: *"Ecce agnus Dei, ecce qui tollit peccata mundi."* Acting on this like St John's

---

[12] Feast of St Clement, Matins, *Lectio* V.

[13] Feast of St Agnes, Matins, *Lectio* IV.

[14] The rubrics instruct the priest to say these words *"intelligibili voce"* (audibly).

disciples, the faithful ratify their own readiness to follow Jesus by responding three times in prayer: *"Domine, non sum dignus ut intres sub tectum meum, sed tantum dic verbo, et sanabitur anima mea"*. As we cannot individually work out the entirety of Christian discipleship, God provides leaders to show the way: *"These follow the Lamb whithersoever he goeth. These were purchased from among men, the firstfruits to God and to the Lamb"* (Apoc 14:4).

St John the Baptist sums up the Old Testament: at first he did not recognise Jesus as the Son of God, repeating: *"And I did not know Him"* (Jn 1:31,33); but when St John baptised his Cousin, God revealed Jesus' identity as His Son (Jn 1:32-34); St John then encouraged his disciples to follow Jesus Who is the New Law; but not all followed.

The same happens today: not all have understood the OT so as to follow Jesus. Jewish men are now being trained as Levite priests to slaughter biological lambs for the Passover and the daily sacrifice.[15] They train in the desert before an image of the Temple which they plan to rebuild, unfazed that for two millennia this has been impossible. They do not yet grasp what St Paul teaches the Hebrews, that the rites of Moses were ordained as a shadow of the good things to come (Heb 10:1-5). Is the mystery so hard to understand? Can a man be redeemed by something worth infinitely less than he: a lamb? Or redeemed by Someone worth infinitely more than he: God acting like a lamb? Which is best? God always does the best.

Finally, as the Lamb was thought of by God before the foundation of the world, so also the priest recalls the lamb before Holy Mass even begins. Vesting in the sacristy, when he puts on his alb he prays: "Cleanse me, O Lord, and purify my heart, that, washed in the Blood of the Lamb, I may attain unto everlasting joys." Before the beginning, the course is set: the Lamb leads us into eternity.

---

[15] Times of Israel, *Passover sacrifice reenacted by Jewish priests-in-training*, 15th March 2015.

The Cross

*The priest signs himself with his right hand from forehead to
breast with the sign of the cross, saying in an intelligible voice:
In the Name of the Father, and of the Son and of the Holy Ghost.*

— *Ritus servandus in celebratione Missæ*, III *De Principio*

Reality abounds with the Cross. This is intensely true of Holy
Mass and Sacred Scripture. The OT announced something
momentous was coming; the New Testament (NT) clarifies
exactly what — the Sacrifice of the Messiah on the Cross. Also
Holy Mass, being Jesus Christ's Sacrifice, contains prolific
reverences to His Cross, so that we may be constantly reminded
of the instrument of our redemption.

Building on patristic teaching, we find the Cross heralded in
the OT too many times to count. The many samples given below
are dealt with thematically: first, the Cross figured by trees; next,
by various instruments of wood; then, by wood used in sacrifices
and in sacred objects; and finally, the Cross may be discerned
through its shape.

This series from the OT is followed by a survey of how Holy
Mass loves to dwell on the Cross.

The general purpose of this chapter is to show the Cross is
everywhere and always. The reader may need stamina for all
these crosses, but we owe as much to Jesus for His stamina on
Calvary. Frequent exposure to imagery of the Cross is training for

our mind. By regularly reading Scripture and often assisting at Mass, we become ever more aware that the Cross stands as the nexus of everything: *stat crux dum volvitur orbis* — "the Cross stands while the earth revolves".

The Cross Concealed in the Old Testament

St Justin Martyr (+165) taught that various biblical trees represent the Cross: the Tree of Life in Paradise, promising eternal life; the Oak of Mamre where God appeared to Abraham, as the place of divine encounter; the seventy palms (or willows) in the desert, signifying life for the Hebrews at their Exodus; and in Psalm 1 the tree which *"shall bring forth its fruit, in due season. And his leaf shall not fall off"* (Ps 1:3).[16] We may infer that Christians who internalise the Cross will be healthy and strong, for the *"just shall flourish like the palm tree: he shall grow up like the cedar of Libanus"* (Ps 91:13).

Proceeding from trees to things made from them, what kind of wood comprised Noah's ark? The original descriptor is the first *hapax legomenon* in the Bible — גֹּפֶר (Gen 6:14). Various translations include: *"Make yourself an ark from smoothed wood"*; *"gopher wood"*; *"timber planks"*; or *"squared wood"*. This last possibility reflects another translation, *"four-cornered"*, which hints at the Cross. St Jerome described it as *"wood covered in pitch"*, that is waterproof, saving us from drowning. Or it might mean durable. It is mysterious. Given the ark is a precursor of the Church, without which there is no salvation, St Justin sees the ark's unique wood as signifying the Cross being essential to the mystery of redemption:

> Christ, being the first-born of every creature, became again the chief of another race regenerated by Himself through water, and faith, and wood, containing the mystery of the Cross... [B]y water, faith, and wood, those who... repent of their sins shall escape the impending judgment of God.[17]

---

16 St Justin Martyr, *Dialogue with Trypho*, 86*ff.*

17 St Justin Martyr, *Dialogue with Trypho*, 138.

Seeing wood instrumentalised for miracles, St Justin writes that the Cross is symbolised by the staff Moses used "to effect the redemption of the people; and with this in his hands at the head of the people, he divided the sea". Moses' grasp on the rod resembles Christ's hands fixed to the Cross; dividing the sea means crossing over death; being at the head of the people signifies Christ Who leads the way. This same staff symbolises the Cross again when used to bring water from the rock (here water symbolising life) and to turn the bitter waters at Marah sweet (turning this vale of suffering into joy).

Once we recognise a sign of the Cross in Moses' staff, then we are primed to see it in other staffs. St Justin includes the rod which Jacob "boasted" was all he had to cross the River Jordan (Gen 32:10), again water symbolising death, specifically as the Jordan is the boundary we must cross to reach the Promised Land, Heaven. So Jesus conquered death with the Cross. Further, Jacob had his flocks regard rods while multiplying (Gen 30:41), as Jesus' sheep must contemplate the Cross for the Church to grow. Aaron's dead rod, which blossomed to identify him as chosen High Priest, indicates the everlasting beauty of the Cross, life from death, and confirms the Eternal High Priesthood of Jesus (Num 17). The stick Elisha cast into the Jordan, thereby recovering the axe used to build houses for the prophets, signifies the Church cannot be built without the wood of the Cross and the initial descent into death (2 Kngs 6:1-7).

Unsurprisingly, St Justin finds the Cross and Passion throughout Ps 21. We encounter it also in Ps 22, in God's staff which comforted David, for the Cross guides, consoles and strengthens us. The Cross really achieves these goods. It helps us maintain a firm will in the face of difficulty, as we understand hardship is not necessarily a sign of error. It consoles and strengthens us to know others have endured and overcome worse suffering than our own, for we can hardly be self-pitiful while meditating on the Passion.[18]

---

[18] St Justin writes that the *"rod"* coming forth from *"the root of Jesse"* (Is 11:1*ff*) as prophesied by Isaiah, signifies Jesus Himself. Ideas overlap.

Trained up by the Martyr's *Dialogue with Trypho*, we notice it was through Judah's rod that his sons were discerned (Gen 38), so true disciples are known by the Cross. We can be struck by Banaias, a mighty man from an obscure end of Judah, who slew a lion (satan) in a wintery pit (hell) and with his rod (the Cross) turned the world's evil (the Egyptian's spear) back on itself, to its total demise:

> *Banaias the son of Joiada a most valiant man, of great deeds, of Cabseel: he slew the two lions of Moab, and he went down, and slew a lion in the midst of a pit, in the time of snow. He also slew an Egyptian, a man worthy to be a sight, having a spear in his hand: but he went down to him with a rod, and forced the spear out of the hand of the Egyptian, and slew him with his own spear. These things did Banaias the son of Joiada.* (2 Sam 23:20-22)

Or why else are these facts remembered forever, if not because they prefigure Jesus? The word used here for *"rod"* is the same, שֵׁבֶט, as the *"sceptre"* which *"shall not be taken away from Juda"* (Gen 49:10). Thus the Cross is constantly at work for Jesus' governance, overcoming His enemies.

Adding a forest of spiritual insights to St Justin's lists of examples, St Gregory of Nyssa writes: "you of course understand the 'Cross' when you hear 'wood'".[19] This is crucial for reading the OT and even understanding nature. Both came before the Crucifixion yet strain to point to it. God wrote them to include this feature. Humble things tell of great things, therefore should not be overlooked.[20]

Bearing in mind St Gregory's important advice (thinking of the 'Cross' whenever we read of 'wood'), we proceed from

---

[19] St Gregory of Nyssa, *Life of Moses*, II, 131-136.

[20] The Fathers teach that Elisha's staff, in the hands of Giezi, his servant literally going ahead of him, was powerless to bring a young boy who had died back to life. But when the great prophet himself came, figuring Jesus, he used his whole being to resurrect the dead son (2 Kngs 4:29-37). So prefigurations of the Cross do not give life, nor do the heralds and prophets of the Messiah, but God Himself raises man.

miracles to sacrifices. The foremost is that of Abraham after he had *"cut wood for the holocaust"* (Gen 22:3), who represents God the Father in a passage which markedly mentions wood a further four times:

> *[Abraham] took the wood for the holocaust, and laid it upon Isaac his son... And as they two went on together, Isaac said to his father: My father. And he answered: What wilt thou, son? Behold, saith he, fire and wood: where is the victim for the holocaust? And Abraham said: God will provide himself a victim for an holocaust, my son. So they went on together. And they came to the place which God had shewn him, where he built an altar, and laid the wood in order upon it: and when he had bound Isaac his son, he laid him on the altar upon the pile of wood.* (Gen 22:6-9)

Five times *"wood"* is specified in Gen 22, emphatically pointing to the Cross. Perhaps even the Five Wounds.

Stressing the lesson that wood is integral to the Lord's sacrifices, God instructed Moses on how Aaron and his priests should make their offerings. They *"shall put fire on the altar, having before laid in order a pile of wood"* (Lev 1:7; cf. 1:12). The wood was not chaotic but orderly, like the Cross.

And what does this fire on the altar mean but divine love, or the Holy Ghost? A holocaust is a whole burnt offering. As a sacrifice entire and perpetual it represents the divine Spirit:

> *And the fire on the altar shall always burn, and the priest shall feed it, putting wood on it every day in the morning: and laying on the holocaust, shall burn thereupon the fat of the peace offerings. This is the perpetual fire which shall never go out on the altar.* (Lev 6:12-13; cf. 3:5)

To stay alive the fire of charity requires sacrifices: *"When the wood faileth, the fire shall go out"* (Prov 26:20). We need to keep making sacrifices if we are to abide in charity. Dying we live. The Cross shall not fail, God's love shall not go out. Elijah saw it envelops all, it is voracious, stronger than all human passion:

the fire of the Lord fell, and consumed the holocaust, and the wood, and the stones, and the dust, and licked up the water that was in the trench. (1 Kngs 18:38)

It was a divine honour for priests and people to carry wood to Jerusalem for the sacrifices, anticipating the itinerary of Jesus Who carried the Cross there in His Heart and then on His shoulders. If they did their duty willingly, glad to serve God, then they participated in Christ's Passion:

We cast lots among the priests, and the Levites, and the people for the offering of wood, that it might be brought into the house of our God by the houses of our fathers at set times, from year to year: to burn upon the altar of the Lord our God, as it is written in the law of Moses. (Neh 10:34; cf. 13:31)

This theme of wood and holocaust is reinforced with the cart and cattle carrying the Ark of the Covenant, that is the Presence of God. The very ones which bore the holy wood were sacrificed: *"they cut in pieces the wood of the cart, and laid the kine upon it a holocaust to the Lord"* (1 Sam 6:14). Another time wood came from the yokes (born on the shoulder like the cross) and threshing sledges (for grinding the wheat, meaning the trials of life unto death, lending a eucharistic connotation), with the beasts of burden for victims:

Take it, and let my lord the king do all that pleaseth him: and moreover the oxen also I give for a holocaust, and the drays for wood, and the wheat for the sacrifice: I will give it all willingly. (1 Chron 21:23; see 2 Sam 24:22 for the yokes)

Wood was essential in seemingly strange ceremonies. In order to purify and make atonement for an unclean house, God designated that the priest shall:

take the cedar wood, and the hyssop, and the scarlet, and the living sparrow, and shall dip all in the blood of the sparrow that is immolated, and in the living water, and he shall sprinkle the house seven times: And shall purify it as well with

the blood of the sparrow, as with the living water, and with the
living sparrow, and with the cedar wood, and the hyssop, and
the scarlet. (Lev 14:51-52)

Without faith in the Cross, this rite might seem arbitrary. With the
Cross, it becomes profound. The living and dead sparrows
indicate this is a matter of life and death. St Justin notes the royal
prophet Isaiah was killed with wood, being cut

> asunder with a wooden saw. And this was a mysterious type of
> Christ being about to cut your nation in two, and to raise those
> worthy of the honour to the everlasting kingdom along with
> the holy patriarchs and prophets.[21]

Here St Justin indicates that by the Cross those who die will live
and those who kill will die. Haman had a scaffold made of wood
on which to execute a *"saviour"* of Israel, Mordecai. The Vulgate
calls this structure a *crux*, that is, a cross (Est 5:14; 8:7; 9:25).
The Septuagint uses σταυροω: to "crucify" (Est 7:9; 8:12r / Vlg
16:18). In the end Haman and his murderous sons were hung on
it, not Mordecai. So it was not Jesus but evil which was defeated
on the Cross.[22]

While Haman prefigures evil being defeated on the Cross,
Esdras the Priest shows the light of understanding which would
shine from Calvary. He *"stood upon a step of wood, which he had*
made to speak upon" (Neh 8:4), and from this *"wooden pulpit"*
(RSVCE) Esdras, like Jesus lifted up from the earth, *"was above*
all the people" (Neh 8:5), and taught them the Law, since they
were ignorant of it. Then *"all the people answered, Amen, amen:*
lifting up their hands: and they bowed down, and adored God"
(Neh 8:6). Did not Jesus reveal the truth of the *Torah, "the book*
of the law of Moses" (Neh 8:1), so that the people adore God?

---

[21] St Justin Martyr, *Dialogue with Trypho,* 120.

[22] The Vulgate reports Haman and his household *"pendet in patibulis"* (Est 16:18).
The latter is the technical term for the horizontal part of the Cross upon which Jesus
hung on Calvary. The *"scaffold"* is variously translated as gallows, impaling pole,
or something made of wood. The Hebrew has עץ (tree, wood), indicating Haman is
cursed (cf. Dt 21:22-23).

What followed symbolises eucharistic feasting: *"all the people went to eat and drink... and to make great mirth: because they understood the words that he had taught them"* (Neh 8:12). This feasting is ours if we understand Calvary.[23]

Wood was notably devoted to holy uses. The Ark of the Covenant and the table for the Bread of Presence were made of incorruptible *"acacia wood"* overlaid with gold (Ex 25:10-13; 23-28). Acacia wood speaks of the Cross as incorruptible and the layer of gold speaks of it as resplendent. Appropriately, acacia was used for the boards and bars of the tabernacle, and the pillars for holding the veil (Ex 26:15,26,32), likewise the altar of holocaust and altar of incense, each with their bars (Ex 27:1,6; 30:1,5). This wood is exceedingly thorny, making it hard to grasp, but is beautiful once worked, and hard enough to withstand extreme winters — all spiritual qualities of the Cross.

On a grander scale, the Temple in Jerusalem was built with *"cedar, cypress and algum timber from Lebanon"*, its nave lined with wood overlaid with gold (2 Chron 2:8; 3:5 RSVCE). This *"algum"* (אַלְגּוּמִּים) wood is elsewhere called *"almug"* (אַלְמֻגִּים), being praised as of unmatched quality:

> *Moreover the fleet of Hiram, which brought gold from Ophir, brought from Ophir a very great amount of almug wood and precious stones. And the king made of the almug wood supports for the house of the Lord, and for the king's house, lyres also and harps for the singers; no such almug wood has come or been seen, to this day.* (1 Kngs 10:11-12 RSVCE)

As Scripture deliberately brings this unique wood to our attention here, might we not think of the Cross again, coming with fine gold and precious stones, supporting the house of the Lord and the house of the king, as the Cross upholds Church and State? Is civilisation not built on the Cross? Is wood ever praised as much as here, except in Holy Week and Feasts of the Cross?

---

[23] What the Hebrew people next did materially, we may do now spiritually, namely to *"dwell in tabernacles"* made with *"branches of beautiful wood"* (Neh 8:14-15, *ligni pulcherrimi*). That is to live in simplicity with gratitude for the Cross.

As they are mentioned, the musical instruments made of wood may stand for the angelic praise of God melodiously offered by those who embrace or kiss their crosses as musicians seemingly do their lyres and lutes:

> *David and all Israel played before the Lord on all manner of instruments made of wood, on harps and lutes and timbrels and cornets and cymbals.* (2 Sam 6:5)

Now all of us, if we practise, may make spiritual music with the wood of the Cross. Taking our lives together God conducts a symphony far greater than the parts.

Abstracting from the material, the Cross is foreshadowed also in its form. The whole People of God formed a vast Cross during the forty years they wandered in the wilderness. Eastwards of the tabernacle, over 200,000 Israelites encamped with Moses and Aaron; to the west some 115,000 camped with the Gershonites; to the north about 160,000 and a similar number to the south with the Merarites and Kohathites respectively. Thus their tents formed a long trunk planted in the east, a top piece rising to the west, and two roughly equal arms of a cross spread north and south.[24]

At the centre was the Tent, the Presence of the Lord, anticipating the Sacred Heart of Jesus on the Cross. Looking down from Heaven, God was pleased with this formation, for which He had given personal instructions to Moses.

Israel's enemies were overwhelmed by it. Balak commissioned Balaam to curse the Hebrew encampment, but standing up on the mountain and seeing them, he could only utter:

> *How can I curse whom God has not cursed? How can I denounce whom the Lord has not denounced? For from the top of the mountains I see him, from the hills I behold him... How fair are your tents, O Jacob, your encampments, O Israel! Like valleys that stretch afar, like gardens beside a river, like*

---

[24] For more precise numbers, see Num 2-3. The family tents did not encircle the tabernacle in rings. Rather, four orderly lines radiating from the centre provided plenty of free space, helping the leaders with an overview, helping everyone with sanitation, and helping children navigate back to their family tent.

aloes that the Lord has planted, like cedar trees beside the waters. Water shall flow from his buckets, and his seed shall be in many waters, his king shall be higher than Agag, and his kingdom shall be exalted. (Num 23:8-9; 24:5-7 RSVCE)

Yes, God's People form *"gardens beside a river"*, Paradise regained and multiplied through an irrigation of grace; like *"cedar trees beside the waters"*, each person growing great who lives the Cross by means of the waters flowing from Christ's pierced side; water wells up from within, the Holy Ghost *"shall flow from his buckets"* (read 'the depths of his soul', cf. Jn 7:38); for *"his seed shall be in many waters"*, which is the supernatural life of Christ we gain in baptism. Thus Christ's *"kingdom shall be exalted"*. It all has everlasting meaning.

How much God packs into a phrase, a word, even a letter. While Hebrew letters are phonetic (representing sounds), they originated from pictographs (representing things). Whatever language God gave to Adam, the Hebrew letter *tav* represents the Cross. In the days of Abraham it was drawn as †, around the time of Moses becoming ✗, developing to ת before the coming of Christ. It is our letter 'T'.

Over many centuries, the initial 'T' of the *Te igitur* beginning the Canon of the Mass was drawn in ancient liturgical books larger than the letters which followed. Gradually it became beautifully decorated, recognised as the Cross, and finally it grew so large that from the Middle Ages until today it is customary for a Missal to have a full-page image of the Crucifixion on the left page facing the *Te igitur* on the right. Right in the middle of the Missal is the big picture depicting exactly what Mass is all about: Christ's Sacrifice. But back now to Sacred Scripture.

The Bible begins: "בראשית ברא אלהים את השמים ואת הארץ" *"In the beginning God created the heavens and the earth"* (Gen 1:1). The letter ת appears three times in these seven words. First, it ends the first word, בראשית, meaning *"In the beginning"*. So the Cross is the end of the beginning. (As Hebrew is written from right to left, then the ת appears to many of us to be at the beginning of the end, which is true too.) But there is much more meaning hidden in this opening word. Its first two letters spell 'Son' (בר).[25] The next letter is assigned to God (א). The next two could mean "lamb of" (שי).[26] And these are followed by the Cross (ת). Thus the very first word of the Bible, בראשית, may be rendered: "Son of God, Lamb of the Cross". Astounding! So deep is the resonance with the revelation: *"In the beginning was the Word"* (Jn 1:1).

The second ת is in the central word of the verse. This word, or particle, את, has no semantic content, but indicates the word following it is the direct object. Still it contains great meaning. Reading right to left, it is the *aleph* (א) and the *tav* (ת), the first and the last letters of the *alephbet*, the Alpha and the Omega, the Beginning and the End, Jesus Christ. In the first sentence of the Bible, the beginning and end stands at the centre. Like the Cross.

The third appearance of *tav* in Gen 1:1 is in ואת, positioned between *"the heavens"* and *"the earth"*. Taking the letters as ideographs: ו stands for the power to unite everything (translated it is the conjunction "and"); א symbolises God (in myth it is pre-creation); and ת is the mark of the covenant or Cross. So the final three words of the first sentence in Scripture can be interpreted: "the heavens are joined to the earth by God with the Cross".

Combining the plain meaning of words with letter combinations and ideographs, the *Torah*'s first sentence reads:

בראשית — Son of God, Lamb of the Cross
ברא — the Son of God
אלהים — God
את — the Alpha and the Omega
השמים ואת הארץ — the All in All

---

[25] The usual term for 'son' is בן (*ben*) but the Aramaic בר (*bar*), as used by Jesus, is universally recognised in Hebrew too.

[26] שֶׂה (*seh*) is the word for 'lamb' used in Gen 22:7-8 (where Isaac asks Abraham *"where is the lamb for the sacrifice"*, to which his father replies *"God will provide the lamb Himself, my son"*). In a clause such as *"lamb of the cross"* the ה (*he*) would be replaced with a י (*yod*), exactly as in the first word of the Bible, בראשית. But here the fourth letter is not שׂ (*sin*), as used in 'sheep' or 'lamb', but is the variation שׁ (*shin*), albeit the two derived from a single, earlier letter.

Many fascinating variations can be found. *"My soul hath fainted after thy salvation: and in thy word..."* (Ps 118:81)! Admittedly it is easy to err here, inventing meanings which are not really there. However, as to the validity of giving microscopic scrutiny to Scripture, St Gregory of Nyssa writes:

> truly, to those who are able to see, the mystery of the cross is especially contemplated in the Law. Wherefore the Gospel says that *not one dot, not one little stroke, shall disappear from the Law*, signifying in these words the vertical and horizontal lines by which the form of the cross is drawn.[27]

This sainted Church Father finds the Cross in the tiniest details. But even when we zoom out from the microscopic to the macroscopic, the Cross remains present, drawn in our imagination by the following description:

> *In the beginning God created heaven and earth... And God made a firmament, and divided the waters that were under the firmament, from those that were above the firmament, and it was so... And God called the dry land, Earth; and the gathering together of the waters, he called Seas. And God saw that it was good.* (Gen 1:1,7,10)

Here a cosmic vertical is traced out from top to bottom in mentioning *"heaven and earth"*. Then comes a horizontal division, distinguishing *"under the firmament, from... above the firmament"*. This cross is planted on *"Earth"*, and at its foot the dry land is divided from the seas. This is precisely what the Crucifixion achieves: dividing life from death, dividing the saved from the condemned, the sheep from the goats. Hence *"God saw that it was good"* (Gen 1:10).

---

[27] St Gregory of Nyssa, *Life of Moses*, II, 151. The 'dot' or Greek *iota* refers to the smallest letter of the Hebrew alephbet, ' (*yod*). The 'little stroke' or 'tittle' is even smaller. It is a mark distinguishing certain letters, for example an O from a Q, or in Hebrew a כ (*kaph*) from a ב (*bet*). In Greek it is called a little horn. In Latin it is the *titulus*, a horizontal accent above a letter to indicate it is long. The *Titulus Crucis* is the sign attached to the Cross announcing in Latin, Greek and Hebrew: *Jesus of Nazareth, King of the Jews*.

Even without recognising the Cross as the key of creation at the beginning of time, it will be unmissable at the end of time, written in the skies for all to see:

> *then will appear the sign of the Son of man in heaven, and then all the tribes of the earth will mourn, and they will see the Son of man coming on the clouds of heaven with power...* (Mt 24:30)

This *"sign"* is traditionally understood to be the Cross. Souls in a state of grace will have a similar sign on themselves. Like the Hebrews keeping the Passover ready for the Exodus, they will be marked with a *tav* by the angels and spared from destruction in the coming cataclysm:

> *And the Lord said to him: 'Cross through the middle of the city, in the centre of Jerusalem, and seal a Tau upon the foreheads of the grieving men, who are mourning over all the abominations which are being committed in its midst'...*

We may be encouraged by those *"grieving"* and *"mourning"* over offences against God, those labouring in sorrow, for these were saved. Continuing the passage:

> *...And he said to the others, in my hearing: 'Cross through the city after him, and strike! Your eye shall not be lenient, and you shall not take pity. Kill, even to utter destruction, old men, young men, and virgins, little ones, and women. But all upon whom you see the Tau, you shall not kill. And begin from my sanctuary.'* (Ezek 9:4-6 SB. See also Apoc 7:3; 9:4; 14:1)

This judgement holds true for all people, of every generation, for we all face the personal cataclysm of death. If we are marked by the Cross, that is if our life has been a sacrifice pleasing to God, then we will come to Heaven.

Reality, visible and invisible, truly abounds with crosses. We should not be surprised that God calls us to carry our own. We will certainly want our soul marked by it in the end. Holy Mass teaches us that His burden is light (Mt 11:30). *Ite ad missam!*

The Cross Revered in Holy Mass

As the Scriptures, nature and human lives are abundantly planted with the Cross, so too is Holy Mass. Creation began with a Cross which none of us could see (Gen 1:1,7,10), and will end at the Apocalypse with one which fills the skies (Mt 24:30). Likewise, Holy Mass begins with a Sign of the Cross which nobody can see (for all are behind the priest who, standing for Christ, signs himself) and it ends with the Last Blessing: the priest turns to face the people and makes a large Sign of the Cross while those present sign themselves, as all wish to be marked by the Cross when the angels come to reap the harvest.

Between this hidden opening and great closing, one is never far from the Cross in Holy Mass. (For what follows here, the reader may need stamina.) Arriving at the steps of the altar for a typical Low Mass, the priest reverences the altar Cross with a profound bow (or he genuflects if the Blessed Sacrament is in the tabernacle). Returning to this place after preparing the chalice and Missal, he reverences the Cross again. Then Mass begins. After the opening Sign of the Cross described above, the priest similarly signs himself during the Prayers at the Foot of the Altar at the *Adiutorium* and the *Indulgentiam*. He makes another Cross at the *Introitus* and bows to the altar Cross during the *Gloria Patri*. He bows to this Cross six more times during the *Gloria*, which he finishes by making the Sign of the Cross on himself. For the *Oratio* he bows to the Cross twice (or up to four times if there are multiple *Orationes*, that is, at each *Oremus* and the doxologies which include the Name of Jesus). He bows to the Cross for the *Munda cor*. When beginning the Gospel he signs the Missal with the Cross, then himself three times: on his forehead, lips and heart. If there is a Creed he bows to the Cross three times, mentions the Crucifixion (*Crucifixus etiam pro nobis*) and ends signing himself with the Cross. He bows toward the Cross at the *Oremus* of the *Offertorium*, and then with the unconsecrated host on the paten he traces a Cross over the corporal, as he will also with the chalice (from the tabernacle toward himself then from the Gospel side to the Epistle side, both strokes showing the hierarchy of reality: God is prior to man; the Gospel is prior to all other Scriptures). Pouring wine and water into the chalice, he blesses the water with a Cross. During the *Veni, sanctificator* he traces a Cross over the bread and wine. He bows to the Cross in the doxology at the end of the *Lavabo* prayer and explicitly recalls the Passion in the *Suscipe sancta Trinitas*. He bows toward the Cross on mentioning *Deo nostro* before the *Præfatio* and afterward at the *Sanctus*, then signs himself for the *Benedictus*. During the Canon of the Mass, the apex of Calvary, the priest makes three Crosses over the gifts during the *Te igitur*, five during the *Quam oblationem*, another during the *Qui pridie*, also during the *Simili modo*, and with the consecrated Body and Blood now before him, five more during the *Unde et memores* (mentioning the Passion), two more Crosses during the *Supplices te rogamus*, and referring to those marked with *"the sign of faith"* — the Cross — in the *Commemoratio pro defunctis*, also bowing to the Cross twice during this prayer, as he had once during the *Commemoratio pro vivis*. The Canon closes with a flourish of Crosses: three during the *Per quem*, five during the *Per ipsum*, and a bow to the Cross before the *Præceptis*. During the *Libera nos* he signs himself with the paten and during the *Pax* makes three Crosses over the chalice with the fractured particle from the Host. He mentions Jesus' life-giving death during the second *Domine Jesu Christe* prayer before Communion, and makes the Sign of the Cross with the Host and then the chalice immediately before receiving them. At the *Postcommunio* he bows to the Cross twice. And after the *Ite missa est* he blesses all present through the Sign of the Cross. For the Last Gospel he signs with the Cross first the altar, then his forehead, then his lips, then his heart.

That is more than seventy crosses (figuratively enough for every nation of the world). As the Lord lives, there is not one too many. All these crosses become second nature to a priest who offers Mass daily. By coming automatically, they serve to hold the form of the Mass together should he be elevated in contemplation of the sacred mysteries or be distracted by something rather less.

As the Cross was intended before the world was made, and will be contemplated after it is gone, so the Cross is honoured in the sacristy before and after Mass.

In a Sung or Solemn Mass there are many more crosses: three times the priest blesses the incense with the Cross; he incenses the altar Cross twelve times and further swings the thurible to make three Crosses over the gifts at the Offertory. The celebrant blesses the sub-deacon with a Cross after the Epistle and the deacon with one before the Gospel. There is a massive multiplication in the Crosses which the deacon and sub-deacon make, and countless more which the servers and faithful make. If there is a homily one hopes it is opened and closed with the Sign of the Cross. A healthy Catholic does not grow tired of any of these. They are part of the fabric and flow of the Mass which fits human nature so perfectly: movement for the body, stimuli for the senses, meaning for the mind, fuel for the heart.

Besides all these, many further crosses may be seen. Just before consuming the Host the priest might glimpse the Cross above the tabernacle, then as he lowers his eyes and head, he might see a cross on the pall, another on the foot of the chalice (engraved there so that he always drinks from the same point, thus facilitating proper purification as the ablutions wash over the same area where the Precious Blood flowed), and another on the corporal (best sewn shallowly into the bottom third so the corporal is always used with the same orientation to protect particles of the sacred species). The faithful can hardly see the Crosses on the chalice or corporal, but might see a Cross on the burse; certainly they should notice a Cross or column on the back of the priest's chasuble (depending respectively on whether it is French or Roman style) and perhaps catch sight of one or two of the three on the priest's maniple. If the nape of the stole is exposed, a Cross is seen there. Most prominent of all, the Crucifix at the centre of the altar is mandatory.

The eyes never tire of these Crosses, nor the mind of finding "wood" in the Scriptures. If searching the Word of God we can find the Cross in the jots and tittles, then there is the equivalent in the more subtle gestures of the Mass. Whenever the priest folds his hands, including when the rubrics instruct him to rest them on the edge of the altar (*manibus junctis super Altare*), then he is to hold his right thumb crossed over his left. This is practical, looks gracious, and as the *Ritus servandus* indicates, it deliberately forms a cross.[28] This happens at least forty times in the Mass. It hardly needs counting. It is more or less constant, save when the Passion is recalled in the *orans* posture, or when the hands rest on the Missal or are otherwise engaged.

A crucial exception to this rule endures from the consecration to purification, when the thumbs and forefingers are not held separated (never mind crossed), but remain pinched together, which is essential to guarding particles of the Host. This is in reverence of that most sublime sign of the Passion given by Jesus Himself: the Holy Eucharist. The separate consecration of the Host and the Chalice, the sign of the Body separated from the Blood, signifies Jesus' death. Insofar as we understand this sign, this Sacrament, this Mystery, we understand the Mass. It is the Holy Sacrifice of Calvary. The Cross, where Jesus was immolated, is His altar.

Every time we read of "wood" in the Scriptures, we may think of Jesus' Cross, His altar. Whenever in life we see wood, a staff or a tree, or even on fire, we may think of the Cross, His altar. And in each Holy Mass, through the scores upon scores of crosses, the Church shows her desire to contemplate constantly the instrument of salvation. The Cross is normal, the shape of each life. It is the actual altar of God.

---

[28] *Ritus servandus*, III, *De Principio Missæ:* "with his hands joined before his breast with fingers extended and together, and with his right thumb over his left in the form of a cross (which form is always to be observed when joining the hands until after the Consecration)".

The Altar

I will go in to the altar of God
— Ps 42:4, Antiphon, Prayers at the Foot of the Altar

Introibo ad altare Dei. These are the words (given above) of the antiphon recited before and after Psalm 42 is prayed at the foot of the altar. The priest must be mindful that he is about to approach the altar of God. An altar has one purpose: sacrifice. Upon God's altar, no sacrifice is worthy now except the one offered on Calvary by His Beloved Son. This offering is accomplished continually by the numerous Masses said around the world. Though few may approach the altar physically, we are all called to go there in spirit, which possibility is open to us always.

The word *"introibo"* means "I will enter". When praying it, the priest is preparing to enter the most sacred space on earth. Jesus uses the same word for entering into our hearts:

> *Behold, I stand at the gate, and knock. If any man shall hear My voice, and open to Me the door, I will come in to him* [εἰσέρχομαι, *intrabo*], *and will sup with him, and he with Me.* (Apoc 3:20)

We enter God's space as He enters ours, the purpose being to *"sup"*, to eat and drink with each other, in fact, to feast *on* each other. This spiritual reality is the foretaste to the nuptial banquet of Heaven. Our being is in God's Being. Our union with God means living by His Substance, which is distantly imaged on earth by a family living from shared sustenance, eating around the table together. To feed a family of billions — the Communion of Saints — no table is great enough. We need something infinitely better. We need to go in to the altar of God.

The Bible hints at how the altar of God developed from the beginning. After considering facets of this, we ponder the Marian meaning of a second altar. Finally we consider the invitation extended in the Mass' multiplication of altars, without which we would starve.

The Altar Develops: Christ

The Hebrew word for *introibo* is from the root בּוֹא, "to come". The first two uses in the Bible of this simple word are when God *"brought"* the animals to Adam and then *"brought"* Eve to him (Gen 2:19,22). How is *"brought"* the same word as *"enter"*? The hiphil form of בּוֹא used here expresses causative action, therefore "to cause to come" is rightly rendered as "to bring".

After God brings to man animals and a bride, next it is man's turn to see what he can bring to God in gratitude. The next two usages of בּוֹא are when Cain and Abel *"brought"* (or *"offered"*) their respective sacrifices (Gen 4:3-4). Did they build altars for these? Either way, Cain's inadequate offering was rejected, but Abel's pleasing sacrifice was accepted. His firstling lamb pointed worthily to Christ.

Long term, no mere animal is sufficient. As Adam found irrational brutes to be inadequate as closest collaborator in his highest work (Gen 2:20) — religion — so God did not intend animals to be the greatest offering in worshipping Him either. Rather, as God gave Adam a bride, so the New Adam, Jesus Christ, would actively cause a Bride to be brought to God — the Church. Jesus first offered Himself as her Head and since then offers the members in His own Name. This calls for our cooperation, offering ourselves in spiritual sacrifice to the Father through Jesus Christ. To prepare for something this stupendous, many more foreshadowings were required. The story of Noah introduces explicitly what until now was only implicit: the altar.

As all types of animals were brought to Adam, so God had Noah bring clean and unclean animals together (Gen 7:2-3). Noah, his family and all the animals *"enter[ed] into"* the ark (Gen 6:18), using the same word בּוֹא for our *"introibo"*, because saints and sinners who enter the holy place in their hearts embark on the ark of salvation. When the time came for their exodus, Noah picked clean animals for his holocaust (suggesting saints suffer the most). And he built something suited to the purpose:

> *And Noe built an altar unto the Lord: and taking of all cattle and fowls that were clean, offered holocausts upon the altar. And the Lord smelled a sweet savour...* (Gen 8:20-21)

That *"sweet savour"* is important. We will return to it.

Noah's sacrifice provided protection for the world (God responded, *"I will no more curse the earth for the sake of man"* Gen 8:21), but not yet redemption. The reward from God is proportional to the gifts offered to Him. A better gift than "clean animals" was needed. Serving the signs to come, Noah, the first man to plant a vineyard, was called אִישׁ הָאֲדָמָה, "man of the earth" (Gen 9:20), which closely resembles "man of Adam". Indeed *"the Lord God formed man* [אָדָם, *Adam*] *of the slime of the earth* [אֲדָמָה, *adamah*]*"* (Gen 2:7). Noah being a vinedresser (tiller of soil or husbandman) is a refinement of Adam's role, whom God appointed to be a *"gardener"* (Gen 2:15). Honing Adam's desire for reconciliation with God, Noah understood God intended to save man, and man for his part should put the earth and its fruits to God's service. But to win redemption, we need an offering far higher than *"the fruit of thy ground, and the fruit of thy cattle"* (Dt 28:4). The needed fruit was indicated by Abraham.

Abraham built four altars to God, each time getting closer to the goal, finally reaching Mount Moriah. Here he offered God something more beloved to him than his own life, namely his son, Isaac. God asked Abraham to give the fruit of his loins, the sole fruit of Sarah's womb. And Abraham was willing to have his posterity cancelled. At the last moment, God sent His angel to arrest Abraham's knife (Gen 22:10-12). God does not desire bloodshed, but a self-sacrificing spirit. Abraham demonstrated that he would hold nothing back from God. That sufficed. In the fullness of time God demonstrated that He holds nothing back from us. The ultimate victim is God's Son, Jesus Christ.

As OT victims approached a likeness to Christ (Abel's animal, Noah's clean animals, Abraham's son), so did the altars. After the Ten Commandments, God's next instruction to Moses was:

> *You shall make an altar of earth unto me, and you shall offer upon it your holocausts and peace offerings, your sheep and oxen, in every place where the memory of my name shall be: I will come to thee, and will bless thee. And if thou make an altar of stone unto me, thou shalt not build it of hewn stones; for if thou lift up a tool upon it, it shall be defiled.*
> (Ex 20:24-25)

Here was progress: altars made not of earth but of stone. The first indicated man's origin from the earth, in fact from their Creator. Earth stands for the *materia prima*, the potential from which living things are created. On an altar things of the earth are raised to Heaven. Stone altars maintain this link, but the solidity and fixedness increase, thereby approaching the Rock Who is Christ. He is not a *"hewn stone"*, cut merely from the quarry of mankind. He is the uncut stone from eternity (Dan 2:34-45).

A Second Altar is Fashioned: Mary

When the time came for building the tabernacle in the desert, the altar of holocaust was made from acacia wood overlain with bronze (Ex 27:1-2). A smaller altar was made of acacia wood overlain with pure gold: the altar of incense (Ex 30:1-3). If the first altar points to Christ, what is the meaning of the second altar? Are there two Christs?

The top surfaces of both altars were squares, signifying balance and being grounded: the altar of holocaust *"five cubits long and five cubits broad; the altar shall be square, and its height shall be three cubits"* (Ex 27:1 RSVCE); the altar of incense *"a cubit shall be its length, and a cubit its breadth; it shall be square, and two cubits shall be its height"* (Ex 30:2 RSVCE). Who then is perfect like Christ, though not matching His magnitude? Who is so precious in God's eyes as to be overlain with pure gold? Perhaps inviting us to make a link, there are striking parallels in the descriptions of the altar of incense and the Ark of the Covenant. Both were made of incorruptible wood and covered, indeed crowned, with gold (Ex 25:10-14; 30:1-5). The Ark famously prefigures the Blessed Virgin Mary. Why not the altar of incense, too?

Following this interpretation, we note the altar of holocaust stood outside the tabernacle in the open air of the court. Jesus was crucified, made a holocaust, outside the city. The altar of incense stood inside the tabernacle, hidden from all but ministering priests. Our Lady sacrificed herself spiritually, interiorly, her soul hidden from all but God. On this second altar the High Priest burned *"sweet smelling incense"* every morning and *"everlasting incense"* every evening (Ex 30:7-8), which corresponds to the sweetness and constancy of the prayers of the Virgin Mary. It was a unique and irreplaceable blend: *"You shall not offer upon it incense of another composition, nor an oblation, nor a victim; neither shall you offer libations"* (Ex 30:9 SB). As Mary was bathed in the Blood of Christ on Calvary, so Aaron was instructed to pray once a year on the four horns of the altar of incense with *"the blood of that which was offered for sin... It shall be most holy to the Lord"* (Ex 30:10).

But if the altar of incense outside the veil represents Mary, and the Ark of the Covenant inside the veil represents Mary, does that mean there are two Marys? No. There is Mary on Calvary, and Mary assumed into Heaven. The tabernacle shows all the highest truths. The altar standing before the veil represents the Our Lady's sacrifice on earth; the Ark hidden in the Holy of Holies represents Our Lady's presence in Heaven (Apoc 11:19).[29]

---

[29] Notwithstanding the *"golden altar"* too has its counterpart in Heaven (Apoc 8:3).

The two altars — Christ and Mary — are described in the Book of Exodus twice. First, the whole project of the tabernacle and Levitical priesthood is presented with detailed instructions in chapters 25 to 30. Then come the incidents of the Golden Calf, Moses smashing the Tablets of the Law, his intercession for his people, the new Commandments (Tablets), the Covenant renewed, the glory of Moses' face, the law for the Sabbath. After all this, in chapters 36 to 39, comes the concrete realisation of building the tabernacle: the precise fulfilment of the instructions given earlier is recounted. Many struggle to read these details once. What is the purpose of this repetition?

It speaks of Christ and the pattern of history, of promise and fulfilment. The significance of the first and the second description is that of the commandment given and then the commandment finally carried out. Lots had to happen in between. History follows the same order of events given in Exodus 25-39: first God gave the Law, then man broke the covenant, yet his punishment was stayed by the pleadings of a selfless intercessor, a new Commandment was given (Jn 13:34), a new Covenant, the intercessor was glorified, the Lord's Day emphasised, and the whole construction of the tabernacle recapitulated, which is the building up of the Church (celestial society) according to God's Plan announced in advance of everything actually happening.

What was first built materially, locally, is now being constructed spiritually, universally. Both Jesus and Mary are at work in the promise and the fulfilment.

Multiplication of Altars: Our Participation

Pointing to the worldwide or spiritual expansion to come, the brazen altar of holocaust made for Solomon's Temple was huge compared to that of the tabernacle, it being *"twenty cubits long, and twenty cubits broad, and ten cubits high"* (2 Chron 4:1). A new perfection exhibited by the Temple altars was their fixedness. Unlike those of the tabernacle, they were not intended to be carried anywhere, for they marked the ultimate destination: the divine Presence in Jerusalem (the holy city, Heaven).

The same understanding is reflected by Pope St Sylvester's (✝355) decree, after the Roman persecutions of the Church had abated, that "altars were thenceforward to be made [not of wood but] of stone only".[30] The proper immovability of an altar should exclude us from categorising it as a table, as an item of furniture. The etymological root of "furniture" in most European languages is *mobile*, meaning moveable in Latin. For example, in German furniture is *Möbel* and in contrast real estate is *Immobilie*. Hence furniture is something added to the immoveable house. But in a church fixedness is the other way around. If by some disaster a church is damaged, for example by an earthquake or bomb, but the altar escapes unhurt, then the walls or roof need only be rebuilt. But if an altar should be broken — *quod avertat Deus* — then once it is replaced the whole church must be rededicated. The ancient rite for the dedication of a Church is more focused on the altar than on the building. This symbology maps our dependency on Christ. The structure exists for the sake of the altar just as communities of Christians live from and for Christ.

Christ reestablishing the Covenant is shown by Elijah, who

repaired the altar of the Lord, that was broken down: And he took twelve stones according to the number of the tribes of the sons of Jacob... And he built with the stones an altar to the name of the Lord... (1 Kngs 18:30-33)

The twelve stones represent the apostles; building the altar with them means celebrating the first Masses with them, establishing the liturgy. By restoring the ancient altar on true foundations, Elijah dramatically overcame idolatry (1 Kngs 18:40).[31] With only a bullock as victim, he defeated hundreds of false prophets. How much more Christ achieves with the apostolic liturgy.

---

[30] Dedication of the Archbasilica of Our Holy Saviour, Matins, *Lectio* VI.

[31] To explain how a sacrifice could be offered far from Jerusalem after the Temple had been built in its designated place, a midrash takes Elijah's words *"according to thy commandment I have done all these things"* (1 Kngs 18:36) to argue that the prophet had a special dispensation from God (*Bemidbar Rabbah* 14:1). Others say it was a case of *epikea* — whereby a law can be overridden to achieve a greater good.

As the altar points to Christ, or Christians, so too do the victims.

Walk in love, as Christ also hath loved us, and hath delivered Himself for us, an oblation and a sacrifice to God for an odour of sweetness. (Eph 5:2)

For *"sacrifice"*, or victim, the Vulgate uses *"hostiam"*, thus we call the Blessed Sacrament the Host. St Paul's phrase *"odour of sweetness"* recalls Noah's sacrifice, the first mention that *"the Lord smelled a sweet savour"* (Gen 8:21). The sweetness and Noah's name come from the same root, נוח, meaning "rest" or "repose", as in heavenly rest. This thought is worth holding onto: sacrifice has the scent of Heaven. Heaven smells of sacrifice. We will recognise it if we get there! Similar phrases occur for the odours of rams offered at the ordination of priests (Ex 29:18), the daily lambs (Ex 29:41), plus dozens of usages in Leviticus and Numbers literally meaning a tranquillising or *"soothing aroma"* (רֵיחַ־נִיחֹחַ) to the Lord. A sacrifice pleases and appeases God because the heart of the one offering ascends. Nothing is sweeter or more restful to God than Christ's Self-oblation and our sharing it, our entering in it.

Besides an altar and a victim, a sacrifice requires also a priest, in Latin *sacerdos*, meaning one who offers the sacred.[32] As Jesus is both Shepherd and Lamb, so He is both Priest and Victim, offering and being offered, in every Holy Mass as once on the Cross. St Augustine writes, "Christ Himself is both the priest who offers it and the victim: the sacred token of which He wished to be the daily Sacrifice of the Church."[33] Going one step further, the Divine Office praises "our Lord Jesus Christ, Who is Himself our Altar, our Victim, and our Priest".[34] The priest alone enters in to the altar to offer this sacrifice *in persona christi* (even if

---

[32] From *sacra* (sacred) + *dare* (to give, offer).

[33] St Augustine, *De civitate Dei*, X, 20. Also Council of Trent, Session XXII, 2 "the victim is one and the same, the same now offering by the ministry of priests who then offered Himself on the Cross, the manner alone of offering being different."

[34] Dedication of the Archbasilica of Our Holy Saviour, Matins, *Lectio* IV.

assisted by sacred ministers), but all the baptised are called to enter the mystery. St Thomas teaches:

'Every visible sacrifice is a sacrament, that is a sacred sign, of the invisible sacrifice.' Now the invisible sacrifice is that by which a man offers his spirit to God, according to Ps 50:19: *'A sacrifice to God is an afflicted spirit.'* Wherefore, whatever is offered to God in order to raise man's spirit to Him, may be called a sacrifice.[35]

Nothing repeatable brings our spirit to a loving contemplation of Christ's Sacrifice as fully as does Holy Mass, for it makes His offering present in reality and sign. A connection runs from the way that the paradigmatic OT offerings — a sheaf, a lamb, flour mixed with oil, wine (Lev 23:11-13) — were *"elevated together"* (Lev 14:24; 23:20), to Christ being elevated on the Cross, to the sacred species being elevated at Holy Mass, so that adoring Him our hearts may be elevated to Heaven. The Hebrew term used for *"elevated"* (נוּף) designates a "wave offering". The victim was held out successively to the four points of the compass, signifying it was offered to the God of all the earth. Thus the victim traced out the form of a Cross, anticipating that Sacrifice to be given to redeem the world. Even more expressively, the offering might be waved back and forth then heaved up and down — indicating a worldwide Cross connecting Heaven and earth.[36] In continuity with the Levite priests and Calvary, at the Offertory in Holy Mass the priest waves the bread and then the wine, elevating them to the Father, lowering them, then moving them east, west, north and south as a Cross reaching the whole world.[37]

This movement with the chalice is accompanied by the prayer: *Offerimus tibi, Domine*:

---

[35] St Thomas, *S.Th.* III Q.22 a.2.

[36] *Mishnah Menahot* 5:5-6 The priest "places the two loaves on top of the two lambs and places his two hands below the loaves and the lambs, extends the offerings to each of the four directions and brings them back, then raises and lowers them". The six directions indicate the whole cosmos. In Mass we avoid offering downwards.

[37] *Ritus servandus in celebratione Missæ*, VII *"elevatam... facit signum crucis"*.

We offer unto Thee, O Lord, the chalice of salvation, beseeching Thy clemency, that it may ascend before Thy divine Majesty, as a sweet savour, for our salvation, and for that of the whole world. Amen.

Evidently this offering has the power to come into the presence of God, to penetrate the Holy of Holies. Thereby each Mass it is capable of reaching the whole world. Its "sweet savour" ascends from earth to Heaven. From terrestrial altars the oblation of our hearts is "borne by the hands of Thy holy Angels to Thine altar on high".[38] The Cross connects earth to Heaven.

By this connection Holy Mass brings heavenly peace to human hearts and heavenly order to human society. The traditional Mass has an organising effect on the people who surround it and thereby on their social conditions, elevating civilisation. People who understand reality is sacrifice make better neighbours and more forgiving enemies. They build a better society.

In the Catholic Church this society is universal. The altar orientates everything by directing us to the holy place. Of all the world God selected Israel; the centre of the Holy Land was Jerusalem; the heart of Jerusalem the Temple; and the chief action in the Temple the offering of sacrifices to God on the altar. This crucial theme develops through the OT, involving great figures: Noah, Abraham, Moses, Solomon, Elijah. There is also development in the scale of the altar services and the culture of the priesthood designated for them. Yet God allowed it all to be suddenly taken away in AD 70. What now? How, o man, will you go to the altar of God? And Christian, for what sacrifice? Pope St Leo tells us that Christ:

> offering Himself to the Father a new and true sacrifice of reconciliation, was crucified not in the temple, whose worship was now at an end, and not within the confines of the city which for its sin was doomed to be destroyed, but outside,

---

[38] Canon of the Mass, *Supplices te rogamus.*

'*without the camp*' (Heb 13:12), that, on the cessation of the old symbolic victims, a new Victim might be placed on a new altar, and the Cross of Christ might be the altar not of the temple but of the world.[39]

Therefore, St Thomas preached that Holy Communion is "the sacrament in which is the term and final realisation of all sacrifices everywhere".[40] Despite the vast scale, Scripture gives us a description fit for God gathering and feeding all His children as tenderly as if

> *one little ewe lamb, which he had bought and nourished up… eating of his bread, and drinking of his cup, and sleeping in his bosom: and it was unto him as a daughter.* (2 Sam 12:3)

This food and drink God gives are to heal the mortal wound self-inflicted in Eden. It is the bread and cup of Him Who made Himself poor for our sake (2 Cor 8:9). In the sermon cited above St Thomas said:

> It is Thou, Who, recalling the memory of former marvels, hast, in this sacred food and supersubstantial bread, wonderfully found means and the way whereby, in the eating of the Lamb without spot or stain, they may be healed who, through the eating of the forbidden tree had been made sick…

Jesus ate of the Eucharist first to open the Way and encourage us. *"Out of the eater came something to eat"* (Jdg 14:14 RSVCE). This is not cannibalism, rather a manifestation of how God mingles His Spirit with ours. The more we return to God, the more He increases His own life in us. When we offer on His altar, that is when we accept our crosses, we are actually receiving.

Holy Communion unites us with the altar: *"Are not they that eat of the sacrifices partakers of the altar?"* (1 Cor 10:18). To be a *"partaker of the altar"* requires bearing whatever crosses God sends us (cf. Apoc 6:9), for Christ's altar was the Cross. We

---

[39] Pope St Leo I, *Homily VIII on the Passion*, 5.

[40] St Thomas, *Selected Writings, Sermon on Corpus Christi*.

cannot separate them. The *doctor angelicus* teaches that our altar "is representative of the Cross", writing of the *ara crucis* — "Altar of the Cross".[41] The Council of Trent adopted the same phrase.[42]

The fact that the Cross is spiritually available to everybody everywhere is symbolised in the marvellous spread of Catholic altars around the world. Each altar is beloved like the Cross which everyone kisses on Good Friday and wherefore in Holy Mass the priest reverently kisses the altar nine times.[43] Stable source of life and light, worthy is the altar to be kissed!

---

[41] St Thomas, *S.Th.* III Q.83 a.1 ad.2; and Corpus Christi, Matins, *Lectio* IV.

[42] Council of Trent, Session XXII, 1; and 2 "in this divine Sacrifice which is celebrated in the Mass, that same Christ is contained and immolated in an unbloody manner, who once offered Himself in a bloody manner on the altar of the Cross..."

[43] The nine kisses occur: upon ascending after the prayers at the foot of the altar; before the Collect; before the Offertory Prayer; before the *Orate fratres*; during the *Te igitur*; during the *Supplices te rogamus*; before the Post Communion; before the *Ite missæ est*; before the Last Blessing. In most cases he kisses the altar as a token of affection before briefly turning toward the faithful, as a 'goodbye' even of a few moments must be soothed. In a solemn Mass an additional kiss occurs before the Pax, for the peace of Christ comes from His altar.

The Light

Send forth thy light and thy truth

— Ps 42:3, Prayers at the Foot of the Altar

Candles are so vital to Holy Mass that the rubrics require at least two be lit at the altar.[44] Mass should not be said without them. Their arrangement, flanking the tabernacle, is alluded to when the priest prays at the foot of the altar: *"Send forth thy light and thy truth: they have conducted me, and brought me unto thy holy hill, and into thy tabernacles"* (Ps 42:3). The candles at Mass show the way up to the tabernacle by giving light and truth, the Psalm expressing visible and invisible realities. St Augustine comments:

> *Light* and *Truth* are two in name; the reality expressed is but One. For what else is the *Light* of God, except the *Truth* of God? Or what else is the *Truth* of God, except the *Light* of God? And the one Person of Christ is both of these. *'I am the Light of the world: he that believes in Me, shall not walk in darkness.' 'I am the Way, the Truth, and the Life.'* He is Himself *the Light*: He is Himself *the Truth*.[45]

The fittingness of identifying light and truth as one reality is manifested in multiple languages when we say "I see" to mean we understand something. To know the truth is to be enlightened.

---

[44] *Rubricæ generales Missalis*, XX.

[45] St Augustine, *Enarration on Ps 42*, 4.

To be ignorant is to be in the dark. The sensible perception of light is a metaphor for the spiritual apprehension of truth: *"The declaration of thy words giveth light: and giveth understanding to little ones"* (Ps 118:130). This is why candles belong to the altar: light is a primary truth. Creation, Scripture and Holy Mass, by testifying truly to light, serve to rescue us from darkness.

Light as Eternal Truth

The light and truth of Holy Mass are older than ancient. From eternity the Son of God is "Light from Light, true God from true God" (*Credo*). He is *"Light"* and He is *"true"*, the Word truly *"with God... in the beginning"* through Whom *"all things were made"* (Jn 1:1-3).

"And God said: Be light made. And light was made" (Gen 1:3). The created mirrors the uncreated, the temporal imitates the eternal. In eternity God speaks His Word, the Father generates His Son, and this reality within the Blessed Trinity is revealed in the very manner of creation. *"Fiat lux" "Be light made"*, was the first order; then, that *"light was made"* communicates this eternal procession insofar as it can be represented materially. An immense brightness containing all. Obviously the difference is infinite. Created light is negligible compared to the Eternal. Yet in our feeble finitude, even created light is too wonderful for us. Let us investigate some of its glories.

The Lord is constant: *"Jesus Christ, yesterday, and today; and the same for ever"* (Heb 13:8). Likewise light is constant, its speed is invariable (3×10^8 m/s). Nothing can overtake it. God created it to be so. According to Einstein, light does not experience time. Suitably, the priest, *in persona Christi*, should not wear a watch in Mass, nor should there be a clock in the sanctuary, for the Mass is timeless, a portal to eternity. Light propagates itself instantaneously as the Gospel fills the world rapidly. Correspondingly, acolytes carrying candles accompany the *evangeliarium* when it is processed and proclaimed in Mass, except on Good Friday when the light of the world went out (briefly).

Theologians, confronted with the data of revelation, deduced that Jesus Christ is the only Person with two natures. The Council of Nicaea (AD 325) dogmatically defined that Jesus is True God and True Man. Some 1,500 years later, physicists, confronted with the data of experimentation, were astonished to deduce the dual nature of light. It is truly a wave and truly a particle. Here we have an image of Christ. The wave, being everywhere at once, represents divinity; the particle, being local and knowing inertia, represents humanity. Supernatural realities are the blueprint for the natural. Creation reveals God.

In writing the book of nature, God made matter capable of being transformed into light ($E = mc^2$). Does this not declare humanity may aspire to divinity, that men are called to be conformed to Christ, even to be deified by seeing God in supernatural light, the beatific vision? What is more surprising: matter becoming light, or men becoming like God? Whether we have the wits to be astonished by the first, we ought to be lost in praise at the second. Supernatural light actually causes deification: *"We know that, when He shall appear, we shall be like to Him: because we shall see Him as He is"* (1 Jn 3:2).

Given that light represents Christ, then so does the sun. The Psalm declares: *"He hath set his tabernacle in the sun"* (Ps 18:5). We cannot gaze on God's glory without being overwhelmed, even dying. Correspondingly, we cannot stare at the sun without pain, even being blinded. So He conceals His glory to protect us. Without the sun there would be no life on earth. Without Christ there is no grace. The sun's light provides warmth and vision indefatigably. Christ is our inexhaustible source of charity and understanding. God created light to glorify Himself and to serve terrestrial life. Christ shows that glorifying God *is* the highest life and the purpose which all lower levels of life serve. With the moon and stars, as with Mary and the saints, the sun sings to God's glory in a language so fundamental it is innate to us:

The heavens shew forth the glory of God... Day to day uttereth speech, and night to night sheweth knowledge. There are no... languages, where their voices are not heard. (Ps 18:2-4)

Accepting that so much meaning is carried by light illumines the words: *"I will open my mouth in parables. I will speak about concepts that are from the beginning"* (Ps 77:2). A parable, in its widest sense, is a parallel in which a sensible thing conveys a spiritual meaning. Each of God's creative decrees, for example *"Let there be light"*, generates being which contains ontological truth. All things bear meaning which is a participation in the eternal *Logos*. Creation is a spectacular parable which speaks of Christ, of God. Different things tell of different aspects of the All in All. Parables conceal meaning which must be sought to be understood. They are told in a manner to awaken our curiosity, to engage our intelligence and our love. Maybe the most encompassing of these ontological parables is light.[46] It is the first and last, history's alpha and omega (Gen 1:3; Mt 24:27).

The first to see Christ's light shining in the darkness was Abraham (Gen 15:17). Afterwards, Moses was instructed to have the Menorah made, the seven-branched candlestick, to stand in the Holy Place of the tabernacle, a light hidden in the desert like the Son of God.[47] Centuries later, giving increase for the Temple in Jerusalem, the Menorah was multiplied: Solomon had ten more made (2 Chron 4:7), so that seventy-seven lights blazed in the sanctuary, saluting the Holy of Holies as the source of true light.[48]

---

[46] Light gives life, vision, warmth; it has the greatest speed, never slows, transcends time; it has a dual nature; and visible light is only a tiny fraction of an infinite electromagnetic spectrum, as Jesus' Humanity lives within His infinite Divinity.

[47] St Bede, *On the Tabernacle*, I, 9 (commenting on Ex 25:40) "For surely the pattern of the lampstand that he was to make was shown to Moses on a mountain because it was on the height of the most secret contemplation that he openly learned the manifold sacraments of Christ and the Church. Nevertheless, he was not able to bring them forth openly to the people whom he was instructing; instead, he signified them by means of a type through the form and the workmanship of the lampstand and its vessels, until such time as our Lord and Redeemer Himself might come in the flesh and disclose the inner meaning of that same form to His Church by conferring the grace of the Holy Spirit."

[48] *Menachot* 98 comments on 2 Chron 4:7-8, that the ten menoroth and ten tables Solomon had made were in addition to the original items. Thus eleven menoroth were lined up on the south side of the holy place, and eleven tables on the north side, five to the left and five to the right of the respective originals, such that the arrangement was in deep continuity with the layout in the tabernacle (see Ex 26:35).

By these God-given stages, the light increased in anticipation of the Eternal Light entering the world, Jesus Christ.[49]

That these lights of the OT signified the Son of God is suggested in that at least one lamp was to be kept burning *"always"* (Ex 27:20), *"a perpetual service and rite"* for Aaron and his generations, so there be light *"before the Lord continually"* (Lev 24:1-4). The trimming of wicks and frequent refuelling was a labour of love. The Temple is gone but as you read these words there are thousands of candles alight at Masses around the world and multiple times more sanctuary lamps testify to God's True Presence in the tabernacles. On this radiance we may reflect when we read God said: *"Be light made"* (Gen 1:3). Christ surrounds us.

Escape from Darkness

The Light and Truth of Christ lead us away from (*deduxerunt*) darkness and falsehood and bring us toward (*adduxerunt*) holiness and truth. Who else can lead us so but God? In the new creation, the Big Bang is not a theory but a fact. It happened two thousand years ago in Bethlehem when the Light of the World was born. This Light is Truth (Jn 8:12; 14:6). Jesus said:

> *For this I was born, and for this I came into the world: so that I may offer testimony to the truth. Everyone who is of the truth hears My voice.* (Jn 18:37 SB)

In nature light effortlessly dispels darkness. This illustrates the defeat of lies by truth, or the desolate flight of non-being before the magnificent advance of being. This story, of sin overcome by grace, plays out through history in much slower motion. Darkness is putting up a fight: the dread darkness which fell upon Abram as God cut a covenant (Gen 15:12); the darkness which fell upon the

---

[49] The Preface of the Blessed Virgin Mary praises her who "gave forth to the world the eternal Light [*lumen æternum*], Jesus Christ our Lord". The Preface of the Nativity lauds "the Mystery of the Word made flesh, the new light of Thy glory hath shone upon the eyes of our mind, so acknowledging God in visible form, we may through Him be drawn to love the Invisible."

Egyptians, full of horrors (Ex 10:21-23; 14:20; Wis 17:1-18:4); the darkness upon the earth at the Crucifixion. These signal the final darkness of the damned in hell. There darkness loses. It never had any chance, for *"the light shineth in darkness, and the darkness did not comprehend it"* (Jn 1:5). Darkness cannot understand truth, therefore it cannot *"comprehend"* (*"overcome"* Jn 1:5 RSVCE) the light. Darkness has had its day. Black holes are nature's illustrations for hell: inexorably shut in on themselves, time dilates to an excruciating standstill; gravity tears apart and crushes; out of which nothing can escape.

Escaping darkness on earth, *"children of light"* (Jn 12:35-36) *"walk in the light"* (1 Jn 1:7; cf. Jn 8:12; Eph 5:11-14; Is 9:2), guided by it into a state of holiness. So the candles at Mass may put us in mind not only of the Second Person of the Trinity but also the Third, the Holy Ghost. The ancient lamps were fuelled with *"the finest and dearest oil of olives"* upon *"the most pure candlestick"* (Lev 24:2-4) made of one piece of *"the finest gold"* (Ex 25:31-40). All these details speak of the Paraclete: oil, purity, unity in multiplicity, lustre, inestimable value, radiance and propagation (procession).[50] The sevenfold Gifts of the Holy Ghost (*sacrum septenarium*) are illustrated by the seven-branched candlestick (Apoc 4:5). This is recalled in Holy Mass by the central crucifix flanked by the Big Six, that is the large candles pointing heavenward. Ideally the seven are of the same polished metal and style, emphasising that Christ on the Cross is the centre and stem whence the Ghostly Gifts are poured upon man.

With light signifying divinity, the candles must be lit before Mass begins and may not be extinguished until it is over. This may symbolise the whole history of sacrifice taking place within the light of eternity. We could not enter this eternity if eternity did not first reach down to us. The words spoken at the beginning of

---

[50] St Gregory of Nyssa, *Life of Moses*, II, 181 "If you hear about lamps which have many branches coming out of one candlestick so that a full and brilliant light is cast all around, you would correctly conclude they are the varied rays of the Spirit which shine brightly in this tabernacle. To this Isaiah refers when he divides the lights of the Spirit into seven." Cf. Is 11:2-3. Visible light comprises a sevenfold spectrum.

Mass, *"emit thy light and thy truth"* (Ps 42:3), are echoed after the end when the Last Gospel professes that Jesus *"Erat lux vera..."* *"was the true light"*. The *"light"* and *"truth"* sent forth by God are one *"true light, which enlighteneth every man that cometh into this world"* (Jn 1:9). The end recalls the beginning.

Evil, too, was flagged at the beginning of Mass: *"ab homine iniquo et doloso erue me"* — *"deliver me from the unjust and deceitful man"* (Ps 42:1). The Last Gospel observes that worldly men refuse to recognise and receive Jesus, Who

> *was in the world, and the world was made by Him, and the world knew Him not. He came unto His own, and His own received Him not.* (Jn 1:10-11)

They shut their eyes or blind their hearts to Christ. Setting out we ask: *"why art thou sad, O my soul, and why dost thou disquiet me?"* (Ps 42:5). We are sad because the world rejected the Son of God and killed Him; and we are sad because we do not know how far we are guilty of the same ourselves. Therefore we ask at the beginning to be delivered of the *"unjust and deceitful man"*, because we want in the end to be counted, as the Last Gospel puts it, among those who received Him, the sons who believed Him:

> *as many as received Him, He gave them power to be made the sons of God, to them that believe in His Name. Who are born... of God.* (Jn 1:12-13)

How shall we believe? The Last Gospel reminds us that St John the Baptist *"was sent from God... to give testimony of the light, that all men might believe through him..."* (Jn 1:6-7). He told us: *"Behold the Lamb of God"*. In Mass we can do this: the *lux vera* is to be apprehended (seen) and believed (because it is true).

Of the saintly Baptist it is said: *"This man came for a witness"* (Jn 1:7). Elsewhere, *"candlesticks"* are the Lord's *"witnesses"* (Apoc 11:3-4). Like John, the candles are witnesses, constantly, with their light, to the truth Who *"walks in the midst of the seven golden lampstands"* (Apoc 2:1). Jesus is there, at the altar. In the end, in the light of eternity, we will understand the beginning.

Mass is our rehearsal for eternity, to learn adoration. We are given many opportunities to grow. We dare not enter eternity as stillborn. It is up to us. St John the Baptist testified to *"the Light of the World"* (Jn 1:8-9), *"the Lamb of God"* (Jn 1:29,36). In God this Lamb is the true Temple and unfailing Light of Heaven:

> *And I saw no temple in the city, for its temple is the Lord God the Almighty and the Lamb. And the city has no need of sun or moon to shine upon it, for the glory of God is its light, and its lamp is the Lamb. By its light... there shall be no night there.* (Apoc 21:22-25 RSVCE)

We must wait until Heaven to see this. But we need not wait to believe it. The elements of light, lamb, altar and cross, though various in this world, coincide in eternity. They are all aspects of Jesus Christ, the *Logos*, the true Word. They are *"parables spoken from the beginning"*. Christ unites what seems separate. When we see Who the Son is, and know in ourselves what He has done, His work, we will realise He unites in Himself not only these four elements, but all things. Eternity literally lives in Him. We see this by faith, especially at Holy Mass.

β) The Immutable Pattern
of the Mass

From the beginning, I announce the last things,
and from the start, the things that have not yet been done,
saying: My plan will stand firm, and my entire will shall be done.
— Is 46:10 SB

Everything visible shows the invisible. The highest reality, Heaven, is so full that, rather than being represented by this thing or that thing, it is better indicated in the relations between elements, the pattern they present. To this end, there is a place chosen by God for the most important events of history and even of creation. The series of events all had aspects of the fullness until the invisible fullness happened there in full view: the divine Self-sacrifice, the Crucifixion.

For us to perceive the immutable pattern we must arrive in Jerusalem, but naturally not that city on earth, rather the heavenly Jerusalem. We spy it from the mountain top (Apoc 21:10). This mountain requires a spiritual ascent. There, as for Moses on Sinai, God shows us the pattern of Heaven: portrayed then to the Hebrews by the tabernacle and today to mankind by Holy Mass.

In our short life here below, we seek the place, to ascend the mountain, to enter the tabernacle, finally to see the Blessed Trinity, living forever. For continuity: the place, the mountain and the tabernacle all share the pattern of the Blessed Trinity.

The Place

ad altare Dei... ad altare Dei... ad altare Dei...
— Antiphon and Psalm, Prayers at the Foot of the Altar

Certain roots of the Mass we have seen are exceedingly long. Altars were built by the first generations. Light was creation's first word. The Cross stands in the first sentence of the Bible. The Lamb was *"foreknown indeed before the foundation of the world"* (1 Pet 1:20).

All the roots are arranged to form a perfect system. We began with particulars to help us understand the whole. A comparison now of the parts reveals an immutable pattern behind everything, our attention drawn to it by "the place". At first, it is best not to try too hard to pin down where or what "the place" is. We may begin with a simple, geographical understanding: Jerusalem. But this is too limited. We progress to a spiritual understanding: God meeting man in the City of Peace. But this is too abstract. Better to combine both in an incarnational understanding — there are real places on earth which connect us with the eternal, with the Self-sacrificial God: namely, consecrated altars. The perfect link of these three perspectives on "the place" (Jerusalem, God-with-man and the altar of sacrifice) is Jesus Christ crucified.

The phrase *"introibo ad altare Dei"* is said three times during the Prayers at the Foot of the Altar. The Psalm was written with Jerusalem in mind and the Church emphasises this phrase because *"the altar of God"* remains decisive. It is "the place" (or adjacent to it). There is an unbreakable continuity about this place, an irrevocable divine decision, the most long-standing tradition conceivable. This place is so foundational that the long series of pivotal events which occurred here in preparation for the Crucifixion stretch back to the first moment of creation itself. In the fullness of time, the original location, a geographical identity, was translated by the Crucifixion into a universal foundation for a new creation so that the whole world has access to it. We reach it through the altar of God at Holy Mass.

"The place" — or to use its blessed Hebrew name, הַמָּקוֹם (*HaMakom*) — is a garden, a field, a mountain, a City, the house of God, the Temple, an altar, the Holy of Holies. These all carry rich theological meaning which we may glean from the events which happened there. Before the Passion, this location, *HaMakom*, was the place of God's Presence. Since the Passion, wherever God is present to meet with man, we may say *there* is the place.

For sceptical readers who doubt what follows is true, there arises a greater conundrum of explaining how the claims about this place ever arose. Satisfying Occam's razor, the simplest answer is that they are historically accurate. But supposing they are not, it is still more incredible that the rabbis who reject Jesus Christ as Messiah and Son of God should be doing more than any others — even Catholic apologists — to honour the long history and future expectation of precisely this place, given that finally it all testifies to the importance of Jesus Christ. Nine tremendous events happened here, each deciphering an aspect of an infinitely greater tenth event which came after them *at the same place*. That tenth event, the most decisive moment in history, the Crucifixion, touches everything.

Geographically speaking, the place is Jerusalem or its vicinity. Our first reaction to the claim that all the events outlined below happened here might be: How can such things possibly be known?[51] I will endeavour to give supporting arguments, mostly from the Scriptures but also from rabbis. The most organised proponent for this thesis is the Temple Institute (TI),[52] though of course they are silent about the Crucifixion. After contemplating the unity and Christocentric implications of all these events, I hope the reader, like me, will ask: How could it not be so?

Meanwhile, Christians need not believe that these events are all supposedly pinpointed on the same eight-figure grid reference. Rather it is the generic unity of the place that matters: Jerusalem and its environs. The precise location of the Temple is not

---

[51] The erection of the Cross on Calvary and the building of the Temple by Solomon both occurred, obviously, in Jerusalem. This is also the place where Abraham bound his beloved son, Isaac, in perhaps the most moving prefiguration of the Crucifixion. And this is the place of Adam's burial, Golgotha. These facts are generally accepted by believers. Proceeding to less evident claims, it is the place where both Adam and Eve were created, close to the Tree of Life. It is the *"field"* where innocent Abel was murdered. It is the *"field"* where Isaac first saw his bride Rebekah. Three more events are said to have happened here, although these are difficult to demonstrate. Rabbis attest it is the place where Jacob dreamt of a ladder reaching Heaven. They also say this is the place where Noah built an altar to God in gratitude for being saved from the deluge of death. Encompassing all, the rabbis teach it is the place where creation itself began.

[52] The Temple Institute, founded in 1987 and based in Jerusalem, is devoted to the rebuilding of the stone Temple on Temple Mount precisely where the Dome of the Rock currently stands, and then the re-establishment of animal sacrifices there according to the laws Moses gave in the *Torah*. The TI are much quoted in this book, as they articulate well what Judaism seeks. When the antichrist comes, he will take his seat in the rebuilt Temple. Does this mean those working to rebuild the Temple work for the antichrist? For many, not willingly, I think. But once they realise he has deceived them, and taken away from them everything for which they have laboured, and expects them to worship him, then who knows if many who have misdirected their efforts will not convert and become great saints?

identical with that of the Crucifixion, but they were within sight of each other.[53]

With this allowance in mind, we are ready to examine how the nine OT events can be said to have occurred in the same place. We begin with the most obvious, the Temple, and journey back in time from there. Afterwards we consider the specific connection each event has with the Crucifixion, and what this means for continuity in Holy Mass as we trace its roots back to Paradise.

Solomon's Temple

Solomon built the Temple one thousand years before the Crucifixion. Scripture tells us the location for it was designated by God Himself, a place with a crucial historical pedigree:

> *And Solomon began to build the house of the Lord, in Jerusalem on Mount Moria, as it had been shown to David his father, at the place [HaMakom] which David had prepared on the threshing floor of Ornan the Jebusite. (2 Chron 3:1)*

No one could think it an accident where the Holy of Holies was built, where God's Presence dwelt among men. *"Jerusalem"* is the Holy City. *"Mount Moria"* is where Isaac was bound. David *"prepared"* this place for holocausts (cf. 1 Chron 21:29-22:2). Being a *"threshing floor"*, it signified trial and judgement, where wheat is separated from chaff. All these factors anticipate the Crucifixion, as the reader can easily verify.

Place matters. Christians rightly think that God is everywhere.[54] But Catholics know how privileged a place is the tabernacle above the altar, where God is substantially present. This local concentration of God's Presence is prefigured in the

---

[53] A deeper analysis might identify the locations of the Holy of Holies in the Temple and the Cross of Crucifixion as those of the Tree of Knowledge and the Tree of Life, both intentionally planted by God in the Garden, Who does nothing without truth.

[54] St Thomas, *S.Th.* I, Q.8 a.3, teaches with precision that God is everywhere: by His Presence (all is laid bare to His inspection); by His Essence (as cause); by His Power (to which all is subject); and also by grace in His Saints.

Holy of Holies. God told Solomon that He is particularly attentive to prayers made at His House:

> *I have chosen this place to myself for a house of sacrifice... If my people, upon whom my name is called, being converted, shall make supplication to me, and seek out my face, and do penance for their most wicked ways: then will I hear from heaven, and will forgive their sins... My eyes also shall be open and my ears attentive to the prayer of him that shall pray in this place. For I have chosen, and have sanctified this place, that my name may be there for ever, and my eyes and my heart may remain there perpetually.* (2 Chron 7:12-16)

God's Name *is* there for ever. His eyes and heart *do* remain there perpetually. But to understand where "there" is, we must rise from a geographical idea to a spiritual. In this place God says prayers are heard because penitential sacrifice is offered and the moral life pursued. Contemplating the continuity of events at *HaMakom* guides us to identify that the perfect sacrifice and perfect morality, better than Solomon's, are those of Jesus Christ.

Failure to admit that the Crucifixion fulfils the Temple's activities risks confining religion to a single locality, sacrifices to materiality, morality to dead letters. On the other hand, dismissing the place and its history — as if we can ignore what God has fixed — risks making religion formless, sacrifices non-existent and morality subjective, relative, empty. We need both the incarnate reality and the transcendent truth. Both are necessary constituents of Holy Mass.

Jacob's Ladder

Hundreds of years before the Temple was built, the Patriarch Jacob woke up in this area knowing that it was the House of God.

> *And when he was come to a certain place [HaMakom], and would rest in it after sunset, he took of the stones that lay there [HaMakom], and putting under his head, slept in the same place [HaMakom].* (Gen 28:11)

Orthodox rabbis connect the place with other key events, linking the stone(s) Jacob took for a pillow with the Foundation Stone:

> …the very same Foundation Stone upon which the Ark of the Covenant rests in the Holy of Holies in the Holy Temple on Mount Moriah in Jerusalem! And the expression *HaMakom* — *The Place* — refers to none other than the place of the Holy Temple… Having dreamed of a ladder planted firmly on the earth and extending to the heavens, with angels ascending and descending, *Yaakov* couldn't have been more on the mark in his realization upon wakening, that this place, this same place where *Avraham* bound his son *Yitzchak* upon G-d's command, and where *Noach* and *Cain* and *Abel* and *Adam* and *Chava* all built their altars in previous generations, was the House of G-d, the property of HaShem.[55]

The *Torah* tells us Jacob called the place *"Beth-el"* (House of God), which before had been called *"Luza"* (Gen 28:19). This lay thirteen miles north of Jerusalem. It seems we need to grant some latitude to accept Jacob's dream as occurring at *"the place"*. But the TI insists that "the very spot that *Yaakov* had laid his head" was later the Holy of Holies on "the Temple Mount".[56]

It is fascinating that orthodox Judaism insists on connecting Jacob's dream with Jerusalem. If we know that Jacob's sleep denoted the Passion of Christ, that the ladder of his visionary dream means the Cross (hence Jacob's fear), that the *"House of God"* means the Church and that the stone Jacob anointed on rising represents Catholic altars, then we may be amazed by what the rabbi teaches about it all:

> We certainly understand *Yaakov's* fright, terrified that one moment he had absolutely no knowledge of where he was and that the next moment he knew exactly where he was: in the

---

[55] TI 6/12/2019. "Chava" is Eve.

[56] TI 2/12/2022. The passage also points to Christ (unintentionally) by going on to say that Jacob had "the first of a series of dreams that changed the course of history, not only for the children of *Avraham*, *Yitzchak* and *Yaakov*, but for all of humanity".

very beating heart of creation — but even more — in the very reason and purpose and inspiration for creation! G-d revealed to *Yaakov* a ladder that binds heaven to earth, that makes G-d, the Creator and Shaper of destinies, approachable, within reach, visible within the mind's eye and the heart's desire. Creation, all of it — its beginning and its conclusion — was all here, focused and concentrated in a simple rock... from this time forth would be known as the Foundation Stone, because in this simple, unimposing rock was the DNA of all creation... *'The place'* — in Hebrew, *HaMakom*... is the very heart and soul of existence — where created man dwells with Creator, where limitless heaven descends to finite earth, and finite earth ascends to the limitless heavens.[57]

O, that Christians would have such an elevated view of Christ, the Rock, Who recapitulates the whole of creation! Should it not pierce our conscience, that some Jews have more wonder for a rock than we Christians have for Christ (cf. Mk 13:1-2)?

Rebekah's Apocalypse

Rabbinic Judaism involves reading the entire *Torah* in Sabbath segments on an annual cycle. The portion about Abraham binding his son Isaac, the *Akeidah* (Gen 22), is followed the next week by Isaac's providential encounter with his bride Rebekah (Gen 24). There are solid reasons to believe the two events happened at the same place.[58]

---

[57] TI 12/11/2021.

[58] Before he met Rebekah, Isaac dwelt far to the south in Beerlahairoi (Gen 24:62). Likely he had news of Abraham's arrangements to find him a wife, and may have travelled up to Beersheba to see his father, and then continued north to encounter the bridal party. Rebekah was travelling southwards from Mesopotamia (Gen 24:10) and she did not delay (Gen 24:55-59), making Moriah a credible meeting point. Furthermore, Isaac stopped to *"meditate"* (Gen 24:63). Where better for Isaac to pause to enter prayer and mourn the loss of his mother than the place of his binding, remembering how he willingly put his own life in God's Hands? And as God had organised the entire success of mission to find Rebekah (Gen 24:42-51), it were a small thing for God to fix the location for their first encounter at the most meaningful place on the planet.

The first event — the Binding — signifies the Sacrifice of Calvary from the aspect of its cause, namely, the Father's willingness to sacrifice His Son, as seen in Abraham's willingness to sacrifice Isaac. The second event — Isaac mourning the loss of his mother and for the first time embracing his wife — is the Sacrifice of Calvary too, but considered in its effect. The death of Sarah represents the passing of the Old Covenant while the union with Rebekah signifies the establishment of the New. Cause and effect are intrinsically linked.

The TI explain that that it was necessary that it be in the same *place* where Isaac was interiorly transformed by his near-death binding that "he would meet his bride *Rivka* for the very first time", for this *place* of God's intimate presence was the ultimate context of their union, for by God's design it was by his meeting with Rebekah (*Rivka*) that Isaac "would create and shape the destiny of the children of *Avraham*".[59]

Indeed in this *place* not one but two new nations were created and their destinies shaped. First there was Israel, biological descendants of Abraham. Then came Christians, spiritual descendants of Abraham. After Isaac met Rebekah, he unveiled her so that she become mother of his children (Gen 24:65-67). An unveiling is an "apocalypse", a revelation. What does Rebekah whisper? In this place the Virgin Mary was declared Mother of God's children (*"ecce mater tua"* Jn 19:27).

Genesis gives gentle hints of the Crucifixion. In a rich line we read Isaac went *"forth to meditate in the field, the day being now well spent: and when he had lifted up his eyes..."* (Gen 24:63). *"[T]o meditate in the field"* can mean "to pray outside the city", as Jesus crucified; *"the day being now well spent"* recalls Jesus' death at the ninth hour; and *"when he had lifted up his eyes"* suggests a liturgical context, the Mass also recalling Jesus' constant regard for Heaven.

As Jesus looked to Heaven, Mary looked to Jesus. Hence Rebekah sensed tremendous significance in *"the man"*. She

---

[59] TI 14/11/2014.

asked, *"'Who is that man who cometh towards us along the field?' [The servant answered] her: 'That man is my master'"* (Gen 24:65). But the servant's master was Abraham, so who is this? The word for *"master"* is *dominus*, κύριός, אָדוֹן, all titles for the Lord God. Here it was Isaac. But it would be heedless to exclude a far deeper sense. Rebekah is looking for her Messiah: *"for one is your master, Christ"* (Mt 23:10; cf. Jn 13:13).

Now why are we told twice that Isaac met Rebekah in *"a field"* (Gen 24:63,65)? We gain a clue when Isaac afterwards says: *"Behold the smell of my son is as the smell of a plentiful field, which the Lord hath blessed"* (Gen 27:27). Ostensibly Isaac was saying this about his son Esau. But Rebekah knew it was their son Jacob dressed as Esau, wearing his goatskins. Here the son Jacob signifies Jesus, the scapegoat, putting on not only our humanity but taking on our sins.[60] This is the most fragrant offering for God. Christ *"gave himself up for us, a fragrant offering and sacrifice to God"* (Eph 5:2 RSVCE).

The rabbi finds the fragrance of Rebekah's son to be timeless. He writes that it the father's discriminating nostrils it signifies Jacob's "spiritual essence". We may think of God the Father knowing the souls of His sons. Yet the mystical field which the father smells in this son is not the profane hunting ground of Esau, nor of the dead animals whose skins Jacob is wearing, but according as the Jewish "sages opine, the fragrance of the Garden of Eden — the fragrance of man's eternal covenant with HaShem!"[61]

Jacob bears the fragrance of Eden, likened to an eternal Covenant! Translated, this means Jesus has the odour of Paradise, cutting that eternal Covenant on Calvary.

---

[60] For the scapegoat ceremony (Lev 16:15-22) one goat was slaughtered and another released into the wilderness to die. Reportedly, one year the scapegoat found its way back to Jerusalem, which was contrary to the desired symbolism, as it seemed to bring the peoples' sins back to them. So in subsequent years the Levite who took the scapegoat out to the wilderness would be sure to 'release' it over the edge of a cliff, ensuring that it would never return. Except Jesus did, and will.

[61] TI 5/11/21.

Does it mean Jacob smelt of flowers and fruit trees? Yes, but spiritually understood this is the scent of saints (flowers) and the holiness of Heaven (fruit trees). The pleasing aroma of Jacob, the son, reminds Isaac, the father, of where he first united with Rebekah, mother of Israel. It is where Adam rejoiced to see Eve, mother of all the living. It is where Jesus' Heart burst for Mary, Mother of the Church. All these couples are interconnected.

Ultimately all people who love are connected with the Cross. Every act of charity unites us to the Tree of Life. Meanwhile Isaac's life shows that though love may be marital, first it must be sacrificial.

Isaac's Akeidah

The surpassing importance of Gen 22, describing Abraham's willingness to sacrifice his beloved son Isaac, is indicated by it being read every morning by pious Jews in their prayers, mirroring faithful Catholics who assist every morning at Mass. The subject of both is mystically one. The *Akeidah* is a prefiguration of the Crucifixion. The imagery, once seen, cannot be unseen. Father and only-begotten son, the wood of the sacrifice, the fire, the angel, the ram, the crown of thorns, the Covenant. Most tellingly, both events happened at the same place: Mount Calvary is part of Mount Moriah.[62]

Here, the three great Patriarchs — Abraham, Isaac and Jacob — had momentous mystical experiences, each uniquely connected with the Crucifixion, even though that would not be seen until long afterwards:

> For all three patriarchs it was a *place* of unprecedented fear and uncertainty, for all three an excruciating test of faith. For all three it was only their total trust in G-d that brought them to *the place* and that sent them from *the place* strengthened

---

[62] In Abraham's day, Moriah was an extensive area which encompassed Calvary, before the distinct peaks were specified. The Book of Jubilee, from the Jewish apocrypha, conscious of offering a different tradition, says Abraham offered Isaac on Mount Zion, not Mount Moriah. In any case, both mountains are in Jerusalem.

and determined to move forward with G-d in His plan for the future. Our sages tell us that *the place* for *Avraham* was a mountain, distant and foreboding, for *Yitzchak*, a meadow, serene and contemplative, and for *Yaakov*, a house, a *place* where G-d and his children could meet together, in every generation, forever...[63]

Is this not how Catholics experience the Cross? First fear and a test of faith, then trust and rising from the ordeal strengthened, all for the unique formation we receive by it — even if we do not understand it!

As a Catholic priest I am awed by the Church Fathers. But how many Christians ever wrote about this *place* with as much reverence as this rabbi, even though we know our Saviour's Sacrifice took place there? How many Saints ever wrote about Abraham, Isaac and Jacob so personally as [I think] Rabbi Chaim Richman, with so much insight born of long study and meditation? How many Christians believe of the Crucifixion what the rabbi believes of the *Akeidah*, namely its power to unite God with His People?

The unnamed author writes that Abraham's act of total dedication on Moriah would bind him forever to God and to the *place*, as also forever binding Isaac to God and the *place*, and likewise all Abraham's descendants through his beloved son. This corresponds beautifully to Calvary. Substitute Abraham for God the Father, Isaac for His Son Jesus, and his descendants' connection to that *place* for Catholics at Holy Mass. It all fits. The more the rabbi writes, the more the connections multiply:

> Where was '*the place*' that G-d sent *Avraham*... and why did the *akeidah* — the binding of *Yitzchak* — have to take place precisely there?... '*On the third day, Avraham lifted up his eyes and saw the place from afar*' (Gen 22:4). What was it that *Avraham* saw that identified that distant hill as '*the place*'.

---

[63] TI 14/11/2014. "[T]hree different sets of circumstances by which they found themselves in *the place*: by commandment [Abraham], by prayer [Isaac] and by Divine appointment [Jacob]."

Was it something fraught with horror, something unlike anything he had ever beheld before? Or was it something dimly familiar, a vision of comfort, that told him *this is the place?*... Ultimately *Avraham*... knew that G-d's test for him was one that would validate his lifelong search for truth. *'And an angel of Hashem called to him from heaven and said, "Avraham! Avraham!"'* And he said, *'Here I am'* (Gen 22:11). *Avraham* knows who he is and he knows where he is. This is the very place where G-d called out to *Adam*, and said, *'Where are you?'* and Adam answered, *'I am hiding'* (Gen 3:9). *Adam* was hiding because he failed to keep the one commandment G-d had entrusted him with. But *Avraham*, who kept to the minutest detail the commandment G-d had given him... answered loud and clear, *'Here I am'*... Clearly understanding the nature of this covenant he has now entered into with G-d, *Avraham* has a new name for the Garden of Eden... Hashem sees me and I see Hashem! (Gen 22:14) No longer does my iniquity create a dissonance between us. This revelation is the foundation stone for the altar that will stand before the Holy Temple bringing together the G-d of Avraham and the children of Avraham. It is in precisely this place that we are the Adam that G-d created, capable and dedicated to fulfilling G-d's command.[64]

Amazing! This is the place where the dissonance of iniquity is overcome, where an altar will stand uniting God with Abraham's children, repairing Adam's fall. What should surprise us more: that rabbis do not make the connection with Christ, or that Catholics do not connect the Mass with the *Akeidah* and the Garden of Eden? The continuity is unbroken. The connections are beyond counting.

The devoted rabbi writes that Isaac "was bound on the rock — the foundation stone of the world which would become the place of the Holy of Holies".[65] How close are Jews and Catholics and

---

[64] TI 7/11/2014.

[65] TI 1/11/2013.

how far! On the same spot but infinitely separated. It is not Isaac's binding and surviving which undoes Adam's fall but Jesus Christ's Death and Resurrection. It is not in Eden we learn to love but now on Calvary. It is not Abraham who links man with God but God's Son Himself is our Emmanuel. It is not the Foundation stone nor Temple altar which unites God with all His children but the one and myriad altars of Holy Mass.

Noah's Altar

Immediately after reading in Genesis that Noah and the animals disembarked from the ark, we read that Noah *"built an altar unto the Lord and offered holocausts upon"* it (Gen 8:20). Can we say where?

> Torah teaches us that G-d's chosen place on Mount Moriah was a central place of worship from the beginning of time: The waters of the Great Flood have receded, and *Noach* and his sons make their way to Mt. Moriah to bring a special offering to HaShem... According to Rabbinic tradition, this altar was built on Mt. Moriah in the same place where Adam had built his altar... (The olive trees seen in the illustration reflect the tradition of our sages that the olive branch brought to the ark by the dove was brought from the 'Mount of Anointment' — that is, the Mount of Olives in the vicinity of Jerusalem.)[66]

This leaves me stunned. That Noah, who saved the world from being totally defeated by death, should erect his altar to the Lord on the self-same mountain where Jesus would be raised on the Cross to save the world from death for ever! That the dove should bring the branch from the same Mount of Anointing whence Jesus ascended to send the Holy Ghost, Who is dove and anointing. That Noah, who became the new father of all men as Adam had been, offered his sacrifice where Jesus, by Whom we are born anew, would offer His sacrifice.

---

[66] TI article with illustration 4/11/2020.

For readers who are not yet convinced by the jaw-dropping mystical connection between Noah and Jesus, which renders the intentionality of God's arrangement undeniable, it is not necessary to prove that Noah built his altar at the place where Christ was to be crucified. What is significant is that orthodox rabbis claim it, even writing that the *"Torah teaches"* it. To follow their arguments one must look at the prestige of the *place* in the Bible as a whole. These who convincingly connect this place with several stupendous events preceding the Crucifixion, events which interpret it profoundly, are the very same who most strongly deny the significance of the Crucifixion itself. This should convince any reader that the whole is no contrivance of Christians or Jews but a work of God, Whom all serve whether they will or not.

Nevertheless, a few considerations might ease objections to the claim that Noah built his altar on Mount Moriah. It is widely held that, after the Flood, Noah's ark landed on Mount Ararat in Armenia. Did Noah and his family really walk one thousand miles to Jerusalem before building an altar of thanksgiving? It seems they did. Perhaps on exiting the ark everyone was elated, exhausted, disoriented? Perhaps the animals were not in the best condition after their confinement and needed to breed so that fresh ones could be had for the holocaust? That Genesis follows one statement (leaving the ark) with the other (building the altar) does not exclude an intermission but suggests a connection in meaning. Noah's sacrifice was to give thanks for salvation, to recognise the God of Life Who abated the Flood. It was a new beginning for mankind. The most appropriate place to celebrate this was the place of the first beginning, Eden. Unknown to Noah, God also intended it be the place of the greatest new beginning, the Passion and Resurrection of Christ. This is the perfect place for God to bring Noah to offer his holocaust, the vinedresser who saved all life on earth by means, like Jesus, of *"contemptible wood"*.[67]

---

[67] *"when water destroyed the earth, wisdom healed it again, directing the course of the just by contemptible wood"* (Wis 10:4).

Another corroborating detail: Abraham gave tithes to Melchisedech (Gen 14:18-20) when Melchisedech was King of Salem, that is of the location where later would arise Jerusalem ("Foundation of Peace").[68] Fascinatingly, Jewish tradition and Church Fathers concur that Melchisedech was none other than Noah's son, Shem. The dates work perfectly, as does the role of Shem — that is, Melchisedech — preserving the sacred memory of the beginnings of the world, of keeping Adam's grave (Golgotha), which information and task he passed on to Abraham, our father in faith. The point here is that if Noah's son Shem settled after the Flood in Salem, later Jerusalem, to serve there as priest, then it is quite conceivable that it was here before the Flood that Shem assisted his father in priestly work, offering sacrifices. Indeed, was there any place more apt than Adam's grave to express gratitude to God that, despite our sins, death has not had the final word? God arranges all things well.

Adam's Skull

Abraham knew Adam's burial place because he met there with its custodian, Melchisedech, also known as Shem, Noah's son. Noah knew the place because Adam's own son, Seth, surely showed him. In any case, Shem was certain because it was confirmed to him by Adam's old friend Methuselah. Adam's grave was an important place to all these men in an age when ancestry mattered. Shem, the first Semite, ensured the place where the head of the human race was buried would never be forgotten — "the place of the skull". In Aramaic: *Golgotha*.[69]

Forty generations later all four Gospels recorded that Jesus was crucified at *"the place of the skull"*, in Latin *Calvaria, Calvary*.[70] That the Church understands Jesus died where Adam is buried is attested to also by ancient icons of the Crucifixion

---

[68] CBN News, 10/7/19 *Archaeologist Says a Stone Pillar in the City of David is Where Abraham Met Melchizedek.*

[69] As it were in gratitude, Holy Mass keeps the memory of Shem alive forever, recalling him — Melchisedech — in the Canon with Abraham and Abel.

[70] Mt 27:33; Mk 15:22; Lk 23:33; Jn 19:17.

which depict Jesus' Precious Blood running down into the rock to reach Adam's bones and redeem him. Today Adam's grave may be visited underneath Calvary in the Church of the Holy Sepulchre in Jerusalem.[71]

Were Adam and Eve not *"cast out"* of the Garden (Gen 3:24)? Yes indeed. More to the point, Paradise was cast out from the earth: παράδεισος (LXX), that state of perfection, of præternatural friendship with God, was withdrawn from man. The geographical location remained but fell into corruption as elsewhere: bringing forth thorns, witnessing death, no longer self-irrigating. How Adam and his wife must have missed it we can scarcely imagine, they who alone among men knew the before and after of sin. It makes sense that in a spirit of reparation they would seek out the place.

The Bible does not say explicitly that Adam made an offering to God after losing Eden by rejecting God's Will, but Judaism holds it to be deep in the 'memory' of Adam's children that he did. Significantly, this was not a response to a new commandment of God, but Adam's own initiative, an "unsolicited gesture toward God, born out of man's longing to… return to the intimacy of his first life-receiving encounter with God".[72] If we wish to avoid notions of a common memory, we can focus instead on man's longing for integration in the divine, in nature and in himself.

In any case, the Temple Institute teaches that the altar on which Adam offered his sacrifices was the Foundation Stone:

> the place of the stone altar, the very place upon which *Adam* was created and upon which he made his first offering to G-d, is itself the very foundation of our memory of who we are.[73]

---

[71] Rabbinic traditions which emerged in the centuries after Christ claim Abraham discovered the bodies of Adam and Eve in the double cave overlooking Mamre. Realising this was the entrance to the Garden of Eden, Abraham chose this place for the burial of his wife Sarah (Gen 23:19) and himself (Gen 25:9). [*Babylonian Talmud, Eruvin* 53a, 6.] Some of these stories are beautiful, but fantastical. The link of Golgotha with Adam is older and theologically more credible.

[72] TI 23/3/2018.

[73] TI 14/3/2014.

The Jewish teaching indicates Adam found his way back to the place where it all began. It seems realistic that Adam and Eve would have wandered in search of their paradise lost, and finding the place if not the pleasures, would have squared up to their sin so as to carry out their religious observance in the place. If they settled hereabouts, their children would learn it was the place to seek or wait for God. Indeed there are hints which connect Seth, Abel and Cain with the place.

If it were on the Foundation Stone that Adam made offerings to God, and around here that his children grew up, then it seems plausible that Adam chose the same environ for the place of his burial, if not under the altar stone itself, then in sight of it — that is, if not on Temple Mount, then on Golgotha. Is this where his son Abel had died? Would Adam not choose a meaningful place?

Jesus chose the time and manner of His death. He chose the place too. With all the earth before Him, it makes sense that God's Firstborn went directly to save God's first-made man. As His brother's keeper, He sought out lost Adam and rescued him. Now He seeks us at Holy Mass, the place of our vivification.

Abel's Death

The first person to die was so like Jesus that the full parallel is arresting. Although the Bible has only a few lines about Abel, still, almost everything we do hear about him points to the Son of God. Like Jesus, Abel is a son of Adam, he is just, a good shepherd who offers God a lamb in sacrifice. Due to envy he is led out to the field and murdered unresisting by his unrepentant brother. His blood cries out to Heaven. In all this Abel points to the Incarnate Son of God.[74]

---

[74] Abel *"was a shepherd"* (Gen 4:2); Jesus is *"the Good Shepherd"* (Jn 10:11). Jesus calls Abel *"just"* (δίκαιος, *justus*, Mt 23:35; Heb 11:4), while Jesus is Himself the Just One (δίκαιος, *justus*, 1 Jn 2:1; Wis 2:12; Is 51:5; 53:11). Truly Abel was a just man; the Lord Jesus, True God, is Justice itself (Est 14:7; Ps 10:8; 1 Cor 1:30). Abel was murdered by his brother (Gen 4:8-16); Jesus by His brothers (Acts 7:52). Scripture tells us Abel's sacrifice was pleasing to the Lord (Gen 4:4) and that *"the voice of [his] blood cries out to [God] from the earth"* (Gen 4:10), while Jesus' Blood cries out *"more eloquently than Abel's"* (Heb 12:24).

In this light, and appreciating the significance of *the place*, *HaMakom*, we are sensitised to the possibility that Abel breathed his last at the same location that Jesus Christ gave up His Spirit. Below are four delicate hints that this is indeed so.

Firstly, Sacred Scripture tells us that the place where Cain slew Abel was *"in the field"* (Gen 4:8). *Torah* gives us to understand not *"a"* but *"the"* field. Immediately we recall it was also *"in the field"* (Gen 24:63,65) that Isaac encountered Rebekah, that is in the place now named Calvary. The key term in Latin is *ager* (field, farm), in Greek, πεδίον (the open, the plain), in Hebrew, שָׂדֶה (field, land adjacent to a city). This last sense — adjacent to a city — is striking.[75] Although in the time of Abel no cities had yet been buil, even so, the Syriac and Vulgate have *"let us go out"* to the field. With all these connotations in mind, we recall Jesus was crucified *"without the gate"* (Heb 13:12), that is, outside the city. It signifies being an outcast on account of sin (Ex 29:14), but in His case the sin is ours.

Secondly, after Abel was murdered by his brother, it is unlikely that Cain, given his indolence, fled very far from the scene. But when, immediately after this, Cain was cast out from God's Presence, the Scripture references Eden: *"And Cain went out from the face of the Lord, and dwelt as a fugitive... at the east side of Eden"* (Gen 4:16). So did the fratricide take place in Eden? This implication adds more weight to the notion from the previous section, that the brothers offered their sacrifices close to the Foundation Stone. Then it follows that the midst of Eden was indeed the place where Abel was killed.

Thirdly, Jesus counted Abel a prophet whose blood was mixed with *"all the prophets"*:

> *That the blood of all the prophets, which was shed from the foundation of the world, may be required of this generation, from the blood of Abel unto the blood of Zacharias, who was slain between the altar and the temple.* (Lk 11:50-51)

---

[75] Cf. Gen 41:48; Lev 25:34; Josh 21:12.

Abel is a prophet because his sacrificial death proclaims Christ. Jesus later clarified: *"it cannot be that a prophet perish out of Jerusalem"* (Lk 13:33). Therefore, despite accidental exceptions which prove the rule, it is most fitting that Abel, whom Jesus names as the first of *"all the prophets"*, perished in the place that would be Jerusalem.

Fourthly, though Abel perished, a living soul was raised up in his stead. Might Eve have chosen this place to give birth? She

> bore a son and called his name Seth, for she said, 'God has appointed for me another child instead of Abel, for Cain slew him'. (Gen 4:25 RSVCE)[76]

This speaks of the Resurrection. The word used for *"appointed"* is ἐξανίστημι, meaning 'to raise up', as in 'raising up seed for a deceased brother' (Mk 12:19). More directly, St Paul uses the same root word for the *"appointment"* (LXX) of Eve's new son specifically to indicate *"the resurrection which is from the dead"* (Phil 3:11). Now we see a seedling of revelation in Eve who lost her innocent son Abel, but soon after was given a son Seth who *"obtained glory among men"* (Sir 49:19). Shall we not think of Mary the Mother of God, who 'lost' her Son Jesus only for Him to be restored to her, and Who obtained the most glory among men?[77] Eve rejoicing was simultaneously natural and prophetic, the unusual phrase *"God has appointed"* making more sense in light of the rejoicing to come in Mary's heart, for Jesus' Resurrection was certainly by God's appointment. If resurrection is a divinely intended connection, why not also the place?

That these clues are all very slight speaks for their authenticity. God does not clamour to demonstrate Himself. He shows Himself to those who seek trusting they will find (Mt 7:7).

---

[76] For something so momentous as the first births, might Eve have gone to the place of the garden? And for Seth, was this close to where Abel died? Jesus rose in the garden owned by St Jospeh of Arimathea, by Calvary (cf. Jn 19:41). Adam had been appointed by God as a gardener (Gen 2:15), then when Jesus, the New Adam, rose from the dead, Mary Magdalene supposed Him to be *"the gardener"* (Jn 20:15).

[77] Jn 1:14; 12:41; 13:31-32; 17:24; 2 Pet 1:17.

Adam's Creation

Jesus was buried in a tomb *"nigh at hand"* (Jn 19:42) to where He died, for it would be unlawful on the imminent Sabbath to have carried His Body far. The Church of the Holy Sepulchre houses the place of Jesus' Death and the stone slab upon which His dead Body was wrapped in the shroud and also that which gives the church its name, the tomb whence Jesus rose. At this site, in AD 326, St Helena discovered the True Cross. The places of Jesus' death, anointing and burial are extremely close together.

If from earlier we accept Jesus died in the same place Adam was buried (Golgotha), could it be that where Jesus arose from the tomb is also the place where Adam himself was created? Is Jesus' rising to new life from the stone tomb *here* not the final sense of Adam being taken from the slime of the earth *here*? Quite possibly, we can find out.

Eden is congruous with Israel. Both lie between Assyria and Ethiopia, with the Tigris and Euphrates to the north, and the Blue Nile (*"Gehon"*) to the south (Gen 2:11-14). God made the Garden for man and placed man in it (Gen 2:8). Very likely God formed man from the very earth of Eden. But where exactly?

God instructed His People through Moses to bring offerings of their first-fruits to the place He would designate for the Temple:

> *Thou shalt take the first of all thy fruits, and put them in a basket, and shalt go to the place which the Lord thy God shall choose, that his name may be invocated there.* (Dt 26:1-2)

By giving the first and the best produce to God, man acknowledges all comes from God, belongs to God, is for God to dispose as He wills. Going deeper, the TI confidently speculates:

> The Holy Temple, we know, was built precisely on the spot of the Garden of Eden. The altar, upon which our thankful pilgrim will place his basket of first fruits, was built where the Tree of Knowledge stood, where Adam was created from the dust of the earth, and the Holy of Holies, guarded forever by the cherubim, was located precisely where the Tree of Life

stood. And so our devoted pilgrim, when placing his first fruit, that is, the first fruit of his harvest in the land of Israel, the soil of Eden, is returning to his Creator His first fruit — the first fruit which G-d forbade man. Man has returned to G-d the forbidden fruit, taken without permission, and now returned to the very place from which it was taken...[78]

The rabbi teaches that Adam was created from the spot where the altar of holocaust stood in the Temple precincts, that is, Jerusalem. If Christians doubt this, or readers of this book want to see better argumentation, or wonder why I make so much reliance on the Temple Institute rather than a broader range of sources, all these objections miss the main point. It is of secondary importance whether or not the claims are factually true. What is fascinating is that orthodox rabbis are making a series of claims which taken together point most meetly to Jesus. From the quotation written immediately above, we may infer Jesus rose from the dead in the same broad place that God breathed life into Adam: Jerusalem. This is eloquent. Whether or not we contest the rabbis' inferences about precise locations (of trees, altars, stones, persons *etc*), it is now breathtaking blindness to deny that the coming to life of the first Adam is a prefiguration of the coming to life of the second Adam. Vitally: the first was to destructible biological life; the second to indestructible life eternal.

This same resurrection is offered to us but we must acknowledge our debt to God. The ritual for the Jewish pilgrim carrying his first-fruits back to Eden required a confession, a recounting of God's gracious acts through history, including deliverance from enemies. Our rabbi speaks almost sacramentally in insisting that thoughts are not enough but the first-fruit must be returned physically: "We live in a material world... A simple apology without physically righting the wrong just won't do."[79]

So a first-fruit and a confession must be offered in the place for atonement. How can we fail to connect this with Christ? He

---

[78] TI 27/8/2021.

[79] TI 27/8/2021.

confessed God most truly in His Sacrifice. He achieved atonement in this place, delivering us from sin. In His own Body rising He promised us victory over death, by which Resurrection He *is* God's First-Fruit (1 Cor 15:20,23).

Jesus is First-Fruit of the Blessed Virgin Mary, too. In his first Hymn of the Nativity, St Ephraim calls Mary "the virgin earth", making Christmas reminiscent of the Garden of Eden itself:

> To Eve our mother a man gave birth, who himself had had no birth. How much more should Eve's daughter be believed to have borne a Child without a man! The virgin earth, she bare that Adam that was head over the earth! The Virgin bare today the Adam that was Head over the Heavens. The staff of Aaron, it budded, and the dry wood yielded fruit! Its mystery is cleared up today, for the virgin womb a Child hath borne![80]

Mary, the Holy of Holies, the Daughter of Zion, is God's Habitation, a Garden Sealed, a Paradise, an Eden. Everything is meaningfully ordered.[81] God announced in advance the advent of the Second Adam through the creation of the First Adam. Just as the whole of Paradise was planted and prepared for Adam to arrive in it, so Israel was planted by God and prepared through the Old Covenant, reaching perfection in the Immaculate Conception of Our Lady, an incorruptible Eden, poised for the arrival of another Adam, the long-promised Messiah, Jesus.[82] Everything in Genesis points to Him.

---

[80] St Ephraim, *Nativity Hymn* I (see also *Hymns* XII and XIII). For the lesser to give rise to the greater requires supernatural intervention.

[81] Did the Cross stand where the Tree of Life once was, or the Tree of Knowledge? Though very much has changed since then, Calvary has, according to some measures, an elevation of 777m (I think here was the Tree of Life) and Temple Mount 740m (perhaps here the Tree of Knowledge).

[82] St Augustine, *On Christian Doctrine*, III, 36, 52 helps us avoid misinterpreting Gen 2:5-15 as if Adam were made before Eden was fully prepared to receive him. Rather, St Augustine explains, Gen 2:8 gives us the headlines and Gen 2:9-15 tells us the whole chronological sequence. This is how God works: announcing the most important things in advance, then working to bring them about.

Yes, I believe Adam came to life *here* in Creation; because Jesus came to life *here* in the Resurrection; this according with the Incarnation, for He took on our life *in the figurative Eden* first, the womb of the Virgin. The Incarnation and Resurrection determine the facts of Creation read in Genesis, not *vice versa*.

The Foundation Stone

In the 1967 Six-Day War, the Israeli army took control of the Temple Mount in Jerusalem. There a rabbi attached to the military sounded the shofar, blowing portentously on the ram's horn. Was history coming to its end? No. Unexpectedly, the Israelis withdrew from the Mount and the Muslims regained control. It was not time for an apocalyptic 'third Temple'.

Today, gaining sovereignty over the Mount is sought with a superhuman desire by elements of the Jewish world. But the realty is jealously guarded by Muslims. The tensions could trigger Armageddon. On the Temple Mount, under the Dome on the Rock, lies a legendary rock. What is this rock that to some means more than the world?

The answer Jewish sages give is astonishing. Atheists might smirk. Christians might think it has nothing to do with them. But let us listen to the rabbis and see if it dawns upon us that every word they say is absolutely true if we are willing to make one substitution: namely, that *"the rock was Christ"* (1 Cor 10:4). Each time the "Foundation Stone" is mentioned here, let us recall St Paul's letter: *"for other foundation no man can lay, but that which is laid; which is Christ Jesus"* (1 Cor 3:11). This is the primary sense. In a secondary sense we may think of each altar upon which Holy Mass is offered. Then what the rabbis write makes perfect sense to us:

> Yom Kippur… is the day that the *Kohen Gadol*, (the High Priest), enters the Holy of Holies, the holiest of places, which is beyond the dimensions of time and space, and lays down the *ketoret* incense offering upon the Foundation stone from which the world was created, and upon which rests the Ark of

the Covenant, the bearer of G-d's eternal bond with Israel. It is here that the *Kohen Gadol* utters a prayer on behalf of the entire nation, on behalf of all mankind.[83]

Can a stone, a rock, transcend time and space? Not an inanimate rock. But close to the Temple, on the neighbouring mountain, Calvary, Jesus was sacrificed. From His Heart went up an aroma pleasing to the Lord, His prayer sweeter in God's nostrils than any *ketoret* incense. It is by connecting with Jesus through His Self-offering that prayers are made for all mankind. He is our *Kohen Gadol*. Such was God's intention from before the beginning, such He revealed to His chosen:

> What *Yaakov* gathered intuitively was that the stone upon which he slept was no ordinary stone. In fact, it was the Foundation Stone, the mythical, but very real stone upon which creation was founded in time and in space. The Foundation Stone, set in place by G-d is the portal through which creation emanated and it is the portal through which G-d nourishes and sustains creation each new day, day after day. The Foundation Stone is where, if all time and all space could be rolled up into one single point of created reality, it would be right there, the place where *Yaakov* laid his head, the right place and the right time, because in reality, it is the *only* place and the *only* time.[84]

Where "*Yaakov* laid his head" and slept is where Jesus "*bowed His head*" and died (Jn 19:30). This, the Crucifixion, is the "portal through which [God] nourishes and sustains creation each new day". Each altar at Mass "nourishes and sustains" us "because in reality, it is the *only* place and the *only* time".

From here the TI puts it poetically in saying the conclusion of Jacob's dream, "*this stone, which I have set up for a title, shall be*

---

[83] TI 29/9/2017. The *ketoret,* from 'bond', was incense consisting of a secret compound of eleven balms and spices used solely for Temple worship. It symbolises the bond between material and spiritual realities.

[84] TI 27/11/2020.

called the house of God" (Gen 28:22), is woven into God's dream that *"they shall make me a sanctuary, and I will dwell in the midst of them"* (Ex 25:8) and that all this becomes a reality once Jacob's distant descendant Solomon builds the Temple in Jerusalem. Unfazed by the building being gone for 2,000 years, the passage quoted above goes on to say:

> the shared dream of G-d and *Yaakov* remains alive to this day, expressed by the prophet Isaiah, *'for My house shall be called a house of prayer for all nations'* (Is 56:7).

Jacob's dream is fulfilled in the Body of Christ, the Catholic Church, evidently *"a house of prayer for all nations"*.

Striving against God for a rebuild, orthodox Jews report that:

> Our sages tell us that when the Holy Temple is rebuilt the color will return to the earth and the taste of the fruits and grains will return to what G-d had always intended for them. This is no surprise for the Holy Temple is the final and ultimate bond between G-d and the world He created. The Holy Temple... opens a limitless portal through which we can acquire that holiness for ourselves right here on this earth, G-d's gift of holiness to mankind.[85]

Is reality not heightened in devotedly consuming the divine tasting grain and fruit called the Holy Eucharist? Is this not how holiness is acquired, through God's greatest gift to mankind? Must World War III be risked to pursue a dream of regaining the Temple Mount so a stone temple may be rebuilt, when already the Living Temple has arisen?

The rabbis tell us that God's key idea in creation, His chief intention in the design of the whole, was the Temple in Jerusalem. Here God could connect with His creatures. For Catholics this is perfectly true, whereby we understand the Temple to be the Body of Christ. When we hear the Foundation Stone called the beginning of all creation, upon which the Holy of Holies would

---

[85] TI 2/5/2014.

be located, we may think: yes, the new creation begins in Jerusalem in the Risen Christ. *In* Jesus God meets with man.

The Foundation Stone is a parable for Jesus' Body. It appeared in creation at a particular point in time — over two thousand years ago in Nazareth at the Annunciation. Yet it underwent a translation in Jerusalem at Easter, putting on immortality, incapable of dying ever again. Hereby His Body transcends, being the foundation in the Flesh for the Church through *all time*. Eloquently, Origen makes the point:

> You must please not think that she is called the Bride or the Church only from the time when the Saviour came in Flesh: she is so called from the beginning of the human race and from the very foundation of the world — indeed, if I may look for the origin of this high mystery under Paul's guidance, even before the foundation of the world. For this is what he says: *'He chose us in Christ before the foundation of the world, that we should be holy and unspotted in His sight, predestinating us in charity unto the adoption of sons.'* (Eph 1:4-5)[86]

Origen teaches us that the Church has *always* existed. That is an awesome thought to bring to the altar at Mass! He continues:

> And in the Psalms too it is written: *'Remember thy congregation, O Lord, which thou hast gathered from the beginning'* (Ps 73:2). And indeed the first foundations of the congregation of the Church were laid at the very beginning; and for this reason the Apostle says that the Church is built on the foundation not of the apostles only, but also of the prophets. And among the prophets Adam too is reckoned, who prophesied the great mystery in Christ and in the Church, when he said: *'For this cause a man shall... cleave to his wife, and they shall be two in one flesh'* (Gen 2:24)... Undoubtedly [Christ] loved [the Church] who did exist; she existed in all the saints who have been since time began.

---

[86] Origen, *Commentary on the Canticle of Canticles*, II, 8.

The Temple which God always intended is made not of stone, but flesh and blood. The foundation for this living Temple is the sacred Flesh which the Son of God assumed in the womb of the Blessed Virgin Mary. Built upon this foundation are all the saints, of all eras: *"Be you also as living stones built up, a spiritual house"* (1 Pet 2:5). We are God's House. The Son dwelt among us as Man so that the Trinity dwell in us as Spirit, Life of our life.

Where is this union made? Where are we built up as His Temple? In the Sacraments: these are our contact with the Sacred Humanity of the Son of God. With His Body, Blood and Soul, Jesus links Earth to Heaven, to His Divinity, to the Blessed Trinity. That such a thing should be is almost too amazing for us. O, far from meaningless is the cosmos! What a plan, what a reality! How can we know it?

It took thousands of years of pedagogy until, in the fullness of time, God judged mankind ready for Him to tell it plainly to His *"friends"* at the Last Supper (Jn 15:15). The goal of Holy Communion throws a new light upon the pedigree of that *place* where Jesus was crucified. Adopting this perspective, reviewing the great events that happened there, we see how finally they point to the greatest event of all.

The Altar at Holy Mass

For this argument to succeed, the individual points articulated should build two ideas in our understanding. First, the striking continuity of *the place*; and second, the common content of the events which marks this continuity. The first thread convinces us that God has chosen Jerusalem since the foundation of the world for His greatest works. He wants the eyes of the world to go there. The second thread reveals that the common content of these great events is life-giving sacrifice.

Both threads converge on the Passion, Resurrection and Ascension of Our Lord Jesus Christ. From the beginning, God has been promising this life-giving sacrifice *for the whole world*.

Revisiting the events chronologically: if the Foundation Stone is the first place of the first creation, then the single stone altar of

Holy Mass is the place where the new creation takes its beginning.[87] Here we are daily made new in Christ. This place, where Adam first awoke, is the place of the Resurrection of Christ, the New Adam. This place is where Adam first saw Eve, and where Christ gazed from the Cross on the beginning of His Church. Here Jesus gave His Mother, representing the Church, to the care of St John, the loyal priest, the day after his ordination, indicating what is essential to the priesthood. And here He gave His beloved disciple to His Mother, indicating Mary is essential for God's children. With significance for everyone, it is the place of Adam's burial and becomes the place where death is buried, overcome in Jesus' rising. For Abel it is the place of martyrdom. At Mass all can follow him spiritually, dying to ourselves for God's sake. For Cain it is the place he was offered escape from sin. Let us not follow his refusal but penitentially hear the *Confiteor*. This place is Noah's *"altar unto the Lord"* and ours; it is the Father's Gift (Abraham) in the willing holocaust of the Son (Isaac); here is communion with the Bride (Rebekah); here is the gateway to Heaven (Jacob's dream); Holy Mass is the House of God at solemn worship, sacrifice (Solomon's Temple). All these events are explanations of the life-giving Sacrifice of the Son of God, the Crucifixion, Holy Mass — they are the same sacrifice.

Given the (same) huge significance of Moses' tabernacle, why is it not in this list devoted to *the place*? Is it simply because the Tent was constructed on the Sinai Peninsula and ended its service in Gabaon? Orthodox Judaism regards the tabernacle as, in a sense, the completion of creation, that eternally intended centre where God dwells with man. This is the real Eden... or is it? Though the tabernacle made its way through the wilderness toward Jerusalem, thereby pointing to it, and though its most sacred contents — the Ark of the Covenant — was brought all the way to its destination on the Temple Mount, it is precisely because Moses' tabernacle was not in the *place*, that it shows Jerusalem is ultimately not a temporal city but celestial.

---

[87] Code of Canon Law, 1236 §1 "According to the traditional practice of the Church, the table of a fixed altar is to be of stone, and indeed of a single natural stone."

Despite its earlier importance, we should not be fixated on geographical place. Geography serves as a launchpad whence our minds should ascend much higher. The wandering of the tabernacle through the wilderness is a sign that our final destination is not in this world: we are just on a journey toward the Jerusalem that is above, the compact city, Communion in Heaven.

But there is One Who is present in both realms perfectly, both the material-temporal and the spiritual-eternal: Jesus Christ, the True tabernacle. He is the meaning of everything that pointed to Jerusalem, of everything that happened in Jerusalem, and of everything emerging from there that today fills the world (Is 2:3; 2 Kngs 19:31; Lk 24:47; Acts 1:8). This latter point, His Gospel and Real Presence spreading to the ends of the earth, is the most convincing parable that Jesus is God, Creator and Pantocrator. No lesser phenomenon is finally worthy of this *place* as that from it God Himself should come, formally (in the Gospel) and substantially (in the Sacrament), to the whole world, offering Himself to all men. This, after all, is the goal of creation: man's union with God.

Inevitably, this end is written into the beginning. While God's intention with the place was revealed in stages through the millennia, now that we know the goal, it is much easier to find the whole hidden in the earlier stages. (Our liturgy runs far deeper than we might think.)

The first time we hear in the Bible of *"place"*, Makom, it is a place of unity:

> God also said: Let the waters that are under the heaven, be gathered together into one place: and let the dry land appear. And it was so done. (Gen 1:9)

Is this not an image of all history? The chaotic waters, representing death, are gathered into one place, they are brought to Calvary, as sin and death are laid upon Christ. There death is defeated and gives way to life, for there appears the *"dry land"*, a place free from *"the waters"*, that is free from chaos and death, a place to live, a place pointing to Heaven. All was gathered in *"one place"* — *locum unum,* מָקוֹם אֶחָד. The term for this *"one gathering"* in Greek is συναγωγὴν μίαν, *"one synagogue"*, which means one assembly, one *ecclesia*, one Church. Now the OT speaks to us newly.

When Abraham *"had cut wood for the holocaust, he went his way to the place [HaMakom] which God had commanded him"* (Gen 22:3). For what purpose had God chosen this place? Scripture answers with a living parable. The place is:

> *where he built an altar, and laid the wood in order upon it; and when he had bound Isaac his son, he laid him on the altar upon the pile of wood.* (Gen 22:9)

The place is for the sacrifice of the Son on the Cross. With new imagery, the same parable is told in Abraham's grandson, Jacob:

> *when he was come to a certain place, and would rest in it after sunset, he took of the stones that lay there, and putting under his head, slept in the same place.* (Gen 28:11)

His sleep is a figure for the Crucifixion. Arranging the stones means making altars for Holy Mass. The wood Isaac carried and lay upon, and the stones Jacob gathered and slept upon, represent respectively the Cross and altars which are for the same single Sacrifice of Christ.

Moses, too, tells us to go to Holy Mass:

> *But you shall come to the place, which the Lord your God shall choose out of all your tribes, to put his name there, and to dwell in it: And you shall offer in that place your holocausts and victims, the tithes and firstfruits of your hands and your vows and gifts.* (Dt 12:5-6)

This advises us to bring our losses and suffering, our duties and blessings, our reparation and thanksgiving, to the perfect Self-gift of Christ: the Mass. Jesus, not Jerusalem, is the way to the Father.

At night, not yet fully clear, God told Solomon the purpose of the location: *"I have chosen this place to myself for a house of sacrifice"* (2 Chron 7:12). It was enough information for the time. Thinking far ahead, knowing not all could travel to a given geographical location, God multiplies the places of the *place*:

> *And if the place [HaMakom] which the Lord thy God shall choose, that his name should be there, be far off, thou shalt kill of thy herds and of thy flocks, as I have commanded thee, and shalt eat in thy towns, as it pleaseth thee.* (Dt 12:21)

Here God has switched from speaking to the whole people together (*"you"* Dt 12:2-12) to addressing us personally (*"thou"* Dt 12:13-32). Our hometown, our parish, is a place for the same worship as Rome, as Calvary.[88] The altar comes to us.

If we cannot get to church at all, God allows that we go there spiritually, that the place come into our hearts. So at Solomon's dedication of the Temple it was recognised that in necessity it was enough to pray in the direction of the Temple, that is to face toward God with our hearts, in order for God to hear us:

> *If, having gone out to war against their adversaries along the way that you will send them, your people adore you facing in the direction of this city, which you have chosen, and of this house, which I have built to your name, you will heed their prayers from heaven.* (2 Chron 6:34-35 SB)

Still, we should desire actual church tabernacles even more than David desired a House for God. David could not rest unless He found a place for God. He *"swore to the Lord"*:

> *he vowed a vow to the God of Jacob: If I shall enter into the tabernacle of my house: if I shall go up into the bed wherein I lie: If I shall give sleep to my eyes, or slumber to my eyelids, Or rest to my temples: until I find out a place for the Lord, a tabernacle for the God of Jacob.* (Ps 131:2-5)

If we prioritise God, we win. At Mass He illumines our souls: *"But where is wisdom to be found, and where is the place of*

---

[88] Cf. 1 Kngs 8:30; 2 Chron 6:20-21.

understanding?" (Job 28:12): Jesus is the place. *"Son of man, the place of my throne, and the place of the steps of my feet, is where I live: in the midst of the sons of Israel forever"* (Ezek 43:7). The "soles" of God's feet indicate His Presence on earth, in church tabernacles where His Humanity and His eternity dwell together.

Can we really make this translation from a geographical place to the transcendent, from the particular to the universal, the temporal to the eternal, the material to the spiritual, from a stone to Jesus Christ? Yes. The centre of the world, geopolitically speaking, is where Asia, Africa and Europe meet: the Holy Land. The centre of the Holy Land is Jerusalem. The centre of Jerusalem the Temple. The centre of the Temple, spiritually understood, is God's Presence. God's Presence is the centre of the world. That is not surprising.

Now through the New Covenant, Jerusalem has been translated to Rome, and through Rome God's Real Presence is geographically 'everywhere', that is in every tabernacle. Rome itself, chosen by Providence, is a practical matter for the Church — an incarnational necessity that *somewhere* be the new centre of operations. The foundational martyrdoms of SS Peter and Paul mark the location. But the wider significance of tabernacles spreading worldwide is that God, the centre of all being, has come to us. He, the Centre, is looking for us.

In 2008, Pope Benedict XVI taught at an Advent *Angelus*:

> although the Incarnation-Redemption occurred at a specific moment in history (the period of Jesus' journey on earth) it nevertheless extends its radius of action to all the preceding time and all that is to come. And in their turn, the final coming and the Last Judgment, which were decisively anticipated precisely in the Cross of Christ, exercise their influence on the conduct of the people of every age.

As Jesus reaches all time, from the centre to the beginning and the end, then so must our liturgy, if it is to be Christian. Given our limitations and weakness, this is impossible unless we maintain great reverence for tradition. The more venerable and long-standing a rite, the more respectful we should be before it. If we do not understand what it means, we should carefully preserve it for later generations. It is not enough to know the origin of a practice to think we can dispose of it; we must understand its future role too, how it might guide Christians in the end times. God lays the elements in place. As we can hardly discern what is what, then our duty is to favour tradition.

I am thinking especially of Jews. If Catholics are faithful to what we inherit, we will make it easier for Jews to convert. If in arrogance we innovate, if we drop timeless traditions in favour of modernity, if we abandon the immemorial even to imitate post-Temple Judaism, then we are failing in charity to the last generations, to those who will need the greatest clarity of all.

Yet it is for our sake too. Indisputably, God can hear our prayers and accept our spiritual sacrifices from anywhere. But we are weak-minded, forgetful and easily distracted, prone to egoism and easily discouraged. Therefore we need stone and mortar, flesh and blood; we need the routine of daily, weekly, monthly and annual cycles; we need the society of men, the order of liturgical services, the magnificence of Gregorian chant, the visual feast of sacred art. All these the Church concentrates around each consecrated altar so that our souls may be rooted in Heaven.

No Christian could be so in error as to think God wants to restrict true worship to geographical Jerusalem. Yet many make the error of spiritualising so much as to forget the material. The purpose of stressing *location* of the place as of definitive importance in the OT, is that we are not to abandon all continuity with the OT — with David, Abraham and Adam — simply because the Temple was taken away in AD 70. Rather, the New Covenant established by Jesus encompasses truths which have been with mankind always, onto which we must hang.[89] The liturgy which the apostles transmitted holds eternity.

---

[89] Jesus was crucified "outside the city", but over the subsequent centuries the city's centre of gravity shifted as it naturally grew to surround the place of His death and resurrection. Now the Church of the Holy Sepulchre is, as it were, at the centre. So the OT too is seen to have shifted around Jesus, the Old being centred on the New.

Our offerings are to be given through all generations: *"But thou, O Lord, endurest for ever: and thy memorial to all generations"* (Ps 101:13). When God had the stone Temple removed some two thousand years ago, it was not so that we cease offering lambs in sacrifice, but so that henceforth none be offered but the true Lamb of God, no sacrificial rites be followed but the Mass:

> God does not permit the lamb of the Passover to be sacrificed in any other place than where His name was named; knowing that the days will come, after the suffering of Christ, when even the place in Jerusalem shall be given over to your enemies, and all the offerings, in short, shall cease...[90]

The Mass, the Sacrifice of the Lamb, entails the lambs of Josiah, Moses and Abel. Thanks to Jesus Christ these are not forgotten but are remembered everywhere:

> *For from the rising of the sun even to the going down, my name is great among the Gentiles, and in every place there is sacrifice, and there is offered to my name a clean oblation: for my name is great among the Gentiles, saith the Lord of hosts.* (Mal 1:11)

The Temple was only ever a preparation, never the ultimate goal. Jesus is the True Temple.

> *But if you turn away, and forsake my justices, and my commandments which I have set before you, and shall go and serve strange gods, and adore them, I will uproot you from my land, which I gave to you, and from this house, which I sanctified to my name, and I will cast it away from before my face, and I will deliver it to be a parable and an example for all the peoples. And this house will be like a proverb to all who pass by. And being astonished, they shall say: 'Why has the Lord acted this way toward this land and toward this house?'* (2 Chron 7:19-21; cf. Jer 7:14)

---

[90] St Justin Martyr, *Dialogue with Trypho*, 40.

If instead of obedience we or our leaders stray from God in our hearts and deeds, we lose the Mass. The destruction of the Temple is meant as a parable to turn our minds to that Temple which, though suffering death, never knew corruption: the Body of Christ. Rising, It can never be destroyed again. This is the cosmic victory. If we are not so faithless as to let it go, then we will taste the victory in full. Mass is offered as a propitiation for sin. It defeats evil. But the Church hierarchy has forgotten this. They have *"turned away"*, remade their ceremonies according to the wishes of the world, to *"serve strange gods"*, instead of being true to what was passed down.

Orthodox rabbis understand the need for tradition but most of our bishops do not. Listen to this rabbi, but apply his words to the Mass of Ages which gathers all generations into itself:

> If Israel strives for a future, it can only do so by recalling its past, and Israel's past can only be recalled by Israel recalling who it is today. Israel's identity is inexorably bound to the Temple Mount and the Holy Temple. It is on that spot that we remember who we truly are and it is from that spot and that spot only that we can *"obliterate the remembrance of Amalek from beneath the heavens"* forever (Dt 25:19).[91]

Mass, Calvary, is the "spot" where we see how loved we are and where Christ conquers our sins. Amalek represents the armies of hell. To resist satan, to fight sin, each must *"remember the rock from which you were hewn"* (Is 51:1). That is, remember Christ. Memorialise Him in Mass. Only Christ gives Christians their identity. This cannot be a work of a few generations, but must encompass all. If we are not united with the saints, we are not united with God.

To remain in the Church we must obey the hierarchy set over the place: *"thou shalt do whatsoever they shall say, that preside in the place, which the Lord shall choose, and what they shall teach thee"* (Dt 17:10). But if the hierarchy themselves are not

---

[91] TI 14/3/2014.

faithful to tradition, then they no longer *"preside in the place"*, rather they have departed to another place of their own devising. For decades the Church hierarchy has been enamoured with the Prince of this World. Though our adulterous generation be destroyed, they that keep faith will see God for ever.

> *Now therefore, let them drive away their fornications, and the ruinous ways of their kings, from before me. And I will live in their midst forever.* (Ezek 43:9)

God does not lie and He does not fail.

We can always reconnect with God, not just spiritually, but in our cult, our public worship, if as a people we seek Him. If we seek to do His will, He will restore the Mass to us:

> *But if you return to me, and keep my commandments, and do them, though you should be led away to the uttermost parts of the world, I will gather you from thence, and bring you back to the place which I have chosen for my name to dwell there.* (Neh 1:9)

This assures us that no matter how much the Church is degraded, even by our leaders, it can always be restored.

What happens at the beginning of the traditional Mass? Representing Him, Christ's priest prays this antiphon before the altar, *"Introibo ad altare Dei"*. Seconds later in the Psalm the server responds, *"Introibo ad altare Dei"*. And after the Psalm the priest prays once more, *"Introibo ad altare Dei"*. They say: HaMakom HaMakom HaMakom. The *place* The *place* The *place*. There is a time and a place for every thing. Better still, for *everything* there is a time and a place. That time is Mass, that place is the altar.

You do not slaughter a lamb just anywhere, but at the place. It was fixed from the beginning. Liturgical changes which do violence to the form of the Mass will disassociate us from one or more of the key events which occurred in the *place*. Such changes are equivalent to rejecting the place chosen by God, disputing its meaning, turning one's back on His Presence.

God's unchanging desire is that we come to the place. The fact that different events are connected to the Crucifixion which occurred long before it, and that various people bear their various relations to Calvary without even knowing it, might help persuade us that our own life is given to touch the Cross. Christ's Sacrifice vivifies our sacrifices; He connects us intrinsically with believers of all generations; His death undoes our death. Jesus is our Foundation and our Temple; He is our Adam and our Moses; He is our lying down and our rising up. When we offer to God, it is in Christ; when we are offered to God; it is in Christ. Our deepest memories are of Him; our best dreams are of Him; our hoped-for future is in Him. He is *the place*. Let us go up to Him, and nowhere else.

The Mountain

in montem sanctum tuum
— Ps 42:3, Prayers at the Foot of the Altar

If we sometimes find it hard to come to the *place*, it is because the journey is uphill work, it is an ascent. The place exists at the summit of the loftiest mountain. While parts of this ascent are steep, and though there be dangers along the way, it is also true that the angels can carry us. While these things are not predictable or under our control, it is certain that our part is to persevere.

A map of reality is offered to those who seek the place. To discern the immutable pattern, we contemplate the heights of the mountain of God, where the pattern is revealed, handed down. But to what mountain is the priest referring, when he prays at the foot of the altar before Mass: *"thy light and thy truth... have conducted me, and brought me unto thy holy hill"* (Ps 42:3)? Congruent answers are given to us by nature, by Sacred Scripture and by the Mass. Combined, their answer is timeless: the holy mountain is Jesus Christ. *Tu solus Altissimus!*

Mountains in Nature

In nature, men dwelling on mountains is associated with abiding in spiritual heights. Besides being 'closer' to God, Whose place is above, the atmosphere is rarefied. Mountains offer a certain solitude, being difficult to reach, therefore few souls dwell there, though many may visit. Likewise many people have spiritual experiences, but few abide in constant spiritual awareness.

Living at altitude contrasts with living in a port city, which is necessarily at sea level, full of bustle, trade and noise. Ports have a high turnover of souls coming and going, of passing strangers, a disconnected society providing cover for sins of the flesh. Fleeing suchlike, the desert fathers found solitude in the wilderness. By religious instinct, communities of monks gravitated against gravity to the mountains: Montserrat in Spain, Mount Athos in Greece, the Hospice at the Great St Bernard Pass in the Swiss Alps, Mount Popa in Myanmar, Paro Taktsang in Bhutan and the world's highest, Drirapuk Monastery in Tibet.

Though mountains have their own storms, one can be so far above the cares of this world as to look down even on the weather — serene stillness above while tempests rage below. Such is the spirituality of nature. The relative permanence of our planet's immense rocks speaks to the absolute permanence of Heaven:

> For ever, O Lord, thy word standeth firm in heaven. Thy truth unto all generations: thou hast founded the earth, and it continueth. (Ps 118:89-90)

Mountains made through the *Logos* silently speak of the Son of God, telling of His immensity, His eternity and of the peace He gives. Ever generous, Jesus reciprocated honours upon them. He went up mountains to pray (Mt 14:23), to teach (Mt 5:1), to heal (Mt 15:29), to appoint His apostles (Mk 3:13), to overcome evil (Mt 4:8), for His Transfiguration (Mt 17:1), for His Death (Mount Calvary) and for His Ascension into Heaven (Acts 1:9,12).

The Collect of the Ascension Octave beseeches the Almighty that as we believe His Only-Begotten Son ascended this day into the heavens, so may we "also in heart and mind thither ascend, and with Him continually dwell". Our spirit is raised to heavenly heights by contemplating Jesus. We cannot see Him directly, Who is hidden under the sacred species. But all nature bears His "footprints", traces of Him, telling us about Him. There are not many things so visible, so pleasant and impressive, as mountains.

St Augustine aptly couples the *"holy hill"* (Ps 42:3) with Christ's Body, the Church:

> He will send out His *'Light'*, and His *'Truth'*; for that they have already *'brought us and led us to His holy hill, and into His tabernacles'*. We possess the 'earnest'; we hope for the prize. *'His holy Hill'* is His holy Church. It is that mountain which, according to Daniel's vision grew from a very small *'stone'*, till it crushed the kingdoms of the earth; and grew to such a size, that it *'filled the face of the earth'* (Dan 2:35)... We are now on His Hill, that is, in His Church...[92]

The holy hill is the Body of Christ and Christ the Head is its summit. We appreciate its celestial elevation in hearing God delegated angels to carry St Catherine of Alexandria's deceased body to Mount Sinai. This signifies her soul being brought to Jesus up in Heaven. The Collect of her Mass reads:

> O God Who gavest the Law to Moses on the summit of Mount Sinai, and didst miraculously place the body of Thy blessed virgin-martyr Catherine in the selfsame spot by the ministry of Thy holy angels, grant, we beseech Thee, that her merits and pleadings may enable us to reach the mountain which is Christ.

St Catherine's Monastery sits between Sinai and Gabal Katrîne, that is, amid the mightiest mountains in Egypt. This is fitting for a woman who surpassed all the philosophers of her day. She draws us to Sinai to ponder the sublime revelation made to Moses.

Mountains in the Bible

On Mount Moriah, thanks to the Patriarchs' love of God, many began to say, *"On this mountain the Lord is seen"* (Gen 22:14 CEB). Four centuries later, on another mountain (Sinai), Moses, being close to God, glimpsed Christ the true tabernacle (Heb 8:5).

---

[92] St Augustine, *Enarration on Psalm 42*, 4-5.

We will look into this presently. Meanwhile, to follow Moses up this mountain required election and purification:

> so that, pure of passion, they might approach the mountain to be initiated, cleansed of every emotion and bodily concern. (The name of the mountain was Sinai.) Persons alone were allowed at that time to approach the mountain, and of them men alone, and of them, only those purified from every pollution. Every safeguard and precaution was taken against the approach of animals to the mountain. If somehow it did happen that any animal showed itself there, it was stoned by the people.[93]

Given bodily purity was required to approach Mount Sinai, a great lump of rock, how much more is spiritual purity required to ascend the holy hill, to increase in conformity to Christ? This is a lesson about reception of Holy Communion. What is our election and purification but baptism and confession? These enable us to follow Jesus to Heaven. For after Moses, prefiguring Jesus, had by himself opened the way up the mountain, he returned with Aaron and the seventy elders, and they feasted with God: *"they saw God, and they did eat and drink"* (Ex 24:11). They represent the divinity (Moses) and humanity (Aaron) of Christ along with all the nations (represented by the number of leaders, seventy) in communion with the Blessed Trinity, sharing life, a feast.

The finality is Heaven; the foretaste which Moses and company point to is receiving Holy Communion on earth. Those who approach without being called will die the death; those who touch the holy heights, the Holy Eucharist, while still impure, will die like beasts. This is what the Scripture teaches. It is futile to protest. It is sensible to go to sacramental confession.

Is it a safe option to cower at the foot of the mountain? No. We are all called to follow. When our Judgement comes, how can one escape calamity except in spiritual heights? This is underscored

---

[93] St Gregory of Nyssa, *Life of Moses*, I, 42.

by Jesus' advice for the Last Days when persecutions will put hearts to the test:

> But when you shall see the abomination of desolation, which has been spoken of by Daniel the prophet, standing in the holy place (let him that reads understand), then let those who are in Judea flee into the mountains… for there shall then be great hardship, such as has not been from the beginning of the world until now, nor ever shall be. (Mt 24:15-16)

When the world is about to end, obviously it will not help to be atop of *"the mountains"*, unless this is spiritually. *"Those who are in Judea"* signifies those still in the Church. The Maccabees give us an example:

> And Mattathias exclaimed with a loud voice in the city, saying, 'All who hold zeal for the law, maintaining the covenant, let them follow me.' And he and his sons fled to the mountains, and they left behind whatever they had in the city. Then many who sought judgment and justice went down into the desert. (1 Macc 2:27-29 SB)

The mountain, or the desert, is the opposite of the city. At Judgement, those who care for the covenant, who follow Mattathias (Christ), will not want to be counted with the crowds of this world.

Mountains, bringing us closer to God, serve also as a figure for the priesthood. Aaron's name, the High Priest, means "mountain" or "strength". St Jerome offers the eminent interpretation: *"Aaron mons fortitudinis"* — "Aaron is a mountain of strength".[94] The dew *"which descendeth upon mount Sion"* is like the precious oils upon Aaron's head, *"that ran down upon the beard, the beard of Aaron, which ran down to the skirt of his garment"* (Ps 132:2-3). This is the blessing of the Lord descending through the hierarchy. Aaron is an immense mountain in the range whereof the Lord is the highest:

---

[94] St Jerome, *Liber interpretationem hebraicorum nominum.*

In the last days the mountain of the house of the Lord shall be prepared on the top of mountains, and it shall be exalted above the hills, and all nations shall flow unto it. And many people shall go, and say: Come and let us go up to the mountain of the Lord, and to the house of the God of Jacob... (Is 2:2-3)

This is the Church. *"His holy mountain, beautiful in elevation, is the joy of all the earth..."* (Ps 47:2-3 RSVCE 48:1-2).

As mountains surround Jerusalem, so the apostles rise around the Lord, providing sure defence for the Church. The very lives of the apostles and holy bishops serve as defences of her doctrines. To keep the Apostolic teachings and traditions is to ascend Truth:

They that trust in the Lord shall be as mount Sion: he shall not be moved for ever that dwelleth in Jerusalem. Mountains are round about it: so the Lord is round about his people from henceforth now and for ever. (Ps 124:1-2)

Mighty landscapes represent holy souls because they excel in drawing forth praises to God from those who see them: *"O ye mountains and hills, bless the Lord: praise and exalt him above all for ever"* (Dan 3:75). This is the landscape of Heaven: not rocks and soil, but great souls!

God appoints apostles as mountains and makes great saints, so that they who attain the heights can share goods from above with souls still below. They irrigate from on high with spiritual aids, with graces and with truth — especially of the Real Presence. The indubitably eucharistic Ps 103 sings of this with its three mentions of mountains plus three mentions of hills:

Thou waterest the hills from thy upper rooms: the earth shall be filled with the fruit of thy works... That thou mayst bring bread out of the earth: And that wine may cheer the heart of man. That he may make the face cheerful with oil: and that bread may strengthen man's heart. (Ps 103:13-15)

If a successor of the apostles should pollute these waters upon which all depend, in God's time he will be uprooted and cast down.[95] Is the shameful fall of cardinals a reason for panic? No, we should not be anxious when we see this happening: *"we will not fear, when the earth shall be troubled; and the mountains shall be removed into the heart of the sea"* (Ps 45:3).[96] The same Psalm assures us that the Lord is exalted above all the earth. Whoever ascends this *"great and high mountain"* will see the *"wife of the Lamb"* in glory at the end:

> *one of the seven Angels, those holding the bowls filled with the seven last afflictions... saying: 'Come, and I will show you the bride, the wife of the Lamb.' And he took me up in spirit to a great and high mountain. And he showed me the Holy City Jerusalem, descending out of heaven from God.* (Apoc 21:9-10)

How can we ascend this mountain, or where will we find the way to this Holy City? The ascent is made at Mass.

God's Holy Mountain at Mass

Ps 42 informs us that we escape the world, we are led up the sacred mountain, by light and truth. If anywhere we reject Christ, truth, we do not ascend. And if we do not ascend, we do not enter His tabernacle. But it is hell outside.

Rather, when we raise our mind to the altar, when we love the sacrifice of the Mass, we ascend His holy mountain, we are conducted up *"montem sanctum tuum"*. This simple truth is presented to us by the altar steps. So vivid is the image that *"introibo ad altare Dei"* is often translated not as "I will go *in*..." but "I will go *up* to the altar of God".

---

[95] Jesus implied this of the Temple Mount (Mt 21:18-23; Mk 11:20-27) for failing to follow Him.

[96] St Bede, *Commentary on St Mark's Gospel* (11:23) "by a mountain is sometimes signified the devil, on account of the pride whereby he lifteth himself up against God, and would fain be like unto the Most High. And when holy teachers, strong in faith, do preach the Word, this mountain is removed, and cast into the sea, that is to say, the unclean spirit is removed out of the hearts of such as are foreordained unto eternal life, and sent free to exercise the wild rage of his tyranny in the riotous and embittered minds of the unfaithful."

To this ascent God has been calling us through all ages. While billions of souls have assisted at Holy Mass, blessed are those few who came to Calvary itself to be with Jesus *"unto the end"*. Blessed are Isaac and Abraham who went up the same mountain for the same reason. Abraham *"lifted his eyes"*, saw the visible mountain *"from afar"*, and in faith perceived the momentous mysteries of God (Gen 22:4). On Mount Moriah, when he offered all, God saw Abraham's heart and Abraham experientially glimpsed God (Gen 22:14). How lovely this mountain which Abraham first saw from afar then ascended and really saw! It is Christ, and His Church, as it were dripping with God's Gifts:

> *The mountain of God is a fat mountain. A curdled mountain, a fat mountain. Why suspect, ye curdled mountains? A mountain in which God is well pleased to dwell: for there the Lord shall dwell unto the end.* (Ps 67:16-17)[97]

This psalm is sung daily at Matins through the Octave of Pentecost. With his commentary on the Douay-Rheims, Bishop Richard Challoner (✝1781) helps us understand it:

> It is here called a *fat* and a *curdled mountain*; that is to say, most fruitful, and enriched by the spiritual gifts and graces of the Holy Ghost.

The greatest work of the Holy Ghost is to provide Holy Communion. When these mountains fill us *"with the fat of corn"* (Ps 147:3), this means with the graces of Holy Communion, as the Feast of *Corpus Christi* makes abundantly clear.[98] This food excels even than that of the Garden of Pleasures.

In Eden the tree of life stood at the top of a hill. Adam and Eve would have been invited up here to eat of the fruit of the Tree of

---

[97] It sounds better in Latin: *"Mons Dei, mons pinguis. Mons coagulatus, mons pinguis: ut quid suspicamini montes coagulatos? Mons in quo beneplacitum est Deo habitare in eo; etenim Dominus habitabit in finem"* (Ps 67:16-17).

[98] *Invitatorium*, Matins, *Corpus Christi*: "Who gives those who feed on Him a spirit of fatness". Also the Versicle in the first nocturn: "And he fed them with the fat of wheat, and filled them with honey out of the rock" (cf. Ps 80:17).

Life if they had waited for God. But they came in disobedience, in rebellion, without the necessary purity of intention. Thanks be to God, in His plan of redemption we now have priests — 'other Christs' — who can go up the mountain (up to the altar), and take the fruit from the tree (the Body of Christ) and bring it to those who come to the mountain spiritually (prepare themselves for Holy Communion). Jesus said:

> believe me, that the hour cometh, when you shall neither on this mountain [Garizim], nor in Jerusalem, adore... God is a spirit; and they that adore Him, must adore Him in spirit and in truth. (Jn 4:21-24).

Mindful that an ascent is needed — up the mountain of God, the climb in Eden, Mount Moriah, Mount Sinai, Mount Sion, the steps of the Temple courts — churches were everywhere built with steps inside. These were thoughtfully placed and became symbolic in number, aiding the recollection and prayers of souls assisting.

Often seven steps rose from the nave to the predella, that is from where the people gather to where the priest officiates at the altar. Whereto he goes physically, all should follow in spirit. We ascend from the world to Heaven by the seven Gifts, beginning with fear of the Lord and working our way up to wisdom. Simultaneously, we reach the Father through the Humanity of His Son, that is through the seven Sacraments. Our entire way to the inner mystery is by the Holy Ghost and by the Son. With seven steps there are eight levels, representing the course of time from the first day to the completion of the world, and the eighth day resurrection.

The steps would be divided between flights. Sometimes two steps lead into the sanctuary, which may be taken as signifying the double commandment to love God and neighbour, or the dual Nature of the Son of God, Who bridges Heaven and Earth (the meeting of the sanctuary and nave), plus five more steps going up to the altar, plausibly signifying the five wounds of Christ.

Or there might be three steps to ascend into the sanctuary and four from the foot of the altar to the predella, still totalling seven. A set of three might suggest faith, hope and charity as the necessary ascent to the Sanctuary, for the theological virtues bring us to heaven. Four typically represents the world (four points of the compass, four seasons, four dimensions of space and time) which only finds its place in Heaven through the Sacrifice of the Altar.[99]

In different churches there might be more steps than seven, or less, but always there is intentionality in sacred architecture. Where there is an opportunity to symbolise saving truths, we do. The exact number of steps might have been determined by architectural limitations, but it is not wrong to invest the result with suitable meaning.

An obvious practical advantage of steps is that those positioned at the back of the Church can more easily see the enhanced elevation of the sacred species. Even in a tiny *oratorium* where there is no room for a step, then a little carpet should be laid before the altar, partly for the priest's physical benefit, but primarily to show an image of that step, of that elevation, of that mountain. The liturgy, the life of the Church, is the highest cultural expression in the world. It is to be held up for all to see, to ponder, to love: *"You are the light of the world. A city seated on a mountain cannot be hid"* (Mt 5:14).

Whether there are steps or not, it is customary that sacred ministers and servers should set off with their right foot when moving in the sanctuary. This signifies prevenient grace — that grace not only builds on nature, but precedes it. How is this signified? The right and left side of the body are similar, almost symmetrical. But the right hand is usually stronger and more dextrous than the left, and the right leg more powerful. This shows that grace does not change our nature, but enhances it. Appropriately for the *"right hand of the Lord"*, the Gospel side of

---

[99] This arrangement allows for a symmetry in a Solemn Mass, with the celebrant on the predella (fourth step), the deacon taking his place on the middle (second) step, and the sub-deacon on the sanctuary plane.

the altar is to Jesus' right as He looks down from the Cross. It has a higher dignity than the Epistle side of the altar.

With similar symbolism, when vesting with the alb, the priest ought to put in first his right arm, then his left, then over the head. Is this excessive control? Not at all. It has meaning. And given how priests struggle to follow some of God's commands, it is kind of Him to give these customs through which we can gain merit by following meekly. Obedience here requires nothing but goodwill.

These details are little steps by which we may ascend the greatest of mountains, God's Son, Jesus Christ. He is God's *"holy hill"* (Ps 42:3). Super-naturalising the natural, we may say that even mountains have long known Jesus is the Holy One. Jacob spoke prophetically: *"until the desire of the everlasting hills should come; may [blessings be] upon the crown of the Nazarite among his brethren"* (Gen 49:26).

This *"desire of the everlasting hills"* is certainly for the Messiah, Jesus, for the hills were made before man, they remember Paradise without sin and therefore long for the restoration of all things in Christ. How happy were the low hills of Judea when the Virgin Mary carried Christ across them. How reverently the holy hills in Jerusalem — Moriah, Sion, Ophel, Olivet — supported the Holy One of Calvary. How beautiful upon the mountains are the feet of him that brings the Gospel.

In the Litany of the Sacred Heart we pray:

Cor Iesu, desiderium collium aeternorum, R. miserere nobis.

Heart of Jesus, desire of the everlasting hills, R. have mercy on us.

If the hills desire Him, so we too may ask to be led to Him Whom we desire, as we kneel on the plains, or stand at the foot of the altar, in Holy Mass. The journey, to the *place* where we are called, is not flat, but it is an *ascent*. The Patriarchs ascended mountains, the Jewish people ascended steps to the Temple, Our Lord conquered Calvary. We too must go up.

Our ascent has stages, a fixed pattern that cannot change. In the next section we will see what this pattern is. In the section subsequent to that, we will see why.

The Tabernacle

in montem sanctum tuum et in tabernacula tua[100]
— Ps 42:3, Prayers at the Foot of the Altar

The purpose of being led by light and truth up the sacred mountain is to enter the tabernacle. We are to penetrate all the way to the Holy of Holies, which finally means the beatific vision, Heaven. But how can our imagination form an image of this transcendent goal?

God revealed His dwelling place to us in stages. He gave it in detail with Moses' Tent in the desert; later the same pattern was magnified in Solomon's Temple; these forerunners were finally fulfilled in the Incarnation, when the Son of God assumed human nature and dwelt among us — God living in a human body and soul. In Heaven God will live in multitudes of human beings, body and soul, all of them united with Christ the Head. To bring us there, Jesus dwells now in the tabernacles of Catholic churches

---

[100] *"unto thy holy hill and into thy tabernacles"* (Ps 42:3). In Hebrew: *"tabernacle"* (singular); Greek and Latin: *"tabernacles"* (plural), for there are many which point to one — not to the one made by Moses, but to one not made with human hands, the pattern from Heaven.

so that adoring and receiving Him we have a foretaste of living with God in eternity. Instituting Holy Communion, Jesus said: *"Abide in Me, and I in you"* (Jn 15:4).

The paradigm for this mutual indwelling is the Blessed Virgin Mary, in whom Jesus literally dwelt, receiving His Flesh while living in the womb of His Mother. And Mary being God's favourite tabernacle entails that, for her part, Mary always lives in God more fully than any other creature ever has. Our Lady illustrates most faithfully that God Himself is the final tabernacle, the Heaven we enter even as the Blessed Trinity fully enters us.

To help us reach Heaven, we will look closely at the aforementioned tabernacles. Before that, we note a feature they all have in common, a threefold distinction which connects the various tabernacles in Christ. The call to ascend the mountain gives the direction in which we should move: upwards. Multiple passages in the Scriptures show us the structure of the journey, that it has three phases. They are clearly distinguished in the tabernacle of Moses and are made universally accessible in Christ. They represent the classical three stages of the spiritual life: purification, illumination, union.

The first time we read the description of the tabernacle in the Book of Exodus, we probably find it laborious. Overwhelmed by details for which we cannot find a meaning, we might not be engaged by it. But once we understand it is all about Jesus Christ, all about our itinerary toward eternal life, then it becomes fascinating, beautiful, exciting. Let us see how God revealed this pattern to man.

God called Moses up Mount Sinai to give him a filtered glimpse of Heaven, which Moses apprehended as informing — like the λόγος — the structure of the entire cosmos. God instructed Moses to represent this in great detail by the construction of the tabernacle and, crucially, God gave the order of rites which would take place therein.

To give us an idea of the height, depth and breadth of this special revelation, St Gregory of Nyssa writes:

Taking a hint from what has been said by Paul, who partially uncovered the mystery of these things, we say that Moses was earlier instructed by a type in the mystery of the tabernacle which encompasses the universe. This tabernacle would be *Christ who is the power and the wisdom of God*, Who in His own nature was not made with hands, yet capable of being made when it became necessary for this tabernacle to be erected among us. Thus, the same tabernacle is in a way both unfashioned and fashioned, uncreated in preexistence but created in having received this material composition.[101]

The pattern seen by Moses is eternal. It surpasses human words. St Paul apprehended it when *"caught up to the third heaven... into paradise"* (2 Cor 12:2-4).[102] The spatial pattern has three stages: the court; the Holy Place; the Holy of Holies. The whole is recapitulated on a larger scale and more solidly in the Temple, it being built according to a divine pattern shown to David (1 Chron 28:10-19): the exterior courts where bloody sacrifices took place (purification); the Holy Place within the Temple building, lit up with sacred lights (illumination); and deep within, the Holy of Holies, almost inaccessible, housing God's Presence (union).

The very same pattern is compacted though discernible in the three types of sacrifice Jesus offered in His single Sacrifice on Calvary: for sin, for peace and for a holocaust. These are to achieve in us the three stages of the spiritual life: namely to purge us, to enlighten us, and to bring us into the divine embrace.

All this is optimally practised at Holy Mass: to persevere up the mountain in spirit (though constancy be arduous); to be conducted by light and truth into the tabernacle (though it be mysterious); and to proceed to the Holy of Holies in the *cor ad cor* union of Holy Communion (though here it be impermanent).

---

[101] St Gregory of Nyssa, *Life of Moses*, II, 174.

[102] St Gregory of Nyssa, *Life of Moses*, II, 178 "Doubtless [Paul] himself had a vision of the tabernacle when he entered the super-celestial sanctuary where the mysteries of Paradise were revealed to him by the Spirit."

This journey is summarised in the prayer *Aufer a nobis*, which the priest utters as he ascends the altar steps shortly after the *Confiteor*:

Take away from us our iniquities, we beseech Thee, O Lord, that we may be worthy to enter with pure minds into the Holy of Holies, through Christ our Lord. Amen.

The Holy of Holies is the goal; our Lord Jesus is the Way, He Who illumines our minds when He purifies us of our iniquities. The priest goes up to the altar in his body to show all should ascend in their soul. The Mass can carry us.

This is the most important journey for man: from life without grace, to a life of grace in the created world, to eternal life in the uncreated, that is in God, Who is Spirit. God has always desired to communicate this to us. Therefore we find it also in the heroic steps taken by Abraham. He left his home, corresponding to our labour of purgation, making a long journey to *"the land of vision"* (Gen 22:2), there being illuminated by God, Who showed him which mountain to ascend for the holocaust, until finally the unitive came in the holocaust itself. The actual sacrifice was not of his son, Isaac, not of the fruit of Abraham's loins, but infinitely better: Abraham made a holocaust of his own heart, for God's sake. This is what each of us should do. Arguably, no one ever did better than Abraham until the Blessed Virgin Mary entered the world. Her part in the three stages is patently unique.

In Eden the journey was made in reverse. After beginning in the union of friendship with God came man's spiritual descent marked by confusion, division and hiding in fear. Lack of purity entailed being *"cast out"*, blocked from accessing *"the tree of life"* (Gen 3:24). Holy Mass opens up the way again to this Tree and its fruit.[103]

---

[103] We might say the first iteration is a positive miniature seen in Eden before the Fall. Adam, in his loneliness, needed to be purged of something, though it was not sin. It was his rib: he had to surrender it, give away something from himself. After this he saw Eve, which corresponds to illumination, a growth in understanding. Then came union, at least a warm embrace.

Having made these huge claims, we turn now to wonder at key details of the five masterworks exhibiting the divine pattern: the Tent, the Temple, Jesus Christ Incarnate, the Traditional Mass, and Mary the Immaculate Conception.

The Tent

During forty days and nights on Mount Sinai, God revealed to Moses the most important pattern of creation: *"And you shall raise the tabernacle according to the example which was shown to you on the mountain"* (Ex 26:30 SB; cf. 25:40). This pattern was given to Moses so that tabernacle and priests under the Law would afford a shadowy glimpse of Heaven. St Paul explains that these Levite priests serve:

> *a copy and shadow of the heavenly sanctuary; for when Moses was about to erect the tent, he was instructed by God, saying, 'See that you make everything according to the pattern which was shown you on the mountain'.* (Heb 8:5 RSVCE)

That the exact arrangement of the tabernacle is of God, is emphasised in the following passage, where eight times we read how the Lord *"commanded"* Moses (or instructed, decreed, *etc*):

> *And Moses did all that the Lord had instructed... [and] the tabernacle was put in place. And Moses raised it up... just as the Lord had decreed... And when he had brought the ark into the tabernacle, he drew the veil before it, in order to fulfil the commandment of the Lord. And he placed the table in the tabernacle of the testimony, at the north side, beyond the veil, arranging before it the bread of the presence, just as the Lord had instructed Moses. And he placed the lampstand in the tabernacle of the testimony, away from the table, on the south side, setting the lamps in order, according to the precept of the Lord. He also positioned the altar of gold under the roof of the testimony, opposite the veil, and he heaped upon it the incense of aromatics, just as the Lord had commanded Moses. And he positioned the tent at the entrance of the tabernacle of the*

testimony, and the Altar of Holocaust in the vestibule of the testimony, offering the holocaust and the sacrifices upon it, just as the Lord had decreed. Likewise, he stationed the [laver] between the tabernacle of the testimony and the altar, filling it with water. And Moses and Aaron, along with his sons, washed their hands and feet, whenever they would enter the covering of the covenant, and when they approached to the altar, just as the Lord had instructed Moses. And he raised up the atrium around the tabernacle and the altar, drawing the hanging at its entrance. After all these things were perfected, the cloud covered the tabernacle of the testimony, and the glory of the Lord filled it. (Ex 40:14-32 SB)

This is an irrefragable demonstration that the details matter to God and therefore they should matter to us. What does it all mean?

The various expressions used above are most often given in the Greek as συνέταξεν, which means "giving order in combinations". We may think of nested systems. In Hebrew צָוָה is used invariably. It is the *"command"* that Adam broke in Eden (Gen 2:16; 3:11,17). Working toward repairing this by choosing obedience to God's commands, *"Noah did all things just as God had instructed him"* (Gen 6:22; 7:5,9 SB). This just man prepared the way for Jesus, Who said: *"I love the Father, I do exactly as the Father commanded Me"* (Jn 14:31; 15:10 NASB).

It is worth comparing Ex 40:1-13 to the verses quoted above (Ex 40:14-32). There is much repetition. Detailed instructions are given by God and immediately the whole programme is repeated under the aspect of Moses complying. Why does the Bible do this? Perhaps to show us how God lays out a plan and then that plan is fulfilled perfectly in His servants? This we understand on one level within the life of Moses, but recognise also that the very biography of Moses is a divine plan later fulfilled on infinitely greater dimensions by Jesus. The pattern is personal. This iconography of souls is at the heart of their eternal conversation in Heaven, as glimpsed on Mount Tabor (Mt 17:3).

Hence we ought to be struck by the beauty of the pattern given to Moses, as St Gregory of Nyssa clearly is as he elucidates:

With his mind purified by these laws, [Moses] was led to the higher initiation, where a tabernacle was all at once shown to him by divine power. The tabernacle was a sanctuary with beauty of indescribable variety — entrances, pillars, and curtains, table, candlestick, and altar of incense, the altar of holocaust and the propitiatory, and the inaccessible and unapproachable Holy of Holies. So that their beauty and arrangement might not be forgotten and might be shown to those below, he was counselled not to represent these things in mere writing but to imitate in material construction that immaterial creation, employing the most splendid and radiant materials found on earth. Among these the most abundant was gold, with which the pillars were overlaid. With the gold, silver also made its contribution by beautifying the capitals and bases of the pillars so that by the changes of colour at each end, I think, the gold might shine forth more brightly.[104]

This must have been of breath-taking beauty for people accustomed to back-breaking slavery then the wilderness. As to the meaning of it all, St Gregory asks:

Of what things not made with hands are these an imitation? And what benefit does the material imitation of those things Moses saw there convey to those who look at it?[105]

He answers, as we have heard above: the tabernacle is an imitation of the λόγος, Jesus Christ; and the benefit for us is salvation:

There is one thing… which both existed before the ages and came into being at the end of the ages. It did not need a temporal beginning (for how could what was before all times and ages be in need of a temporal origin?), but for our sakes, who had lost our existence through our thoughtlessness, It consented to be born like us so that It might bring that which

---

[104] St Gregory of Nyssa, *Life of Moses*, I, 49.

[105] St Gregory of Nyssa, *Life of Moses*, II, 173.

had left reality back again to reality. This one is the Only Begotten God, Who encompasses everything in Himself but Who also pitched His own tabernacle among us.[106]

This is summarised by the crux of the Last Gospel: *"And the Word was made flesh, and tabernacled* (ἐσκήνωσεν) *among us"* (Jn 1:14).

If we can get to know this Person, Jesus, we get to know the highest reality, the pattern which informs the rest of reality. He is our purgation, the Lamb of God Who takes away the sins of the world on the altar of the Cross. He is our illumination, the Light of the world Who teaches us the truth of God's Love by His holocaust. He is our union, Who bodily makes us one with God (see *The One Perfect Actor* below). All this occurs in Holy Mass.

The process of purging is the beginning of illumination, as we learn our sinfulness, our helplessness, but learn in parallel His mercy. This illumination is the beginning of our union with Him, learning His form (His soul), which He reveals only to those who are conforming themselves to Him, because becoming like Him *is* the only true knowledge of Him. And the Blessed Sacrament is the pledge of our final union.

The angels are there already. They are His tabernacle too. They form a template for our imitation. St Bede writes:

> the angelic powers [are their Creator's] perfect tabernacle in every way, for the one by whom they were made never ceases to remain and dwell in them... Now if we aspire to fellowship with the angels in heaven, we who are on earth should always imitate their life...

If we imitate the angels in doing God's will, we build up a tabernacle for Him, the Church, making visible life "on earth as it is in Heaven".

Perhaps you are asking how you, a fleshly human being born from the earth, can possibly imitate the celestial tabernacle

---

[106] St Gregory of Nyssa, *Life of Moses*, II, 175.

114

which is spiritual. They love God and their neighbours; imitate this. They come to the aid of the unfortunate [humans]; imitate this. They are humble, they are gentle, they are peaceable toward one another, they obey the divine commands; how well would you do to imitate this! They neither speak, nor do, nor think anything that is evil, or useless, or unjust, but assist at the divine praises with speech and thought that are unwearied; as far as you are able, imitate this. Build a sanctuary for the Lord in accordance with the pattern that was shown to Moses on the mountain, and when our Lord and Saviour comes He and the Father will make a home with you, and then after this life He will bring you into that blessed tabernacle which you have always imitated.[107]

The Venerable Bede knows this is true because he lived like this! He wrote his beautiful works in eighth-century Northumberland, when it was a patch of Heaven on earth. A few hundred years before this, St Gregory of Nyssa wrote in the same vein, referring to a revelation given earlier still to St Paul:

We can gain clarity about the figures pertaining to the tabernacle from the very words of the Apostle. For he says somewhere with reference to the Only Begotten, Whom we have perceived in place of the tabernacle, that *in Him were created all things, everything visible and everything invisible, Thrones, Dominations, Sovereignties, Powers*, or forces. Then the pillars gleaming with silver and gold, the bearing poles and rings, and those cherubim who hide the ark with their wings, and all the other things which are contained in the description of the tabernacle's construction — all of these things, if one should turn his view to things above, are the heavenly powers which are contemplated in the tabernacle and which support the universe in accord with the divine will.[108]

---

[107] St Bede, *On the Tabernacle,* I, 3 commenting on Ex 25:8-9.

[108] St Gregory of Nyssa, *Life of Moses*, II, 179.

Christian tradition clearly conveys that the entire cosmos is structured like Moses' tabernacle, purposefully: creation reveals God; and history reveals Him even more, especially through His servants.

St Bede regards the two sets of five curtains, forming the front and the rear of the tabernacle, as representing the two Testaments, coming before and after the Lord. In this the physical layout of the material tabernacle illustrates Jesus Christ reaching backwards and forwards through time to all God's elect:

> All the curtains were embroidered with one and the same handiwork and colours but they were joined together in [groups of] five, because all the worshippers in both testaments believed in one and the same God and served Him with works of one and the same piety and charity, but in the celebration of the sacraments each people played its own separate part. For they celebrated the sacrament of the Lord's Passion... in the flesh and blood of sacrifices, but we celebrate it in the oblation of bread and wine. They believed in and confessed as things to come the Lord's nativity in flesh, His preaching, His working of miracles, His temptation, His Passion, His burial, His Resurrection and Ascension, as well as the coming of the Holy Spirit and the faith of the Gentiles, but we believe and confess that all these things have already happened... Nevertheless, at the time when the tabernacle was being erected all the curtains were fastened to one another, because when the beauty of the whole Catholic Church from the beginning unto the end of the world is considered, it is assuredly as if ten curtains joined together into one adorn the tabernacle of the Lord.[109]

This unity of the Old and New Covenants in Christ is testified by the two angels placed on the Ark of the Covenant:

> the two testaments can be figured through the two cherubim; one of them proclaims the incarnation of the Lord as future,

---

[109] St Bede, *On the Tabernacle*, II, 2.

the other as having been accomplished. They look toward one another because they do not disagree with one another at all in the attestation of truth which they preach. They turn their faces to the propitiatory because they vigorously commend the Lord's mercy, which is the world's only hope. For this reason they are on each side of the mercy seat, because they fill the times preceding the Lord's incarnation, as well as those that follow, with the preaching of spiritual knowledge.[110]

Faithful commentators are free to suggest a better interpretation of the cherubim than that which St Bede offers. Seemingly, nobody ever has. But it is not admissible, if the arrangement is too obscure for us, to dismiss it as meaningless. God never commands arbitrarily. Rather the spiritual knowledge which goes out from the tabernacle, such as identifying Christ as the centre of history, shows the way to Heaven.

This way to Heaven is also given in the tabernacle's three-phase structure. The outer court, with its screens of posts and drapes, represents withdrawal from the distractions of this world, the purgative stage of the spiritual life. There is the great sea for the ritual washing, the purification of the priests. There is the suffering of the victim, its bleeding, its death, its holocaust. The hangings of skins dyed red prefigure the Passion of Christ.[111]

Beyond this, through the *"gate"*, is the inner court, covered overhead, containing the Shewbread and lights. This is the place of apprehending the Truth, Jesus Christ, recognising He is the form and meaning of creation. The Bread symbolises His Body incarnate, the Lamp the seven Gifts of His Holy Spirit. This is the stage of spiritual illumination. The altar of incense speaks of the accord between interior and exterior worship, that is the golden altar within and the bronze altar of holocaust outside in the court,

---

[110] St Bede, *On the Tabernacle*, I, 5.

[111] St Gregory of Nyssa, *Life of Moses*, II, 183 "if one sees skin dyed red and hair woven... For the prophetic eye, attaining to a vision of divine things, will see the saving Passion there predetermined. It is signified in both of the elements mentioned: the redness pointing to blood and the hair to death. Hair on the body has no feeling; hence it is rightly a symbol of death."

in the world. The exterior sacrifices we make for anyone are worthless without an interior willingness, an offering of ourselves out of love of God.

Finally the Holy of Holies represents Heaven itself, to us as yet unseen. The High Priest entered once per year to represent Jesus, Who had access to Heaven always but entered once (in His Ascension). After describing the brilliant colours and beauty of the artistically woven curtains which veiled this area, St Gregory writes:

> The curtains divided the tabernacle into two parts: the one visible and accessible to certain of the priests and the other secret and inaccessible. The name of the front part was the Holy Place and that of the hidden part was the Holy of Holies.[112]

Here we have the summit of the mountain, the fulfilment of the threefold pattern. Everything about the tabernacle was well ordered and its beating heart, *Person(s)*. The Divine Presence was served by a triple Levite ministry, named because *persons* will never be forgotten:

> On the inside perimeter of the tribal encampments were the dwelling places of the tribe of *Levi*, the families of *Kohat, Gershon* and *Merari*, protecting the sanctity of the tabernacle, attending to the service in the tabernacle, and overseeing its transport... across the wilderness. And actively conducting the service within the tabernacle, the offerings and the ceremonies, were, once again, individuals, each with a name: *Aharon*, the *Kohen Gadol*, (High Priest), and his sons *Elazar* and *Itamar*.[113]

It is Trinitarian: three families of Levites sharing one life. Three heads are named to stand for the trinitarian activity within: worship (love).

---

[112] St Gregory of Nyssa, *Life of Moses*, II, 172.
[113] TI 27/5/2022.

The Temple

This same pattern was the body and soul of the Temple in Jerusalem, yet scaled up in important regards. Like the tabernacle, vitally, the Temple was built according to divine specifications. God showed David the pattern, and he instructed his son, Solomon, how to proceed. The detailed description following becomes infinitely interesting in light of its last line:

> Now therefore seeing the Lord hath chosen thee to build the house of the sanctuary, take courage, and do it. And David gave to Solomon his son a description of the porch, and of the temple, and of the treasures, and of the upper floor, and of the inner chambers, and of the house for the mercy seat, as also of all the courts, which he had in his thought, and of the chambers round about, for the treasures of the house of the Lord, and for the treasures of the consecrated things, and of the divisions of the priests and of the Levites, for all the works of the house of the Lord, and for all the vessels of the service of the temple of the Lord. Gold by weight for every vessel for the ministry. And silver by weight according to the diversity of the vessels and uses. He gave also gold for the golden candlesticks, and their lamps, according to the dimensions of every candlestick, and the lamps thereof. In like manner also he gave silver by weight for the silver candlesticks, and for their lamps according to the diversity of the dimensions of them. He gave also gold for the tables of proposition, according to the diversity of the tables: in like manner also silver for other tables of silver. For fleshhooks also, and bowls, and censors of fine gold, and for little lions of gold, according to the measure he gave by weight, for every lion. In like manner also for lions of silver he set aside a different weight of silver. And for the altar of incense, he gave the purest gold: and to make the likeness of the chariot of the cherubim spreading their wings, and covering the ark of the covenant of the Lord. All these things, said he, came to me written by the hand of the Lord that I might understand all the works of the pattern. (1 Chron 28:10-19; cf. 2 Chron 4:7)

God wrote instructions, leaving to chance nothing that mattered!

While the Temple's continuity with the Tent is significant, so also are the distinctions. The Venerable Bede gives faithful interpretations, telling us both tabernacle and Temple represent "the Holy Church universal". Whereas the tabernacle speaks of Christians who labour on earth, journeying through the wilderness on their way to the Promised Land, the Temple represents those already in Heaven, for Solomon raised this edifice after having "taken possession of the same promised land and the kingship in it" — symbolising Jesus seated at the Right Hand of God.

In support of this reading, that the Temple represents those in Heaven, St Bede points out that the construction of the house was silent, perfectly peaceful, for it:

> *was built of stones hewed and made ready: so that there was neither hammer nor axe nor any tool of iron heard in the house when it was in building* (1 Kngs 6:7).[114]

This is a remarkable historical phenomenon. God meant something by it. The materials comprising God's House in Heaven are perfectly purified souls who do not need to be worked on or formed further by the blows and trials of this life.

Besides taking the transition from tabernacle to Temple as representing the transition of souls from earth to Heaven, our venerable monk offers another reading. He says that the development highlights key differences between the Old and New Testaments, such as the former being realised by one people, while the latter is given for all peoples:

> the workmanship of the tabernacle is the time of the synagogue (that is, of the ancient people of God), but the workmanship of the temple signifies the Church (that is, the multitude of the elect which has come to faith after the Lord's

---

[114] There was an intermediary stage between tabernacle and Temple, when the Ark was stationed in Shiloh, with a dramatic history (Josh 18:1; 19:51; Jdg 18:31; 21:2; 1 Sam 1:24; 4:3; Ps 77:60; Jer 26:9). It was housed within solid walls but having the roof of a tent. Perhaps like Purgatory?

incarnation). For Moses completed the tabernacle with the people of the Hebrews alone, but Solomon finished [building] the temple with a multitude of proselytes gathered together, and also with the help of the king of Tyre and his artisans, who were Jews neither by birth nor by profession.[115]

The Temple is a universal work. By it all peoples are made one. This key helps us to see at a still higher level how Jews and Gentiles are made one in Christ:

> If we consider them more carefully, the building of both houses mystically represents the state of the whole present Church, which never ceases to be built from the beginning of the world's creation up until the last elect person who is to be born at the end of the world. In the wondrous truth of their figures, they also depict the glory of the life to come, which the Church enjoys now in part but will enjoy forever in all its members after the end of this age. Hence as we embark on saying some things with the Lord's help concerning the tabernacle, we first invoke Him with humble prayer to unveil the eyes of our hearts so that we may be able to consider the wonders of His law, and so that we may understand that in the beauty of precious metals and vestments we have been advised to make our character illustrious with the ornamentation of faith and devotion...[116]

St Bede tells us here that the precious materials, intricate order and God-orientated life of the Temple point higher than themselves to the personal and supra-personal. First, they point to Jesus Christ, and then, to all who live like Him and in Him. He continues:

---

[115] St Bede, *On the Tabernacle*, II, 1, refers to the growth of the early Church from Hebrew roots and leaders to soon including non-Jews, "even St Luke the evangelist himself, and the apostolic men Timothy and Titus, attained to their jurisdiction from the calling of the Gentiles".

[116] St Bede, *On the Tabernacle*, II, 1 "...and what John heard, *'a great voice from the throne, saying: Behold the tabernacle of God with men, and he will dwell with them'* (Apoc 21:3)."

Otherwise, unless we imitate the material ornamentation of the tabernacle or temple by the devout and pure adornment of heart and body, there cannot apply to us that word of the Apostle, *'For you are the temple of the living God; as God saith: I will dwell in them, and walk among them.'* (2 Cor 6:16)

How does the Temple show Christ? His Body is the true Temple, accordingly it is strong, well proportioned, structurally perfect. Jerusalem's Temple was decorated with gold, inspired artistry and wondrous furnishings, mirroring Christ Who is full of glory, grace and virtue. Every day, prayers of praise and sacrifices of supplication went up from the Temple courts and Holy Place to Heaven, as every moment Jesus is in loving conversation with the Father, putting His Body and Soul at the service of His Mission. The Temple was the centre of Jerusalem, centre of the Holy Land, centre of the world, as Jesus is the real centre of all. The Temple was destined to become a house for all nations (Is 56:7). Jesus achieved that translation in Himself. Pope St Leo preached that as all sacrifices end in Christ's Sacrifice, so all the nations are made one in His Kingdom.[117] The Temple was the only *place* for worship; so Jesus is sole Mediator.

Altogether the Temple is an intense parable, packed with meaning, prefiguring the Hypostatic Union. Christ's Humanity, that is His Body (the building), Blood (sacrifices) and Soul (the psalms, incense, rites of atonement, the teaching, judging) are united with His Divinity (as the Temple housed the *Shekinah*, God's presence) for the sake of salvation. The Temple gently announces Jesus' eternal Priesthood.

---

[117] Pope St Leo I, *Homily VIII on the Passion*, 7: "You drew all things unto You, Lord, for the veil of the temple was rent, and the Holy of Holies existed no more for those unworthy high-priests: so that type was turned into Truth, prophecy into Revelation, law into Gospel. You drew all things unto You, Lord, so that what before was done in the one temple of the Jews in dark signs, was now to be celebrated everywhere by the piety of all the nations in full and open rite... Now, too, the variety of fleshly sacrifices has ceased, and the one offering of Your Body and Blood fulfils all those different victims: for You are the true *'Lamb of God, who takes away the sins of the world'*, and in Yourself so accomplish all mysteries, that as there is but one sacrifice instead of many victims, so there is but one kingdom instead of many nations."

Christ is the beginning, the head, of billions who join Him. In its day the Temple drew pilgrims to Jerusalem for feasts. Analogously Christ draws us, chiefly through Mass to the heavenly City of God for the spiritual banquet.

Not only Jews knew that the Temple was the greatest building on earth — if not in size, then in its quality, order and purpose. The Queen of Sheba fainted when she visited Jerusalem. The reaction of this extravagant queen was entirely appropriate, for if we decode the biblical description, it seems she was appraising the blueprint of Holy Mass one thousand years in advance:

> *all the wisdom of Solomon* [Christ], *and the house which he had built* [the Church], *and the meat* [βρῶμα, Body of Christ] *of his table* [the banquet on the altar], *and the apartments* [καθέδρα, seat, see, cathedral] *of his servants* [saints], *and the order of his ministers* [λειτουργός, liturgists, ministers, sacred orders], *and their apparel* [vestments], *and the cupbearers* [chalices], *and the holocausts* [Calvary, the Holy Eucharist], *which he offered in the house of the Lord* [Holy Mass]*: she had no longer any spirit* [רוּחַ] *in her.* (1 Kngs 10:4-5)

It is enough to take anyone's breath away (רוּחַ, spirit, breath). The old expires when the New comes to life. The Septuagint says she was ἐξ ἑαυτῆς ἐγένετο — outside of herself, beside herself, we could say ecstatic. Elsewhere Scripture adds that there:

> *was no more spirit* [πνεῦμα] *in her, she was so astonished. And she said to the king: The word is true which I heard in my country of thy virtues and wisdom.* (2 Chron 9:4-5)

So ought we think of the Mass! Despite Solomon's great wisdom, One much greater than he has come (Mt 12:42). Jesus Christ is the Wisdom of God (1 Cor 1:24). The first verse of one of the most astute books ever written asserts: *"All wisdom is from the Lord God, and hath been always with him, and is before all time"* (Sir 1:1). Here Jesus ben Sirach speaks of the eternal *Logos*, preparing the way for St John who wrote: *"In the beginning was the Word, and the Word was with God..."* (Jn 1:1).

All things speak of this Wisdom. All. Some more eloquently. It was literally by the רוּחַ חָכְמָה (*"spirit of wisdom"*), with human cooperation, that the vestments for Aaron were made (Ex 28:3). To construct the tabernacle, the *"Spirit of God... wisdom"* filled Beseleel, who was grandson of Hur and great-grandson of Miriam (Ex 31:3). Likewise his helper Ooliab of Dan (Ex 31:6), which tells us that the construction of the tabernacle was literally inspired by God. For continuity, חָכְמָה is the same *"wisdom"* Moses passed on to his people from God (Dt 4:6); the *"angelic wisdom"* of King David (2 Sam 14:20); Solomon's *"surpassing wisdom"* (1 Kngs 4:30). What has this wisdom done?

"Wisdom hath built herself a house, she hath hewn her out seven pillars" (Prov 9:1; cf. 24:3). This *"house"* is recognisable in the Church with seven Sacraments, above all the eucharistic sacrifice, as the subsequent words imply:

> She hath slain her victims, mingled her wine, and set forth her table... Come, eat my bread, and drink the wine which I have mingled for you. (Prov 9:2-5)[118]

The Queen of Sheba, seeing Solomon's order of service, was wise enough to know that the wisdom of the world was nothing compared to divine Wisdom (1 Cor 3:19), for *"who shall know thy thought, except thou give wisdom, and send thy holy Spirit from above"* (Wis 9:17).[119]

The marvels of the Temple were exceeded in the Virgin Mary when "the womb of her that knew not a man is become the

---

[118] Antiphon I of Laudes and Vespers through the Octave of *Corpus Christi* rejoices: *"Sapientia ædificavit sibi domum, miscuit vinum et posuit mensam, alleluja"*.

[119] The divine Wisdom required for this universal work of building the Church is not less than the Son, of Whom Mary is the Seat: *"The Lord possessed me [wisdom] in the beginning of his ways, before he made any thing from the beginning. I was set up from eternity, and of old, before the earth was made. The depths were not as yet, and I was already conceived... I was with him forming all things: and was delighted every day, playing before him at all times"* (Prov 8:22-30; cf. Wis 9:9). At play *"at all times"* includes in Eden, a hide-and-seek, foretelling there in figures the end to come: *"we speak the wisdom of God in a mystery, a wisdom which is hidden, which God ordained before the world, unto our glory"* (1 Cor 2:7).

temple of God".[120] The continuity of Eden, tabernacle and Temple is fulfilled and infinitely exceeded in the Incarnation. Compare Eden's guardian cherubim (Gen 3:24) and the completion of works when God descended to take possession of His new dwellings:

> *After all things were perfected, the cloud covered the tabernacle of the testimony, and the glory of the Lord filled it. Neither could Moses go into the tabernacle of the covenant, the cloud covering all things, and the majesty of the Lord shining, for the cloud had covered all... and a fire by night.* (Ex 40:31-36)

The same key themes are related at the dedication of the Temple:

> *When Solomon had made an end of his prayer, fire came down from heaven, and consumed the holocausts and the victims: and the majesty of the Lord filled the house. Neither could the priests enter into the temple of the Lord, because the majesty of the Lord had filled the temple of the Lord.* (2 Chron 7:1-2)

Both accounts say all this took place before all the people of Israel, who

> *falling down with their faces to the ground... they adored and praised the Lord:⁻ because he is good, because his mercy endureth for ever.* (2 Chron 7:3)

Now we Christians are supposed to read all this and adore, for we see in the descent of the *Shekinah* a prefiguration of the Baptism and Transfiguration of Jesus as the heavens briefly opened, the hidden truth of the Incarnation being made manifest in stages to man.[121] Pentecost is prefigured here too, when the

---

[120] Circumcision of Our Lord, Vespers, Magnificat Antiphon *"templum Dei factus est uterus..."*

[121] Octave of the Epiphany, Matins, *Lectio* VI — St Gregory Nazianzus, *Discourse on the Epiphany*, II says that at His Baptism Jesus "saw the heavens opened not divided, even those heavens which Adam had once shut upon himself and us his descendants, when the cherub's fiery sword barred the gates of Paradise."

Spirit filled the Church, all fire and divine majesty, an outpouring on earth reflecting the happenings in Heaven. Jesus, having *"accomplished"* (Jn 19:30) His work, was glorified above. So the Spirit poured out.

A key difference with the OT accounts above is that when the *Shekinah* descended on the tabernacle and Temple, nobody could then enter in but Jesus, being the first to enter Heaven, has opened it for a multitude.

God first descends, so we can ascend; He condescends so we can rise with Him (con-ascend). We begin now with small steps, an ascent easier to represent in the architecture of the Temple than in the collapsible tabernacle of the wilderness. To reach the Holy Place, first one must ascend Mount Moriah to come to the Court of the Gentiles. From there, twelve steps lead the pilgrim into the Women's Court. Going through the Nicanor Gate, a further fifteen steps lead Levites into the Priests' Court. *Kohenim* with duties in the Temple climb twelve more steps to reach the vestibule through to the Holy Place.

The soul needs such ascents in virtue and grace — in holiness — so that while the eyes of the body look upon the ordered ceremonies given by God then the eyes of the soul can see their eternal meaning. The meaning of it all is sacrifice, Calvary, Christ's Sacred Heart. The soul must reject sin to see this. God designed the Temple and its vessels and services to communicate the meaning of life to us. It is a picture of the ceaseless activity of Heaven, as revealed to and described by St John: the liturgy centred on the lamb that is slain but stands; the altar; incense (prayers); vestments; choirs singing; angels ministering; crowds adoring (Apoc 4:1-11; 19:1-10).

To understand this life of Heaven is the life of Christ, Head and Members, is to understand the form of Holy Mass. Our Mass is designed by the same God Who inspired the tabernacle and the Temple. God's intention with these earlier and latter works, His work which they either prepare for or since continue, is the Incarnation — God's dwelling with us here so that we might dwell with Him in Heaven.

The Incarnation

Before considering how tabernacle and Temple illustrate the Incarnate Lord in Himself, we can begin by reflecting on how they depict His goal of living not only among us, but within us.

When the Tent was pitched in the desert, the Levites would surround it by erecting their family tents closest. In the Temple they got even closer. The assigned *Kohanim* of a given month's rota had their sleeping quarters in three levels of cubicles built *into* the walls of God's House (1 Kngs 6:5-9). They literally dwelt and slept with God in their midst, separated only by a wall. Imagine their prayers! This intimate arrangement is one way to interpret the Psalm: *"an abundant vine on the sides of your house. Your sons... surrounding your table"* (Ps 127:3).

Another personal aspect of the Temple was that the two great pillars at its entrance were actually given names: Jachin and Boaz (1 Kngs 7:21; 2 Chron 3:17). Perhaps they stand for the two great pillars of the Church, SS Peter and Paul? We approach the Holy Place with the Menorah and Shewbread — that is the Gifts and Sacraments — by way of SS Peter and Paul, patrons of Rome and the universal Church.

Many stones making one building illustrates a multitude of souls made one in Christ. So does the abundant use of gold. If gold is a fit material to anticipate The King, its multifarious uses in the Temple suggest the varied lives of the saints harmoniously reflecting God's glory. Scripture stresses that *"the purest gold"* was used for furnishings, utensils, decoration and structurally.[122]

Certain items had to be made of *"beaten work"*, that is *"hammered gold"* (Ex 25:31; 37:7,17; 39:3). St Bede writes how these represent the suffering of saints following Christ, enduring their trials, being tested and forged into unity:

---

[122] *"Solomon made all the vessels for the house of God, and the gold altar... of the purest gold, the lampstands with their lamps... and certain flowers, and lamps, and gold tongs. All these were made from the purest gold. Also, the vessels for the perfumes, and the censers, and the bowls, and the little mortars were from the purest gold. And he engraved the doors of the inner temple, that is, for the Holy of Holies. And the doors of the outer temple were of gold."* (2 Chron 4:19-22)

And because something is made of beaten work by being smitten, aptly was the [lampstand] made of beaten gold. For our Redeemer, Who from His conception and birth existed as perfect God and perfect man, endured the pains of sufferings and thus came to the glory of the resurrection. *All who want to live godly in* Him *suffer persecution;* it is through the blows of suffering that they make progress toward the grace of immortality, just as metal is stretched out by being smitten.[123]

St Bede understands that the faithful of both the OT and NT are *"one work"*. Joseph, Job and Jonah all suffered mighty smitings, and great is their glory in Heaven. How Abraham was stretched out for God when his beloved son was stretched out on Mount Moriah. All who accept suchlike instruction become the glorious Temple erected in Heaven. God lives in them.

The excellence of God's pedagogy through the OT is not measured by those who rejected it, but finally by that inspired generation of Jews who became the first Christians.[124] For them the examples of patriarchs and prophets as well as the life of the Tent and Temple were powerful in preparing their hearts for Christ. Reading the OT can help us keep our bearings today, in this time when the Church hierarchy neglects tradition.

Besides speaking of Christ's many members, the tabernacle and Temple speak also of Christ in Himself. Jesus always is perfect. He needed no purgation or illumination to achieve union. Yet it pleased Him to illustrate the spiritual phases to show their importance and His closeness to us. His Circumcision and fasting

---

[123] St Bede, *On the Tabernacle*, I, 8. Continuing: "the Church... says to her Redeemer, *'In distress you have enlarged me'* (Ps 4:1), as if beaten gold should say to its maker, 'With a metalsmith's pummelling you have stretched me out, and by pounding me you have afforded me greater progress.'"

[124] St Augustine, *On Christian Doctrine*, III, 6 "These men, because they had been very near to spiritual things (for even in the temporal and carnal offerings and types, though they did not clearly apprehend their spiritual meaning, they had learned to adore the One Eternal God,) were filled with such a measure of the Holy Spirit that they sold all their goods, and laid their price at the apostles' feet to be distributed among the needy [Acts 4:34-35], and consecrated themselves wholly to God as a new temple, of which the old temple they were serving was but the earthly type."

speak of purging our flesh, His Baptism of purging our souls. The illuminative phase is represented to us by the evident growth of His sacred Humanity: *"Jesus advanced in wisdom, and age, and grace"* (Lk 2:52; cf.40). Now He sits at God's Right Hand in Heaven, demonstrating the unitive goal.

More compactly, we may see the phases contained in Christ's one Sacrifice on Calvary, which accomplishes three types of sacrifices which man is required to offer (Num 6:14): for remission of sin (Lev 5); for peace of salvation (Lev 3); and so man's spirit be wholly accepted by God, a holocaust (Lev 1).

> Now these effects were conferred on us by the humanity of Christ. For, in the first place, our sins were blotted out: *'Who was delivered up for our sins'* (Rom 4:25). Secondly, through Him we received the grace of salvation: *'He became to all that obey Him the cause of eternal salvation'* (Heb 5:9). Thirdly, through Him we have acquired the perfection of glory: *'We have a confidence in the entering into the Holies [i.e. the heavenly glory] through His Blood'* (Heb 10:19). Therefore Christ Himself, as man, was not only priest, but also a perfect victim, being at the same time victim for sin, victim for a peace-offering, and a holocaust.[125]

Thereby Calvary covers the three phases. It is a sacrifice for sin to purge us. It is an offering for peace to illumine us. And for our ultimate unity, a total holocaust, Jesus gave all. This succeeds so comprehensively because Jesus is the all: He is the all giving all.

Besides being the whole, Jesus is all the parts. He identified Himself as Absolute Being, saying: *"before Abraham... I Am (ἐγώ εἰμί)"* (Jn 8:58), the final phrase echoing the most important words God spoke to Moses (Ex 3:14). St John reports seven further times Jesus said "ἐγώ εἰμί", qualifying these with highly significant elements from the operations of Tent and Temple:[126]

---

[125] St Thomas, *S.Th.* III Q.22 a.2.

[126] With thanks to dispensationalist Charlie Garrett for suggesting parallels between the items of the tabernacle and the seven *"I am"* statements in St John's Gospel. This acknowledgement is no endorsement of Garrett's non-Catholic teaching.

• Jesus said: *"I am the bread of life"* (Jn 6:35 cf. 41,48,51). In the Tent and Temple we find the warm loaves of Shewbread. God instructed Moses to set upon the table *"loaves of proposition in my sight always"* (Ex 25:30), לֶחֶם פָּנִים, *"Bread of the Presence"*.

• Jesus said: *"I am the light of the world"* (Jn 8:12; 9:5). In the tabernacle we find the Menorah, the lampstand with sevenfold light.

• Jesus said: *"I am the resurrection and the life"* (Jn 11:25). This is symbolised by incense on the golden altar. It is consumed yet rises. The scent of solid grains is relatively weak, not reaching far, but when immolated this sweet odour becomes strong and omnipresent, even penetrating the veil to the Holy of Holies, that realm of divine life, as the Risen Jesus. So in His public ministry, in the Body, Our Lord reached tens of thousands. Risen, He now reaches billions (Jn 12:32).

• Jesus said: *"I am the door"* (Jn 10:7,9). The true shepherds enter *"by this door"*, so in Exodus we read of those priests called by God: *"thou shalt bring Aaron and his sons to the door of the tabernacle of the testimony"* (Ex 29:4; 40:12). All who look can see God's presence there: *"And all saw that the pillar of the cloud stood at the door of the tabernacle"* (Ex 33:10).

• Jesus said: *"I am the good shepherd"* (Jn 10:11,14). This is the One High Priest Who lays down His life. He was foreshadowed in the OT by a multitude of Levites who point hierarchically through their families and grades to one greater than all: the Son of God.

• Jesus said: *"I am the way, and the truth, and the life"* (Jn 14:6). Exodus tells of the laver for priests to purify themselves on the way to offer sacrifices or enter the tent: *"lest perhaps they die. It shall be an everlasting law"* (Ex 30:21). In this water is everlasting life in Christ, as it stands for Jesus purifying souls with Truth, washing them in the Word of Life: *"that He might sanctify [the Church], cleansing it by the laver of water in the word of life"* (Eph 5:26).

• Jesus said: *"I am the true vine"* (Jn 15:1,5). The true wine He gives is His Most Precious Blood, anticipated by the endless blood which was poured, sprinkled and dabbed round the tabernacle.

Seven times St John reports these *"I am"* statements of Jesus, and seven times we find their allegory in the tabernacle and Temple. How deeply Christ connects us with the OT.

The Traditional Mass

The seven essential elements of the tabernacle and Temple which manifestly speak of Christ's work remain present in the rites of the New Covenant, in the traditional Mass, translated by Jesus:

- The Shewbread is fulfilled in the Holy Eucharist.
- The seven-branched candlestick is replicated in the supernatural light of the crucifix plus the Big Six.
- The unique *ketoret* blends itself with Christian incense, both of which symbolise the Resurrection and the Life by being immolated yet captivatingly rising heavenward.
- As tabernacle and Temple each had gateways to their courts, so each church has its door, a holy portal which may even bestow indulgences on those who enter by it.[127]
- The High Priest was a forerunner of the Good Shepherd, seen in the celebrant of Holy Mass, who by ordination is indelibly marked in his soul as an *alter Christus*.
- The laver, or ancient bronze sea, for washing before worship is now found in the baptismal font — *"He saved us, by the laver of regeneration and renovation of the Holy Ghost"* (Tit 3:5) — and is finely recalled in each Mass by the priest at the *lavabo* (Ps 25).
- The blood poured out of old heralds Christ pouring out His inebriating Blood, in Mass under the accidents of wine. Drinking it (spiritually), we are living branches of the True Vine.

Whether or not St John was conscious of all these connections when he recorded the seven *"I Am"*'s in his Gospel, he was the man who knew Jesus best, the saint who rested on Jesus' Heart (Jn 13:23). It was the piercing of this Sacred Heart on the Cross (Jn 19:34) that opened the depths of the mystery at the heart of

---

[127] Or as tabernacle and Temple also had a doorway to the inner sanctuary, so churches properly have a gate for ministers in the altar rails.

the tabernacle, the divine Presence in the Holy of Holies. When this happened: *"behold the veil of the temple was rent in two from the top even to the bottom, and the earth quaked, and the rocks were rent"* (Mt 27:51). Creation was rent, and death too was rent (Mt 27:52), as God's plan to give His Life for us was revealed. This elicited a saving confession from a soldier watching Christ on the Cross (Mt 27:54), for once we perceive the goodness of what God offers us — everything — we are only a breath away from giving our consent.

Savouring these truths, the hymn *Cor arca,* sung on the Feast of the Sacred Heart, praises God's plan which Tent and Temple foretold, which Jesus fulfils by making mansions for us in Heaven:

O Heart, Thou Ark... Thou new, immaculate sanctuary...
Temple more sacred than of yore... Veil more profitably rent...
Who would not choose to dwell in this Heart, eternal tabernacle

Likewise the Litany presents Jesus' Sacred Heart Itself as connecting these major OT types with our heavenly destination:

Heart of Jesus, Sacred Temple of God...
Heart of Jesus, Tabernacle of the Most High...
Heart of Jesus, House of God and Gate of Heaven...

To enter the Holy of Holies means to enter His Heart, Heaven, sanctuary of the Holy Trinity, dwelling place of the saints.

The Mass keeps the essential elements of tabernacle and Temple fully operative in Christ and achieves their high purpose. Their triple structure of courts, Holy Place and Holy of Holies is built into our churches and made accessible in Mass. Architecturally, the nave represents the world (courts), made through the *Logos*; our sanctuary (Holy Place) represents the meaning of the world, which is Christ, where everything is brought into order; then the predella and altar, including the Real Presence of God on the altar or in the tabernacle (Holy of Holies), presents us with Jesus in Heaven.

At the beginning of Mass, we are given a hint of how we are to penetrate this structure spiritually. Three times it is prayed: *"Introibo ad altare Dei"*, prompting us to expect a threefold movement which maintains a certain continuity within its actions. The three are linked.

The first phase, corresponding to entering the outer court, is purgative. The *Asperges me* of Sunday Mass is our soul being washed by grace. At each Mass we ask God to deliver us from the corruption of this world: *"ab homine iniquo et doloso erue me"*. We are fully aware the focus is our own sins: *"quia peccavi nimis cogitatione, verbo et opere: mea culpa, mea culpa, mea maxima culpa"*.[128] In the *Kyrie* we beg nine times for mercy, and there are multiple prayers throughout the Mass when priest and people lament their sins, asking God for forgiveness and purification. One of the most intense of these penitential prayers comes shortly before the priest washes his hands at the *lavabo*, when in preparation for the Offertory he prays:

> Accept, O holy Father, almighty and eternal God, this unspotted host, which I, Thy unworthy servant, offer unto Thee, my living and true God, for my innumerable sins, offences, and negligences, and for all here present: as also for all faithful Christians, both living and dead, that it may avail both me and them for salvation unto life everlasting. Amen.

While engaged in purgative toil, the illuminative phase commences. The Epistle teaches us truth, and more so the Gospel, each enlightening our understanding with God's Word. Symbolically, the *evangeliarium* is accompanied by candles. Indeed all the prayers and rites of the Mass are good for our instruction, ideally the homily too.

---

[128] The *Confiteor* guides through all stages of ascent as we combat our sins of thought, word and works (*cogitatione, verbo et opere*). To overcome sinful actions (*opere*), through purification and sacrifices, is like ministering in the outer courts. To have no errors of understanding or expression (*verbo*), to know and witness to Truth, is to stand in the Holy Place. To be free from sinful thoughts (*cogitatione*), to be fixed in contemplation, is to enter the Holy of Holies.

The purpose of it all is the unitive, entering the Holy of Holies. This means worthy reception of the Blessed Sacrament (or by necessity spiritual communions). The High Priest entered once per year; now Christ invites us to enter daily so that in the end, on One Day, we may enter once and for all bodily.[129]

Typically we do not maintain or even attain perfect union on earth. Nor do we pass through the three stages neatly, but throughout life are in need of constant purification, illumination and ever closer union. Even so, every one of us can aspire to the Holy Place. Purged in baptism, purified through sacrifices, advancing in spirit through steady prayer, being illumined by meditation on Christ, approaching union in the love of Him: finally in receiving Holy Communion sacramentally or spiritually. If from these we do not depart, but remain in grace, we will enter the beatific vision after we die.

The only failure is failure to make this pilgrimage: from life in the created world to eternal life in the uncreated, in God. Freedom is the transformation from being dominated by matter to becoming dominated by the Word of God, the Lord. It is a progress from worldly concerns to spiritual concerns. The Spirit leads us from mundane experiences, the outer courts, so we may enter the Holy Place — encountering Christ — and He shows us the unseeable in the Holy of Holies — the Father. It cannot be surprising that the greater part of this mystery remains beyond us:

> If the interior, called the Holy of Holies, is not accessible to the multitude, let us not think that this is at variance with... what has been perceived. For the truth of reality is truly a holy thing, a Holy of Holies, and is incomprehensible and inaccessible to the multitude. Since it is set in the secret and ineffable areas of the tabernacle of mystery, the apprehension of the realities above comprehension should not be meddled with; one should rather believe that what is sought does exist,

---

[129] St Thomas, *S.Th.* III Q.22 a.5 "Christ entered into the Holy of Holies (Heaven) and prepared the way for us, that we might enter by the virtue of His Blood, which He shed for us on earth."

not that it lies visible to all, but that it remains in the secret and ineffable areas of the intelligence.[130]

Our failure to understand life does not mean life cannot be understood, only that on this side of eternity certain depths must remain hidden. But this does not mean we should not search.

God gives us the material to help us understand the greater realm of the immaterial. In any case, that we should not absolutise matter ought to be obvious. Even the tabernacle of Moses with its bronze altar was left in Gabaon while David brought the Ark from Cariathiarim to Jerusalem (2 Chron 1:3-6). This shows the importance of the interior over the exterior.

After this, even the material Ark was lost when the Temple was destroyed by the Babylonians. The rebuilding of the Temple was not for its own sake, but is a prefiguration of Jesus' Resurrection, Who called His own Body the Temple (Jn 2:21).

Finally the rebuilt stone Temple was itself destroyed by the Romans, not one stone left upon another, showing that the time of figures passes to give way to reality.

The many stages of this single revelation include Eden, Mount Moriah, the Tent, the Temple, all leading to the first Easter Triduum. In perfect continuity from here, Holy Mass brings us to Heaven. The whole of history hangs together, all these layers essentially congruent, the same DNA being transmitted through the different phases. There must be much to say here, for after visiting 'heaven', St Paul spent years expounding to scriptural experts how the OT speaks of Jesus' Passion and Resurrection:

aided by the help of God, I stand unto this day, witnessing both to small and great, saying no other thing than those which the prophets, and Moses did say should come to pass: That Christ should suffer, and that He should be the first that should rise from the dead.[131]

---

[130] St Gregory of Nyssa, *Life of Moses*, II, 188.

[131] Acts 26:22-23.

Therefore, to be Christian, we should be attentive to the OT. We might not understand it, but if we reject it then we reject Christ. If our religion is unrecognisable in it, then we are unrecognisable in Christ. Moreover, the OT warns us what to expect if we deviate from tradition into our own fabrications:

> *But thou, son of man, shew to the house of Israel the temple, and let them be ashamed of their iniquities, and let them measure the building: And be ashamed of all that they have done. Shew them the form of the house, and of the fashion thereof, the goings out and the comings in, and the whole plan thereof, and all its ordinances, and all its order, and all its laws, and thou shalt write it in their sight: that they may keep the whole form thereof, and its ordinances, and do them. This is the law* (תּוֹרָה, *Torah*) *of the house at the summit of the mountain, with all its parts all around. It is the Holy of Holies. Therefore, this is the law* (תּוֹרָה, *Torah*) *of the house.* (Ezek 43:10-12)

Who can read this without shuddering if they have rejected Tradition?

The rule of life in Heaven, as seen by Ezekiel in this vision, is according to a law (*Torah*), a pattern, which God gave to Moses on the mountain. This same form was inherited in the Temple and testified to by the prophets. Jesus destroys not an iota but fulfils it all (Mt 5:17). The same pattern, the Life of Christ, is transmitted to us by Tradition, by the Mass of Ages. This means Holy Mass must be true not only to Trent but also to the tabernacle. Otherwise it departs from Christ, has not the pattern of Heaven, cannot draw us there. The engulfing, catastrophic, pole-axing tragedy of our time is that the New Mass is man's own design, not God's.

We are not alone. We have assistance to find the way, aided by a living tabernacle closer to Jesus than any other: Mary, Mother of God.

The Immaculate Conception

In a surpassing and primordial way, Mary lives in Jesus and Jesus lives in Mary. God prepared "the body and soul of the glorious Virgin Mother Mary to become a worthy dwelling for [His] Son".[132] Mary was made to be His *habitacalum*, His habitation. But transcending all categories, her divine Son is Himself the very tabernacle containing the universe:

> [Jesus] is given the predicate 'tabernacle' in accord with a signification fitting to God. For the power which encompasses the universe, in which lives the fulness of divinity, the common protector of all, who encompasses everything within Himself, is rightly called 'tabernacle'.[133]

While Mary is contained by her Son, this same Jesus dwelt in Mary, spiritually and bodily: "O Virgin, Mother of God, He Whom the whole world cannot contain, shut Himself in your womb, becoming Man. Alleluia."[134] The best house God built for Himself is Our Lady.

When one hears how some rabbis praise the tabernacle, it is striking how perfectly their words fit the Virgin Mary. The rabbis say the tabernacle was God's first and fullest idea for creation, His intention being to meet there with man, as He did with Moses, and indeed God desired to dwell among us, as the *Shekinah*. Yet God went further than this. In the Virgin Mary the Incarnation took place — divinity and humanity were perfectly united, so that indeed God met man. He came to dwell among us, bodily, in the flesh. To be fit to be Mother of God, Our Lady was immaculately conceived. God's principal idea for creation is flawless to the power flawless.

As Jews hold the tabernacle to be the perfect plan of the entire cosmos, so Pope Pius IX taught:

---

132 Oration following the *Salve Regina*.

133 St Gregory of Nyssa, *Life of Moses*, II, 177.

134 Feast of the Nativity of Our Lady, *Graduale*.

the very words with which the Sacred Scriptures speak of Uncreated Wisdom and set forth His eternal origin, the Church, both in her ecclesiastical offices and in her sacred liturgy, has been wont to apply likewise to the origin of the Blessed Virgin, inasmuch as God, by one and the same decree, had established the origin of Mary and the Incarnation of Divine Wisdom.[135]

Here the pope explains that certain passages of Scripture which are properly applied to the Eternal Word (for example, Prov 8:22-36) are also used by the Church in Masses and the Divine Office to praise Mary the Mother of God, for she is the created expression of uncreated wisdom, she is the creature closest to Jesus, so close that the Incarnation is inconceivable without her. God's decision to create anything at all was a free decision. But we cannot think of God doing this work badly. On the contrary, He necessarily does it excellently. And the best demonstration of this is His greatest masterpiece, the Blessed Virgin Mary, His own Mother.

Fr Serafino Lanzetta writes something which Catholics might find difficult to conceptualise, but which is easy for us to believe. I think for those rabbis who speak of the primacy of the tabernacle, it is an idea perfectly easy to conceptualise, though at present something they are not prepared to believe:

> Mary is the first idea of God the Father when planning all things in Christ... Our Lady is in God's original plan, in his mind – *together with* and *in* Christ – when He made all things. Mary is foreseen, foreloved and hence pre-destined with Christ to be his Mother. Therefore, as Christ holds a primacy over all creation, so does his Mother. There is a "primacy of Mary", as a unique share in the primacy of Christ... Mary shares through Christ in the excellence of being generated first, before all others, for the sake of God's love, as perfect resemblance *ad extra* of God's love. "Jesus and Mary", their

---

[135] Pope Pius IX, *Ineffabilis Deus,* 8th Dec 1854.

communion in the one eternal predestining love, outside God, is the most intimate and perfect resemblance of God's inward love. Our Lady mirrors the Most Holy Trinity, she is God's heaven.[136]

The Immaculate Conception is not like us.

Yet she is like us. St Bernard extols Mary, whose life-giving motherly love reaches all generations:

the angel Gabriel was sent to the Virgin, to the most worshipful of women, a woman more wonderful than all women, the restorer of them that went before, and the quickener of them that come after her.[137]

We rightly think it is Christ Who gives life, Who restores and quickens. But He chooses to do so, by divine decree, through Mary His Mother. As a token of this joint action, we may regard the altar of Holy Mass. Above, it was argued that Christ is represented by Temple's altar of holocaust because His sacrifice is bloody, mortal, in the outer court where many see it. Meanwhile, Mary is like the altar of incense because her sacrifice is spiritual, interior, unseen by the world.[138] In the Church we have not two altars but one, for the two of the OT are fused, united. This speaks of Our Lady uniting her whole heart, mind, soul and strength to the Sacrifice of her Son on Calvary, willingly offering Him even as He willingly offered Himself. They made one Sacrifice: Christ as Priest, Mary as the most faithful. They made it as One Body: Christ as Head, Mary as the Church.

Necessarily then, each Holy Mass — each renewal of Calvary — is offered not only in worship of God but also in honour of Our Lady. This is made explicit in the prayers.

---

[136] Fr Serafino Lanzetta, *Primacy of Mary as Immaculate Conception*, 7th Dec 2022.

[137] St Bernard of Clairvaux, *Homily* II on Lk 1:26.

[138] The Canticle alludes to the movements of Our Lady's soul with *"she that goeth up by the desert, as a pillar of smoke of aromatical spices, of myrrh, and frankincense"* (Cant 3:6).

Our Lady's place above all the angels and saints is six times acknowledged in the threefold *Confiteor*, her name having priority. Every Offertory observes that the oblation is made "in honour of Blessed Mary, ever Virgin..." The Canon includes the *Communicantes*, which — ahead of twenty-four named saints, including the Apostles — venerates the memory of, "in the first place, the glorious ever Virgin Mary, Mother of God and our Lord Jesus Christ".

Following the Canon, the *Libera nos* asks "the intercession of the Blessed and glorious ever Virgin Mary, Mother of God" for peace, freedom from sin and from disturbance, acknowledging her power. There are numerous Masses with a supplementary *Postcommunio* asking for the intercession of "Blessed Mary ever Virgin, in veneration of whom we have offered up these gifts to Thy Majesty". And scarcely a month passes without a great liturgical feast dedicated to Our Lady.

Many saints are named in the calendar. Indeed all the saints are honoured in each Mass because by participating in Mass we admit our debt to them who passed this greatest of treasures on for us (see the *Suscipe, sancta Trinitas*). Yet for Mary, the honour is highest, intrinsic to the Mass, for Our Lady of Sorrows, uniquely, participated on Calvary itself with the theological virtues of faith, hope and charity. Therefore wherever the Sacrifice of Calvary is renewed, then Mary's love is necessarily present, for it cannot be fully represented without them.

This is why the golden altar was essential to the service in the Temple and before that in the tabernacle. The gold speaks of Mary's immaculate holiness; the altar's operation, for immolating incense, makes Mary our guide and model in the imitation of Christ, Who immolated Himself; the position of this altar by the Veil shows Mary is closer to the Holy Trinity than the Shewbread and Menorah, that is, even dearer to God than the Sacraments and the Spiritual Gifts. Being Full of Grace, she is the original 'created uncreated'. So St Peter Damian is in holy awe of Mary's place in the tabernacle, who works the altar of incense as our sovereign Queen, who even has, so to speak, leverage over God:

For how can that Power ignore thy power, when it received its fleshly origin from thy flesh? Thou standest before that golden altar of reconciliation, not only asking, but commanding, as mistress rather than handmaid.[139]

With the golden altar standing for Mary, we recall that in the House of God one was surrounded by gold, *"the purest gold"*, representing the saints. Some of these uses of gold were structural, some were for holy vessels, some were decorations of stunning beauty. But we may say all of them were coloured after the golden altar, like Mary. Whatever they had been through to win their Christian glory, Our Lady led the way. In a sense Mary is the totality, not as excluding others, but as providing the pattern for all. The whole Church is Marian. The Litany of Loreto entitles the Queen of Saints "House of Gold" — *Domus aurea*.

Bodily Mary was a house for Jesus, and Mary made a home in Nazareth for Jesus to bodily dwell. Now even we are called in our own way to receive Him tenderly. St Ephraim, Doctor of the Church, concludes His long Homily on the Lord with this:

So He, Who came to make our bodies abodes for His indwelling, passed by all those dwelling-places [of the proud]. Let each one of us then be a dwelling-place for Him Who loves me. Let us come to Him and make our abode with Him. This is the Godhead Whom though all creation cannot contain, yet a lowly and humble soul suffices to receive Him.[140]

God does not despise little beginnings. He loves whom the world overlooks. In Walsingham one thousand years ago, at Our Lady's request, a replica of the holy house of Nazareth was built. This was in order to put men in mind of the Incarnation, that God was pleased to make a home among us. It was signalled long in advance by God's little Temple in Jerusalem, by His foldable tent in the wilderness. And long before these, the plan was sketched out faintly but indelibly in the Garden of Eden.

---

[139] Octave of the Assumption, Day IV, Matins, *Lectio* VII, *Homily*, St Peter Damian.

[140] St Ephraim, *Homily on Our Lord,* 57.

Eden was laid out to show the 'structure' of Heaven, which God wishes to communicate to us. So *"the Lord God had planted a paradise of pleasure from the beginning: wherein he placed man whom he had formed"* (Gen 2:8). As Heaven is a banquet wherein God Himself provides our substance, so in Eden His trees offered fruits pleasant to eat. As *"the tree of life was in the midst of Paradise"* (Gen 2:9), accordingly St John saw in the midst of Heaven *"the Tree of Life"* (Apoc 22:2). The True Cross marks the Throne of Jesus. To those who overcome, Jesus will *"give to eat of the tree of life, which is in the paradise of my God"* (Apoc 2:7).

The virgin earth from which God formed the trees and animals and which bore Adam himself is seen by Tertullian as an analogy of the purest flesh of the Virgin Mary from which Jesus Christ was born.[141] St Jerome concurs.[142] On the Feast of the Immaculate Conception, "Paradise" is mentioned at Matins six times in the First Nocturn's readings. St Germain (✝733), Patriarch of Constantinople, teaches that the Blessed Virgin Mary is that *"Eden, wherein hath sprung that Tree of life, Whereof if any man eat he shall live for ever."*[143] As Mary conceived Christ first in her heart, then the newly created earth represents the immaculate soul of Mary.

This analogy speaks to us too. For as the earth can receive a seed to germinate unto fruit, at a higher level of life so do female

---

[141] Tertullian, *Conversion of the Jews*, XIII "elsewhere the Prophet has announced the fruit of this tree saying: *the earth has given her blessings* (Ps 66:7). This was, indeed, that virgin earth not yet irrigated with rains nor made fecund with showers, out of which in the beginning Ada was perfectly formed, and out of which now Jesus Christ was born through the flesh of the Virgin. He says further: *And the tree has brought forth its fruit,* not that tree in Paradise, which gave death to the first-formed man, but the tree of the passion of Christ, from which *life was hanging, and was not believed by you* (Dt 28:66)."

[142] Feast of the Immaculate Conception, Matins, *Lectio* V, Sermon from St Jerome, *On the Assumption*, identifies the Virgin Mary in Cant 4:12, *"Hortus conclusus, fons signatus, emissiones tuæ paradisus"* — "A garden enclosed is my sister, my spouse, a garden enclosed, a fountain sealed, thy perfumes are a garden of delights."

[143] Feast of the Immaculate Conception, Matins, *Lectio* VII, Homily by St. Germain, Patriarch of Constantinople, *On the Presentation of the Blessed Virgin Mary.*

animals; and higher still, female humans; and higher again, any human soul in whom, by the incoming Word, truth and grace are conceived. This participation in divine life is higher in the hierarchy of being than our biological life. The persons who remain in grace populate Heaven.

All creation speaks these truths to us. Light is the fundamental creature which means Christ. Fire means the Spirit. Mountains means the Church. What does 'water' mean? From nature we understand it means life and death. Without water, there is no life. We need it to drink. But you can drown in it, leaving no trace. In Christ these waters of death and life are in Baptism. In this Sacrament begins our life in Heaven. *"And a river went out of the place of pleasure to water paradise"* (Gen 2:10). This speaks of the grace which gives life to the world, seen in that water which issued from Christ's pierced Heart and is present also in Heaven: *"a river of water of life, clear as crystal, proceeding from the throne of God and of the Lamb"* (Apoc 22:1).

We read that the first river, Pishon

> *runs through all the land of Hevilath, where gold is born; and the gold of that land is the finest. In that place is found bdellium and the onyx stone.* (Gen 2:11-12)

Is this water not grace, which *"runs through all the land where gold is born"*? Is this gold not the holiness and glory of the saints, for *"the gold of that land is the finest"*, gold of such quality as would cover the Ark of the Covenant (Ex 25:11) and decorate the Temple? How overwhelming must have been the impression upon entering the Temple to see all those surfaces covered in gold. How much more glorious to enter Heaven. The summation of all acts of love will be visible all at once. Holiness, not gold, is much to be desired!

The *"onyx stone"*, שֹׁהַם (Gen 2:12), which first appears here in Eden, is a fascinating mineral: even when black it seems to shine. Is this the subtlest of nature's allusions to the Resurrection, to light conquering darkness? Suitably the Scriptures next present onyx on the ephod and breastplate of the High Priest (Ex 25:7), who anticipates Jesus, the Resurrection and the Life. Onyx was laid up by King David for adorning the Temple (1 Chron 29:2) then was later seen by St John in the Heavenly City (Apoc 21:20). We have a link running from Eden through the priesthood of the tabernacle to Solomon's Temple and finally Heaven itself — and in the midst of it all is Christ, for understood in the light of Heaven, the onyx shines like the Resurrection.

This trail or trial made of precious stones is the only one worth walking. It was laid by God Himself in Creation and in Scripture to show us that, wherever we find ourselves now, the way from the beginning to the end is through the Risen Christ.

In Eden Adam rejoiced over his bride Eve (Gen 2:23) as in Heaven Christ will behold His Church (Eph 5:25-27; Apoc 21:2). In Eden satan was cursed and doomed (Gen 3:14-15), so he and his angels have no part in Heaven, being cast out (Apoc 12:7-9). Iniquity, too, has no place in Heaven, so once sin slithered into material creation, the remedy was established in Eden forthwith: God promised the victory of His Messiah. It would be through the Immaculate Conception the triumph is achieved (Gen 3:15).

Whole chapters could be written about how Eve's part in the fall of mankind is turned around by Mary's part in our redemption. When we sin we might choose to blame the devil, or the world, or ourself. These three are represented by the serpent, by Eve and by Adam. It is true that the devil has corrupted the world as the snake deceived Eve, but our sin remains entirely our own, as Adam's was for him. It makes no sense to blame anyone else. But as the fallen world is full of temptation, thanks be to God it is even more full of our heavenly Mother's care for us. Mary teaches us that the many goods we receive are all chances to magnify God, and *all* the evils are chances to offer ourselves up in sacrifice. This vale of Eva's tears gives access everywhere to Christ our Redeemer and to Mary our Co-redemptrix.

The Virgin conceiving Christ was the beginning of the end for the serpent. Even the name of *Eva* is reversed by the *Ave* received by Mary when the Archangel Gabriel announced the Incarnation (as sung in the *Ave, maris stella*). We love to hear *Ave Maria*.

The point is that there are many details woven by God into the account of Eden which gently anticipate the pattern which would become more explicit in stages: in the tabernacle and the Temple as shadows, then as full colour in the Incarnate Christ, Who continues His work in Holy Mass though His substance remain hidden, until the ultimate reality, being no mere image, the divine liturgy of Heaven.

Our imitation of Christ can begin through our imitation of Mary, in humility fulfilling our duties of state as she did, before we realise it is precisely this that conforms us to Christ. If the Virgin Mother seems too far away for our eyesight, we may begin with those around us who set a holy example, who inspire. We work our way up through the saints as we come to know them. They form a chain linking us to Christ. The Christians in Thessalonica became *"a pattern for all who believe in Macedonia and in Achaia"*, because they learnt to imitate St Paul and through him the Lord (1 Thes 1:6-7). The saints are the pattern of Christ, shirking not to *"give ourselves a pattern unto you, to imitate us"* (2 Thes 3:9). St Peter exhorts the priests be *"made a pattern [for] the flock from the heart"* (1 Pet 5:3). But the pattern closest to Jesus is Mary.

To spell it out: the immutable pattern of reality is sacrifice. If that is difficult to conceptualise, we can simply ask: What works? What gives life, what guarantees growth, what is the way for the soul to ascend, to be more alive? Sacrifice. So testify Temple and tabernacle, prophets and patriarchs.

King David discerned that the core sacrifice pleasing to God is *"an afflicted spirit: a contrite and humbled heart"* (Ps 50:19). This comes into focus with Jesus and with Mary. They were deeply *"afflicted"*; though sinless they were *"contrite"* on our behalf; they *"humbled"* themselves so perfectly that none could humiliate them.

More germane here, they specified that the ultimate sacrifice is self-sacrifice. Motherhood or Crucifixion, living for the other or dying for them, in all cases willing their good first. Heaven has this priority of the other before oneself; entering Heaven is the fruit of sacrifice; it is actual, boundless life. This is counter-intuitive to fallen man, but it is the law of reality. Nothing else works. Life comes from giving one's life, even if while on earth that means death. To God such giving is life itself. The reason this cannot be otherwise is because this is how the three Divine Persons always treat each other, as we will see.

To depart from this pattern, in our daily business or in liturgy, is to become ineffective, to approach nothingness. *"He that loveth his life shall lose it; and he that hateth his life in this world, keepeth it unto life eternal"* (Jn 12:25). Mary is proof.

The Blessed Trinity

Gloria Patri, et Filio, et Spiritui Sancto.
Sicut erat in principio, et nunc, et semper:
et in sæcula sæculorum. Amen.

— Doxology after Psalm 42, Prayers at the Foot of the Altar

Holy Mass references the Blessed Trinity at least forty times, paying ardent honour to a mystery intimated in the OT then revealed in the NT: the Divine is One God in Three Persons. To know these Persons is to have eternal Life. Their Self-gift takes Self-sacrifice to another level.

How shall we get to know the Persons of the Blessed Trinity? How shall we learn about their Self-sacrifice? How shall we imitate it? Relying on the revelation of Jesus Christ in the NT, this chapter ventures to say something about the presence of the Trinity in the OT, in Holy Mass and in Heaven.

The Trinity in the Torah

Assuredly, it is impossible to recognise the Holy Trinity in the OT without the light of Christ. Some of *Torah's* apparent references to the Trinity can be reasonably doubted. Other references give sheer delight. Some manage both, as in a game of hide-and-seek.

CREATION — בראשית ברא אלהים

Genesis tells us: *"In the beginning God created..."* (Gen 1:1). The first three letters are ברא, which are the initial letters for Son (בר), Spirit (רוח) and Father (אב).

The second word of the Scriptures consists of the same three letters, ברא (*bārā,* created). Again the Holy Trinity is playfully present, though hidden.

The third word is *"God"*, אֱלֹהִים (*Elohim*), the plural form of אֱלֹוהַּ (*Eloah*, God). It is used over 2,500 times in the OT while the singular appears only sixty times. There is never any doubt in the Bible that God is One. Why, then, is the plural form preferred?

God says in Genesis: *"Let us make man to our image and likeness"* (Gen 1:26), using the plural terms *"us"* and *"our"* (also in Gen 2:18; 3:22). What is the image in which we are made, our blueprint? The spirit of each human enjoys being, understanding and loving. Imaging our Creator, these constitute within us three relations yet only one substance. That requires some pondering!

To explain away the plurality revealed in Genesis, it is plausibly asserted that it is a usage of the *pluralis majestatis*, the "royal we", wherein a monarch's pronouns are plural. If earthly monarchs can use "we, us, our", why not God?[144] But the next two verses of Genesis contain a subtle distinction of Persons.

The second verse of Genesis refers to the Holy Ghost: *"the spirit of God moved over the waters"* (Gen 1:2). The third verse

---

[144] As a rich example, Pope St Pius V wrote in *Quo Primum* (1570), "in virtue of Our Apostolic authority, We grant and concede in perpetuity that, for the chanting or reading of the Mass in any church whatsoever, this Missal is hereafter to be followed absolutely, without any scruple of conscience or fear of incurring any penalty, judgment, or censure, and may freely and lawfully be used... It is Our will, therefore, and by the same authority, We decree that, after We publish this..."

of Genesis says: *"And God said: 'Be light made'"* (Gen 1:3). God Who spoke is the Father while the Word He speaks is the Son. God speaking 'externally' is the work of creation, with the Holy Ghost already named, assuring us of His constant cooperation with Father and Son.

So full are Genesis' first three letters, first three words and first three verses — each layer already implying one God and three Persons. We could say the same for the first three chapters, for wherever the one Name יְהֹוָה (YHWH) is used in Gen 1-3, it is always compounded with the plural אֱלֹהִים (Elohim), as in *"the Lord God"*, referencing both the unity and plurality.

ABRAHAM AND SARAH

Various Church Fathers interpret God's appearing to Abraham at Mambre (Hebron) as Trinitarian.[145] The Bible reports:

> *And the Lord appeared to him in the vale of Mambre... there appeared to him three men standing near him: and [Abraham] adored down to the ground.* (Gen 18:1-2)

Abraham would not adore men. He understood this was *"the Lord"*. In the light of Christ, we understand *"the Lord"* is Three Persons. When the three speak, they do it together, with one voice, as Scripture makes explicit: *"they said"* (Gen 18:5,9). This is unusual. When they come or go, eat or turn, they do it together (Gen 18:2,9,10,16,22,33).

Once we are open to the Trinitarian possibility, then a rich revelation dawns. We discover the whole passage abounds with references to Jesus and to Mass. Here is the opening of the scene:

> *And the Lord appeared to him in the vale of Mambre as he was sitting at the door of his tent, in the very heat of the day. And when he had lifted up his eyes, there appeared to him three men standing near him: and as soon as he saw them he ran to meet them from the door of his tent, and adored down*

---

145 St Augustine, *De Trinitate*, II, 10-11; Cyril of Alexandria, *Contra Julianum*, I; Maximus the Confessor, *Quaestiones ad Thalassium*, 28.

to the ground. And he said: Lord, if I have found favour in thy sight, pass not away from thy servant: But I will fetch a little water, and wash ye your feet, and rest ye under the tree. And I will set a morsel of bread, and strengthen ye your heart, afterwards you shall pass on: for therefore are you come aside to your servant. And they said: Do as thou hast spoken. Abraham made haste into the tent to Sara, and said to her: Make haste, temper together three measures of flour, and make cakes upon the hearth. And he himself ran to the herd, and took from thence a calf very tender and very good, and gave it to a young man: who made haste and boiled it. He took also butter and milk, and the calf which he had boiled, and set before them: but he stood by them under the tree. (Gen 18:2-8)

Abraham is at the *"door of his tent"*, the same words used for where God meets man — speaking face to face with Moses at the door (פֶּתַח) of the tabernacle (אֹהֶל) (Ex 33:9-11). Recalling Jesus is both Door and Tent, next we see Abraham prefiguring Jesus, conforming his will to the Divine Will, fulfilling His God-given mission.

Abraham *"lifted up his eyes"*, which indicates contemplating God, specifically in the liturgy. A meal is prepared by mingling *"three measures of flour"*, as in the Holy Eucharist the Three Persons are present (the Son substantially, the Father and Spirit through their inseparable union with Him, that is by περιχώρησις, *circumincession*). The meal is not bread alone, but involves flesh from a calf *"very tender and very good"*. This is Jesus, the One selected to be slaughtered, Who is very *"tender"* and *"good"*. The meal includes *"milk"*, so it is flesh and drink from an animal, while in Mass we consume flesh and drink from Christ's Sacred Humanity. Abraham provides all this in collaboration with Sarah, his bride, as the Mass is the work of Christ ordering His Bride, the Church (v.6). Each does their work in *"haste"* (מָהַר is used three times in v.6-7), indicating the redemption of the world, for Church history is never for a moment aimless or stalled. *"Surely"*, says Jesus, *"I come quickly"* (Apoc 22:20).

150

The same haste, מְהַר, characterises the work of Rebekah and Jacob in preparing a meal for Isaac (Gen 27:20). This mirrors the devotion of Jesus' (Jacob's) work with Mary His Mother (Rebekah) and His desire to complete it (Mal 3:5) for the sake of the Father (Isaac). Again the slaughter of a kid, a young victim, to provide a meal, speaks of the Holy Sacrifice of the Mass.

Returning to Abraham, we find him *"sitting"* (v.1) and *"standing"* (v.8) and he *"adored down to the ground"* (v.2) — like Holy Mass: sitting, standing, kneeling. Abraham calls himself the Lord's *"servant"*, the term used for the Messianic Suffering Servant, as also for Levitical ministers and the prophets, and generally for worshippers of God. In fact, Abraham distinctly calls himself *"thy servant"* (v.3) and *"your servant"* (v.5), addressing the Lord as singular and as plural, as if recognising the One God is Triune.

Crucially, the Lord is to *"rest ye under the tree"* (v.4) and Abraham *"stood by them under the tree"* (v.8). This tree signifies the Cross. It happens *"in the heat of the day"* (v.1), when Jesus was crucified. The shade *"under the tree"* represents the darkness which covered the land at the Crucifixion. While the three men *"rest"*, Abraham *"stood"*. So the Trinity is at peace, resting in Heaven, while Jesus assumes His office on the Cross. Abraham's eager service of His three heavenly visitors is an image of the human will of Jesus being perfectly united with the One Divine Will shared by the Three Persons of the Trinity. This unity of purpose is praised in every Holy Mass. Prior to receiving Holy Communion the priest whispers:

O Lord Jesus Christ, Son of the living God, Who, according to the will of Thy Father, with the cooperation of the Holy Ghost, hast by Thy death given life to the world...

All Three Persons acted together. How sad that some imagine the death of the Son on Calvary was due to indifference from the Father or abandonment by the Spirit. The celestial visitation to Abraham shows the magnificent cooperation between the Holy Trinity and the Incarnate Son.

SARAH LINKING THE TRINITY TO THE INCARNATION

This same collaboration between the Holy Trinity and the Incarnate Son for the redemption of the world is found very subtly in the key event of the OT: the *Akeidah*, the binding of Isaac.

Initially, there was Abram, אברם. The first two letters of his name spell *"father"* (אב). The middle two letters spell *"son"* (בר). The next two letters (רם) are the first and last of *"Spirit of God"* (רוח אלהים), the Holy Ghost, Who is self-effacing and content to be abbreviated here.[146] So Abram represents the Holy Trinity, his very name being an interlocking of the letters for Father, Son and Spirit of God.

When ready to herald the Incarnation through the birth of Isaac, God changed Abram's name to Abraham, meaning *"father of a multitude of nations"* (Gen 17:5). The change is achieved by inserting the letter ה (*h*) to give אברהם. The basic meaning does not change, but there is a revelation, for the origin of this letter (ה) is a window, with the sense "Behold!". At what shall we look? Abraham being promised many descendants through a son, his beloved son, Isaac, whom later he would be willing to offer as an oblation. All this is a figure of the Holy Trinity (אברם), giving a new revelation (ה), to be *"father of a multitude of nations"* (אברהם) through offering the promised son for a holocaust.

Through the same revelation — that is the addition of ה, "Behold!" — Sarai (שרי) becomes Sarah (שרה) (Gen 17:15). We may take Sarah to stand for the Virgin Mary saying *"Behold the handmaid of the Lord!"* (Lk 1:38). All in one chapter, God changes Abraham's name (Gen 17:5), promises the seed and the covenant (v.6-14), then changes Sarai's name (v.15). There is much in a name!

There is much in Isaac's name too. When the good news was announced Abraham *"laughed"* (Gen 17:17). When Sarah heard of it, she *"laughed behind the door of the tent"* (Gen 18:10). Sarah *"laughed"* secretly (Gen 18:12), God knew she *"laughed"*

---

146 With thanks to (alas not Catholic) John Kostik for these insights into Hebrew.

(Gen 18:13), and asked why she did *"laugh"* (Gen 18:13). Sarah had a moment, think Calvary, feeling she should not *"laugh"* (Gen 18:15), but God affirmed she did *"laugh"* (Gen 18:15). Accordingly, they named their promised son *"Isaac"* (Gen 21:3), which means "one who laughs" or "one who rejoices". Sarah said: *"God hath made a laughter for me: whosoever shall hear of it will laugh with me"* (Gen 21:6). Why all this laughing?

There is *"laughing"*, that is "rejoicing", because it is all about the Incarnation! Hence Sarah *"laughed"*. When Sarah heard she would miraculously conceive a son, she asked, *"shall I give myself to pleasure?"* (Gen 18:12). The word for *"pleasure"* derives from עֵדֶן, Eden. Her words were prophetic: indeed yes, through Isaac her son would come Jesus, the New Adam, to establish the New Eden. St John Damascene tutors us that Mary, herself a new Eden, by her glorious Assumption into Heaven enters the ultimate Eden:

> This day the Eden of the new Adam receives the living garden
> of delight [Mary], wherein the condemnation was annulled,
> wherein the Tree of Life was planted, wherein our nakedness
> was covered.[147]

The original garden indicates the ultimate garden, and does so by way of Mary and even Sarah. In the very first, *"the Lord God produced every tree that was beautiful to behold and pleasant to eat"* (Gen 2:9). As the beatific vision is the sight of God and His banquet, so was Eden pleasant to look at and eat from — clearly not an ecstasy, but pointing in that direction. Now Jesus opens the way not merely to pleasure but to the joy of salvation and the rapture of Heaven. Overcoming seemingly impossible obstacles, this is indeed worth a spiritual "laugh", or rejoicing.

If with Sarah's help we accept that Isaac's name speaks of the Incarnation, then it is easy to accept that Abraham's name tells of the Trinity. They also, at the *Akeidah*, did their work with wills united — *"together"* (Gen 22:6,8).

---

[147] St John Damascene, *Oratio II de dormitione Beatae Mariae Virginis.*

THREE GREAT PATRIARCHS AND A FOURTH

Proceeding a generation, there are countless reasons to consider the lives of the Three Great Patriarchs — Abraham, Isaac and Jacob — as altogether Trinitarian. The three men form an endlessly rich image of the One God. Abraham stands for the Father, being recognised magnificently as the *"father of us all"* (Rom 4:16). Isaac stands for the Son, being ready to be immolated on Mount Moriah (Gen 22:6,8), which is Calvary. Jacob, who descends from Abraham and Isaac, stands for the Holy Ghost Who proceeds from Father and Son, and is ever fruitful no matter the obstacles (Gen 30). Hence the designation *"the God of Abraham, Isaac and Jacob"* is profoundly personal, the earthly reflecting hidden depths in the Triune God.

Or why is the description of the God of Israel as the God of *"Abraham, Isaac and Jacob"* used by Scripture so prolifically? The phrase is foundational, being stressed in every book of the *Torah* (Gen 31:53; 32:29; 48:15; 50:24; Ex 2:24; 4:5; 6:3, 8; 33:1; Lev 26:42; Num 32:11; Dt 1:8; 6:10; 9:5, 27; 30:20; 34:4) as well as numerous references in the Prophets and Writings. The three synoptics show Jesus identifying God as the God of *"Abraham, Isaac and Jacob"* (Mt 22:32; Mk 12:26; Lk 20:37). The early Church witnessed to the same, which we hear from St Stephen (Acts 7:32), St Peter (Acts 13:13) and St Paul (Heb 11:8-9,17-21; Gal 4:21-31; Rom 9:7-13).

Why are the lives of the three Patriarchs given to us in such detail? Along with a fourth, Jacob's favourite son Joseph, these persons thoroughly dominate three quarters of the Book of Genesis. Why? God inspired Moses to record the beginnings of creation and history. Much is unlocked if we accept Abraham, Isaac and Jacob as figuring the Father, Son and Spirit; and Joseph, who came after and from them, as figuring the Incarnate Son, Jesus Christ (parallels for which are super-abundant). We remain flexible, for in certain respects each of these four men symbolises Jesus. But the overall picture, once seen, is unmissable: our origins are Trinitarian and Incarnate.

The Trinity in the Prophets

Some places where the Trinity is hidden in the OT may be plausibly explained away by non-believers. Other places cannot be unlocked by any other key. Here we look at an example of each kind, given by the first of the major prophets, Isaiah.

THE TRIPLE SANCTUS

Isaiah reports his vision of Heaven where the second highest choir of angels, the Seraphim, sing: *"Holy, holy, holy, the Lord God of hosts"* (Is 6:3). Linguists may say the triple *"holy"* is not Trinitarian, for Hebrew expresses superlatives not with distinct words such as "good, better, best" or "holy, holier, holiest", but a threefold repetition of the same word: קָדוֹשׁ קָדוֹשׁ קָדוֹשׁ, *holy, holy, holy*. Biblical Hebrew, being so ancient, has a limited vocabulary, capturing high truths with simple words. Therefore some say this repetition is not an adoration of Three Persons, but simply honours the superlative holiness of the One God. This is plausible, but is there more to it?

Christians see both aspects honoured: distinguishing a triad in the Godhead while praising their substance as identical. The three Persons are distinct yet alike, so one word is repeated thrice.

We garner more clues from the opening context Isaiah gives concerning the death of Judah's king: *"In the year that king Ozias died, I saw the Lord sitting upon a throne high and elevated: and his train filled the temple"* (Is 6:1). Here Jesus is figured as the King of Judah Who dies; that same year He ascends on high to His throne in Heaven; and His train fills the Temple. What train? His saints, who adorn Him as royal vestments and who adore the Trinity through the Sacred Humanity of the Risen Son: *"Holy, Holy, Holy... Heaven and earth are full of Thy glory"*. On earth this *Sanctus* is sung in churches during Holy Mass, joining the seraphic song of Heaven. With it is sung the *Benedictus*, offering like praise to *"He Who comes in the name of the Lord"* — Jesus — just as to the Trinity: *"Hosanna in the highest"*.

The triple *Sanctus* invites us to the Trinity. Without faith, one will not admit it. With faith, one hears what the prophet hears.

ISAIAH IS EXPLICIT

For those open to the inner truth of the OT, Isaiah refers to the Trinity in another passage which, once the matter is pointed out, it becomes undeniable can only be explained by the Trinity, and this only in retrospect, now that Jesus has opened the ancient Scriptures by His Incarnation-Ascension.

The prophet attests: *"now the Lord God hath sent me, and his spirit"* (Is 48:16). Obviously, the first Person mentioned here is Divine: אֲדֹנָי יְהוִה, *"the Lord God"*.

The second Person referenced here is also Divine: the *"me"* does not refer to Isaiah, but it is the voice of the Son of God. That the voice is divine is absolutely clear from the verses before and after, for it is only God Who may say: *"for my own sake will I do it, that I may not be blasphemed: and I will not give my glory to another"* (Is 48:11). God alone says: *"I am he, I am the first, and I am the last"* (Is 48:12; cf. Apoc 1:8; 22:13). It is the λόγος Who speaks: *"My hand also hath founded the earth, and my right hand hath measured the heavens"* (Is 48:13). The next words, immediately before the phrase, are from One Who is present through all time:

> I have not spoken in secret from the beginning: from the time before it was done, I was there, and now the Lord God hath sent me, and his spirit. (Is 48:15-16)

Immediately following this Trinitarian finish we read: *"Thus saith the Lord thy redeemer, the Holy One of Israel: I am the Lord thy God that teach thee profitable things"* (Is 48:17). As the voice saying *"I"* and *"me"* in this passage is manifestly divine, then *"the Lord God hath sent me"* means God has sent God, the Father has sent the Son.

Accepting that there are at least two Persons Who are God in this line, the third becomes obvious: *"now the Lord God hath sent me, and his spirit"*. The *"spirit"* referred to by Isaiah is the Holy Spirit, sent by God after sending His Son. God's Spirit is a Person and cannot be less than God. It was forgivable before Pentecost not to believe this. It is sinful to actively deny it now.

The Trinity in the Writings

The OT verse most quoted in the NT is from the Psalms, the largest book in the collection of the *Ketuvim* (Writings). It is the verse which has always formed the cornerstone of the entire Divine Office, the hinge upon which the weekly cycle of the 150 Psalms turns. It is a verse Jesus Christ used to reveal His Divinity to all who will listen and to silence those who will not. There is no cogent explanation for this verse except by accepting the Dogmas of the Holy Trinity and Incarnation. It is: *"Dixit Dominus Domino meo: Sede a dextris meis"* — *"The Lord said to my Lord: Sit thou at my right hand"* (Ps 109:1).[148]

Evidently, there is here more than one Person Who may be addressed as Lord (God) given that *"The Lord"* spoke to *"my Lord"*. Jesus presented this startling conundrum to the Pharisees and Sadducees after they discovered they could not trap Him with any of their contrived and vexed questions. Jesus asked them about the Messiah: *"If David then call him Lord, how is he his son?"* (Mt 22:45). Jesus' enemies could not bear to even begin to admit or even to hear that the only way David can call his own distant descendant *"my Lord"* is that this Messiah have two natures: divine and human. Regarding Jesus' divine Nature, David calls Him *"Lord"*. Regarding His human nature, Jesus is a son of David.

Jesus knew His question was decisive because being the Messiah, being the Son of God, only He and Mary knew the answer. Nobody else had ever thought to even frame the question. Accordingly, after Jesus raised this question, *"no one was able to answer him a word, nor from that day did any one dare to ask him any more questions"* (Mt 22:46 RSVCE). This revelation of the Incarnation is the beginning of the defeat of evil in the world, hence the same Psalm verse predicts: *"Sit thou at my right hand: Until I make thy enemies thy footstool"* (Ps 109:1).

---

[148] Quoted in Mt 22:44; Mk 12:36; Lk 20:42; Acts 2:35; 1 Cor 15:25; Eph 1:20; Heb 1:13; 10:12-13. There are unmistakeable allusions to the same in Rom 8:34; Acts 5:31; 7:55-56; Col 3:1; 1 Pet 3:22; Heb 1:3; 8:1; 12:2; Apoc 3:21; 5:7.

As mentioned, it is also a revelation of the Blessed Trinity, for the sublime Psalm implicitly involves a third *"Lord"*. Or how could David know what God the Father was saying to God the Son? How did David hear the Divine conversation? Jesus asserts it was by the inspiration of the Holy Ghost, saying: *"David, inspired by the Spirit, calls him Lord, saying, 'The Lord said to my Lord...'"* (Mt 22:43 ‖ Mk 12:36 RSVCE).

To deny that the Gospels' treatment of Ps 109 is about the Blessed Trinity and Incarnation is to deny God's Self-revelation. There is no other coherent way to subscribe to Jesus' words.

Tanakh, Tanakh, Tanakh

Given the Blessed Trinity is present to everything, it follows that It is discernible not only in the details of the OT, but also in the structure of the whole. The examples looked at above are found in the Law, the Prophets and the Writings. Taking the Hebrew initials for these three, we have *Tanakh*, the name for the Hebrew Scriptures. It is three in one — **T** for *Torah* (the Law of Moses); **N** for *Neviim* (the Prophets); and **K** for *Ketuvim* (the Writings): **Ta-na-kh** (תָּנָ"ךְ).

Investigating this structure further, there are countless reasons to associate the *Torah* with the Father, the Prophets with the Son, and the Writings with the Holy Ghost — albeit the same One God inspires every word throughout the Bible.

Torah concerns creation, the origins of all, including the Patriarchs as the princes of God's People, and unbroken genealogies from Adam. These themes speak of the Father. The Prophets prophesy the coming of the Son in the flesh and His Passion, doing so with words and with signs, ultimately by their own sacrificial deaths in Jerusalem. They give the "Word of the Lord", which is the Son. The Writings, wisdom literature, are especially attributed to the Holy Ghost as their inspiration. In these ways the three parts represent three Persons.

Despite these distinctions, the three parts of the Tanakh have the same substance and are equal in majesty. For perfect unity, the parts harmonise completely and explain each other. They cover the same material. St Justin Martyr observes that exactly the same is taught by the prophets as was taught by Moses.[149] Jews agree.[150] As for the Spirit, reading the Sapiential books one notices that besides countless echoes from the *Torah* and Prophets, they are full of couplets. A single idea is expressed in two ways, so that between these the sense is secured in clear focus. There is an implicit communication between two sides, safeguarding the meaning. Indeed the *Ketuvim* contains the fruits of deep meditations on the Law and the Prophets. This may be likened to a procession from the Father and the Son.[151]

Further, as the *Torah* is associated with the past and the Prophets with the future, so the Psalms prefer a mystical tense, not easily tied down to past or future, rather speaking from eternity, or the *nunc stans*. Thus the threefold division of the Tanakh covers all time: the past, the future, the constant present. Eternity is Being at its Highest, it is divine Life, and it is Three-in-One.

Jesus' division of the OT, after He had risen from the dead, into *"Moses, the prophets and the psalms"* (Lk 24:44) is, like everything He does, a Revelation of the Unity of the Holy Trinity and even the Incarnation. As indicated earlier, *"Moses"* is said not of the man alone, but he is named as a principle to represent

---

[149] St Justin Martyr, *Dialogue with Trypho*, 27.

[150] Talmud, Megillah 14a: *"48 Propheten und 7 Prophetinnen haben den Israeliten geweissagt, und sie haben nichts vermindert und nichts vermehrt an dem, was in der Tora geschrieben steht, ausgenommen die Verlesung der Estherrolle."*

In certain synagogues readings from the Prophets came under the name *Haphtorah*. The likeness in sound to *Torah* is coincidental, but the passages were selected to follow and reflect whichever portion of the *Torah* was first read out on any given Sabbath. In periods when the *Torah* was banned, the readings from the *Haphtorah* served as a replacement. It includes portions from Isaiah, Jeremiah, Ezekiel, Amos, Malachi, Hosea, Obadiah, Zechariah, Micah. The prophets tell what the *Torah* tells, or in our analogy, the Son does nothing but what He sees the Father do (Jn 5:19).

[151] In Masoretic manuscripts, the books of Job (א), Proverbs (מ) and Psalms (ת) are presented in a special two-column format to accentuate this parallelism. The initials of these three books form an acronym for Truth (אמת), so the collection is known as the Books of Truth. Immediately one thinks of the Holy Ghost proceeding from the Father and the Son, the Spirit of Truth communicated by them.

the entire Law. He wrote the *Torah*, so the first five books of the Bible are called the Books of Moses. The *"Prophets"* stands for all the books of the Prophets, Minor and Major. And as the principal part of the Sapiential books, *"the Psalms"* stands for the entire *Ketuvim*. There we have the whole OT, three-in-one.

But Jesus had said that these OT works were about Him. Unforgettably, He taught His disciples that they concerned His Passion, Resurrection and the worldwide mission of His Church (Lk 24:25-27, 44-47). Since then, fascinatingly, for whatever reasons, the Church categorises the various books of the OT differently to Judaism, dividing them not into three parts but into four: the Law of Moses, the Prophets, the Wisdom Books and the historical books. It is as if Jesus' explanation has shown how the saints and the Incarnation (the historical) were always laid up, pre-planned, in the vast trinitarian eternity. Right at this point St Luke tells us: *"Then He opened their understanding, that they might understand the scriptures"* (Lk 24:45).

The Triplicate Temple

As the threefold pattern is pervasive, we are not surprised to find it made visible, concrete, in the life of Israel. It is most obvious in that structure which God had guided man's hands to build as His Hands and their hearts to love with His Love: namely, the tabernacle, or which is like it, the Temple. This makes sense, for the Temple was designed to showcase Heaven. The Holy Ghost inspires couplets correlating the two: *"The Lord is in his holy temple, the Lord's throne is in heaven"* (Ps 10:5). Here the *"temple"* parallels *"heaven"*.

The idea of the Temple beckons us on a pilgrimage to perfection, that is through the purgative, illuminative and unitive stages. But what have these to do with the Trinity? It is by no means suggested there is need of purification in God, nor is any possibility of growth implied within the Godhead, Who is immutable and perfect, always the fullness, to Whom nothing can be added. Nor is any inequality among the Three Persons suggested. All Three are likewise Holy, Holy, Holy.

Rather the three phases of the spiritual life refer to the Most Holy Trinity as encountered by us. To be ignorant of God is to be far from the Temple, far from the Holy Land, drowning in the sea: *"without faith it is impossible to please God"* (Heb 11:6). But to confess there is One God is a beginning of life. St Paul continues: *"For he that cometh to God must believe that He is, and is a rewarder to them that seek Him"* (Heb 11:6). Such a soul seeks to please God. Responding then to an inchoate call which prioritises the spiritual over the carnal, the pilgrim enters the purgative phase. Discovering more of their sins, their helplessness, they learn in parallel the mercy of God, His willingness to help us. Recognising that Jesus is the Son of God is the beginning of illumination. Straining toward the light requires conforming oneself to Him, which being perfected brings one into the unitive phase and ends in Heaven with the beatific vision of the Holy Trinity. God indeed rewards those who seek Him.

Or if this is too obscure, there is a more obvious way that the three phases present themselves in connection with the Temple and its surrounds. This is apparent on the macro and micro scales.

First we may think of the whole world, noticing there are three levels for land: that under the waters (death); land above waters (natural life); and better still, the Holy Land (supernatural life).

Or selecting the Holy Land to begin with: there is Israel (the territory renamed Samaria after the ten tribes fell away from their inheritance); this was distinguished from Judea and Benjamin (chosen to keep the Promises alive); and within this Jerusalem (the Holy City).

Or regarding Jerusalem, we find the same pattern: in the fields surrounding Jerusalem (which belong to it and sustain it, yet where belong thorns, labour and sweat: purgative); then within the walls of the Holy City itself (built compactly, adorned with towers for defence and beauty: illuminative); and at its heart the Temple compound (the holiest part of the holy city in the holy land: union with God).

Or in the precincts of the Temple were three levels of courts: the Court of the Gentiles (where even the uncircumcised entered);

next was the Court of Women (for Hebrews only); and beyond this, the Priests' Court, where the holocausts took place (only Levites entered).[152]

The same pattern is in the Temple building: first the vestibule; then the Holy Place; then the inner sanctum, the Holy of Holies.

However near we zoom in or out, we find, as with a fractal, the pattern. Whether macro or micro, we see a first stage which represents being, a second stage for growth, and a third which stands for perfection. Regardless of the scale, there is a threefold division which represents man's spiritual itinerary from further away to closer, from death to life, from sin through purification to holiness. Such is the itinerary on which the Blessed Trinity calls us: the Spirit of purity whispering to lead us to the Son; He, the Light of the world, illuming us; finally presenting us back to our ur-origin, who we did not know, the Father. This is what it is all about. Only the Blessed Trinity can give us eternity.

It was always God's intention to bring us to Him and the sin of Adam did not alter this, only deepened its manner of accomplishment. This is indicated by the pattern's presence pre-Fall. There was the whole world, representing the Temple Courts; then there is the Garden itself, a paradise planted by God to represent the Holy Place; and within this the unapproachable, the Tree of Life, the Holy of Holies. As this existed before the Fall, then our journey is not just about purgation and redemption from sin, but something more foundational: a learning about, an apprehension of, the eternal pattern, the Holy Trinity. We came from God as unknowing creatures; we return seeing as sons.

This is Whom we hope to see in Heaven, God Himself, in the beatific vision, not mediated by senses or imagination. This is the reward of those who seek God. After the Temple was taken away, there exists no better place to look than Holy Mass.

---

[152] We are all called to a lifelong ascent — to enter through the Courts, rising from being uncircumcised, foreign to God (Court of the Gentiles); to living with natural virtue, concerned for the things of this world (Women's Court); to living with supernatural virtue, concerned for the things of God (Priests' Court). Spiritually, all these levels are open to Jews and Gentiles, to men and women alike (Gal 3:28).

Holy Mass: Entirely Trinitarian

Scarcely a minute goes by in Holy Mass without an explicit reference to the Holy Trinity.[153] This sacred saturation is inevitable given the Mass is the highest reality on earth, our umbilical cord bringing grace from Heaven.

As the very first words of the Bible speak of the Trinity, so do the very first words of the Mass: *"In nomine Patris, et Filii, et Spiritus Sancti. Amen."* Here the priest expresses the Three Persons ("Father... Son... Spirit") in one Name ("In the name of..."), while making a sign of the Cross, thereby honouring the collaboration of the Three Persons in the Passion.

The Three Divine Persons are named again in the doxology of Psalm 42, and again in the *Introitus*.

After this comes the ninefold *Kyrie eleison*. Three times three the Lord (or the Christ) is invoked. For the first set of three, our mind can run from imploring mercy from the Father in Himself, then as Father of the Son, then as Co-Principle of the Spirit; in the next three asking mercy from the Son as generated by the Father, then in Himself, then as Co-Principle of the Spirit; and for the third three to turn to the Spirit as proceeding from the Father, from the Son, and then in Himself. All these are sources of mercy, freely given. Admittedly to run through them quickly enough takes practice, but daily Mass helps, and the *Kyrie* at a sung Mass affords ample time.

In the *Gloria*, with a fourfold action we praise, bless, adore and glorify the One God (*Gloria in excelsis Deo*); then the Father is named (*Deus Pater omnipotens*); the Son is named (*Domine Fili unigenite*); and the Spirit is named (*cum Sancto Spiritu*). Thus there are named in order the One God and the Three Persons.

The first *Oratio* ends with a doxology venerating the Three Divine Persons (as does also, if there are more, the last *Oratio*).

---

[153] Besides these, there are at least seventy references to the Holy Trinity daily in the Divine Office, which is to the Mass what geography is to Calvary, or what the calendar is to Good Friday — that is to say, it encompasses it as leading to it and flowing from it.

The Creed consists of three sections: first for the Father, then the Son, then the Spirit. A bow of the head is made to reverence each Person: God the Father implicitly during *"Credo in unum Deum"*; God the Son at the Holy Name *"Jesum Christum"*; and the Holy Spirit during the words *"simul adoratur et conglorificatur"*.[154]

The Offertory is thoroughly Trinitarian. The Father is named in the *Suscipe, sancte Pater* — "Accept, O holy Father, almighty and eternal God". In the following prayer (*Deus, qui humanæ*) the Son is named (*Jesus Christus, Filius tuus*), followed by explicit mention of the Holy Ghost (*Spiritus Sancti Deus*) and again the Spirit honoured and invoked in the *Veni, sanctificator*. The Three Persons are named again in the doxology at the end of the *lavabo*; and after this the Trinity addressed directly as "O holy Trinity" (*Suscipe, sancta Trinitas*).

The Preface of the Holy Trinity, typically used for Sunday Masses, tells us three facts from which we should never stray: God is absolute unity of Essence; utter distinction of Persons; and among the three Persons is complete equality of Majesty. It is true that to us the Holy Trinity is an unfathomable mystery, but anyone who holds onto these three facts has a higher level of science than can be found in any secular discipline (because everything flows from first principles).

The Canon is addressed to God the Father through the Son. Within it is a reference to the Trinity so profound it is almost hidden. After the consecration, the priest implores God the Father with the *Supra quæ* to look upon the Body and Blood of His Son, and to accept them as He was graciously pleased to accept the sacrifices of Abel, Abraham and Melchisedech. Now these three are figures of the Three Divine Persons: Abel is a type of the Son, Abraham of the Father, and Melchisedech of the Holy Ghost.

---

[154] A genuflection is made to honour the Incarnation at *"Et incarnatus est de Spiritu Sancto ex Maria Virgine: Et homo factus est"*. The Crucifixion is mentioned and at the end of the Creed a Sign of the Cross is made during *"vitam venturi sæculi"*.
Thus the Creed honours the Trinity, the Incarnation and the Passion, not only with words but with bodily gestures (bows, genuflection, Sign of the Cross). It is genius.

While this book has already presented Abraham as a figure for the Father, and Abel for the Son, it is worth dwelling here on how Melchisedech figures the Holy Ghost, given that elsewhere he is convincingly compared to the Son.[155]

Like the Holy Ghost, Melchisedech is mysterious. Sacred Scripture purposefully describes him as

> *without father or mother or genealogy, and has neither beginning of days nor end of life, but resembling the Son of God he continues a priest for ever.* (Heb 7:3)

This is a perfect type of the Holy Ghost, Who is not created, not begotten, and not generated or born, therefore has no genealogy. Rather the Holy Ghost "proceeds from the Father and Son" (as the Creed affirms). This Procession is from all eternity, so has *"not beginning of days"* and likewise He has *"no end of life"* but rather is the very Lord and Giver of Life. Of course the Holy Ghost resembles the Son of God, being of identical Substance. And as Melchisedech uniquely could make of bread and wine a most pleasing offering to God, so the Holy Ghost, the Spirit of the priest, is invoked over the bread and wine in Holy Mass so they may become the perfect offering, namely the Body, Blood, Soul and Divinity of Jesus Christ.

In praying the *Supra quæ*, the Church is not asking that as the offerings of old were pleasing to God, so He might find something in Holy Mass which pleases Him in a similar way. Rather it is prayed with absolute confidence, knowing that the very reason the former sacrifices were pleasing to God is precisely because they anticipated the Sacrifice of Jesus Christ. Everything created is made through the Son of God, including human actions. With their offerings, Abel, Abraham and Melchisedech acted with high rationality, paying due homage to divine realities, and seeking in their own obscure way to offer the whole of creation back to God from Whom everything came. The highest, indeed perfect, expression of this return offering is Jesus

---

[155] See *Quæstiones Veteris et Novi Testamenti*, CIX for Melchisedech's likeness to the Holy Ghost.

Christ's Self-sacrifice on Calvary, and our Old Testament saints were straining virtuously toward this.[156]

By averting to Abraham, Abel and Melchisedech, the prayer appeals to God's consideration of Himself as Father, Son and Spirit. This is the Supreme reason and cause for everything. Just as God swears by Himself when He considers Abraham, Isaac and Jacob, and swears and will not change His mind in regard to Melchisedech, so the *Supra quæ* appeals to God as the Highest reason for His own diffusive Goodness. Hence we have total confidence in the efficacy of Holy Mass, for God cannot be untrue to Himself.

At the end of the Canon, the Trinity is praised with a perfect prayer, *Per quem hæc omnia*:

> Through Whom, O Lord, Thou dost ever create, sancti ✠ fy, quick ✠ en, ble ✠ ss, and give unto us all these good things. Through ✠ Him, and with ✠ Him, and in ✠ Him is to Thee, God the Father ✠ almighty, in the unity of the Holy ✠ Ghost, all honour and glory. World without end. *R.* Amen.

To "create" is attributed to the Father; to "sanctify" to the Son; to "quicken" is attributed to the Spirit. To "bless" is Divine. So we have the three-in-one. With the Christological description "by (*per*) Him, and with (*cum*) Him, and in (*in*) Him", we may think respectively of all creation being done through (*per*) the Son; then the Son coming to dwell with (*cum*) us as Emmanuel; and then our living in (*in*) Him by baptism. These three great works of the Son are all done in perfect Trinitarian collaboration, as the prayer acknowledges by proceeding to say "all honour and glory" goes to the Father with the Holy Ghost. Honour belongs to high office, and God has the highest office. And glory belongs to the highest achievement, and God's is the highest achievement: in creation,

---

[156] It is not that ancient works of sacrifice bestow goodness on the Mass, but the reverse. The Holy Trinity bestows goodness through all creation, and precisely insofar as some*thing* participates in the λόγος, or for humans, insofar as some*one* is conformed to Jesus Christ.

in the Incarnation and in our redemption. All this is *"Per omnia sæcula sæculorum"*, eternal.

Before Holy Communion the Trinity may be honoured in the threefold *Agnus Dei*: the Lamb sent by the Father, the Lamb Himself, the Lamb sending the Holy Ghost.

The threefold *Domine, non sum dignus*, besides being addressed with a threefold love to Jesus Whom we are about to receive, invites God to "enter under my roof", that is to dwell in the recipient's soul. Jesus distinctly told us that this indwelling is the Will of all Three Persons (Jn 14:16-17,23; 15:4). This we may quietly contemplate after receiving.

When the Mass is ended, there is whispered to the Holy Trinity the *Placeat tibi, sancta Trinitas*, followed by a final blessing: "May almighty God bless you, Father, Son, ✠ and Holy Ghost". From beginning to end, the traditional Mass is Trinitarian, and must be so, because the Mass looks to Heaven.

The Heavenly Mystery

The Scriptures and the Mass present us with the Mystery of the Holy Trinity, which receives us as far as we love to enter. The highest reality is a communion of Persons Who offer us entry into their eternal life. It is for this we live at all.

The absolute Unity of God does not mean solitariness or uniformity. It means everything works together. There is nothing the Father withholds from the Son, nothing the Son refuses from the Father. All that the Father is, He gives, and all this the Son receives. Therefore they are Identical in nature, consubstantial. The perfect bond arising is the Holy Ghost, Who is One with the Father and Son. The Spirit adds nothing to either, and of course takes nothing away. Father could not exist without the Son (or He would not be Father); Son could not exist without the Father (or He would not be Son); and neither could exist without the Spirit (for the Spirit is the seal of their unity; an absence of seal would indicate Father and Son were not consubstantial, in which case one would be greater than the other, or that there were two Gods, all of which scenarios are impossible). There must be Three Persons or else there is no God at all.

A correlate of this absolute Unity is the utter distinction of divine Persons. Without distinction, what could unite? The unalloyed distinction of Persons demonstrates that identity is incommunicable. For every person this is true: we are who we are and we can never be any other person. Yet the union of the Trinity shows we live for each other, cannot live without each other. Yes, each of us humans is a substance, but the measure of our being, the degree to which we are alive, the intensity of our existence, is nothing other than how much we love others. Just as the Three Divine Persons love completely and exist completely, so we, the more we love, the higher we ascend up the hierarchy of being, the more we exist. Moreover, we must love now. The Trinity will not come into existence, it cannot pass out of existence, it is only present. So love must be actual love, in the present moment, or else the lover is not living.

As the Three Persons are equal in Majesty, let us not scorn any person made in their image. We know that in the body the brain needs the stomach, the heart needs the bones, the skin needs the blood. So it is with society. Creatures have not the same status, but each is indispensable to the perfect functioning of the whole. God made each soul for Himself, and died for all. Scorning a neighbour makes us distant from God and reduces our fitness for Heaven. God's Plan is that billions of spirits become one.

What is Spirit? The form of the mind is the ideas it has, and this is the extent of its being. For an idea is not a separate substance from the mind, but is its measure: great minds have great ideas. Great ideas presented to our contemplation are much loved; much love is much being. When the idea is perfect and perfectly apprehended, that is God from God, Father and Son; and the unity of this, the compatibility of Knower and Knowledge, the act of Knowing, is Love, the Holy Ghost, Their bond: the perfect Goodness of apprehending the perfect Idea and of being perfectly apprehended.

Knowledge has to be active, alive, to be Knowledge. It is not enough to have known yesterday but to have forgotten now, nor to be able to look it up tomorrow. In these cases it would not be the form of the mind. But one must advert to it, pay attention to it. It must be actual knowledge. More so with love: it is not enough to say "I loved you last year" or "I will love you when we are older". It has to be love now in order to be perfect. If it can grow cold it is not real love, which is forever. Real love involves actual advertence to the Beloved. And because these are distinct (lover, beloved, loving) we have distinct Persons, yet without separation. There must be a Knower, or none of this works. There must be Knowledge to be known, or the Knower were empty. There must be Knowing, or it all collapses (if the Knower does not Know the Knowledge, then we cannot call anything by these names).

Notwithstanding these distinctions between Persons, the Substance of each of the Three is identical. Rejoicing in the revelation thereof, in her Epiphany Octave the Church celebrates "O Christ, Thou Light of Light".[157] If we see the Son then we see the Father also. If we understand that the first act of creation (*"Let there be light"*) showcases Christ, then we follow Him to know the Father. The Father, too, is eternal Light — *"the Father of lights, with Whom there is no change, nor shadow of alteration"* (Jas 1:17). Darkness has no part in light. This is why darkness cannot *"comprehend"* light (Jn 1:5), while God Himself Understands, and is Understood, and this in Understanding.

When we say, rightly, God is Love, the Lover must have a massive ability, an infinite power, to love; and the Beloved must be infinitely lovable. If the Goodness of the Beloved were only in measure, or if the Beloved were so Good as to exceed the power of the Lover to love, then there would be a mismatch — no perfect union, no Spirit. Likewise with Knowledge: if the One could know more than the Knowledge presented to them, or if the Knowledge exceeded the intellect of the Knower, then one would be better than the other, and the act of Knowing could only be the

---

[157] Magnificat Antiphon, Day III, Octave of the Epiphany.

equal of the least of them. Yet the Son as the fullness of Being can be known to infinity, and loved to infinity; and the Father as the fullness of Being is able to know infinitely and love infinitely. Equally infinite is the Union, the Spirit, proceeding. And these Three are One. For the Power to love (the Father) is the same as being lovable (the Son), for the more we do love (the Spirit) is precisely how lovable we are (alive).

As we search for the real distinction between the First and Second Person, Father and Son, Knower and Knowledge, Lover and Beloved, we can scarcely find anything truer to say than that the First Person is active in respect to generation (Paternity) and the Second Person passive in respect to generation (Filiety). The Spirit is the perfect correspondence of the two, therefore is equal to both, for if it were less in any regard then it could not testify to their correspondence in this regard. And as there cannot be correspondence between 'one', then the Spirit cannot proceed from one or the other but can only proceed from both as a single principle (*Filioque*).

The truth of the *Filioque* is seen everywhere in nature: a child is not begotten by its father through its mother as if the father is sufficient, but the child's genetic identity proceeds equally from both father and mother. The present cannot exist without both past and future, so the Spirit is inconceivable without the Son. A directional dimension cannot be defined unless two others fix the perpendicular plane: if only the first dimension is given then the third remains unknowable until the second is known. The Spirit is not simply the love of the Father for the Son, but the mutual love of Father and Son. Love is giving *and* receiving, not half-half, but always wholly both. You cannot give what is not received. Hence contraception is anti-love, an inherently blasphemous disaster.

We find the Trinitarian relations at the deepest level of created existence. The one, the true and the good are each convertible with being, as Father, Son and Spirit have identical substance. Every creature declares being is triune: being as indivisible (*unum*), being as known (*verum*), being as loved (*bonum*). The hierarchy of origin within the Trinity is mirrored in the metaphysical priority of unity before truth and these before goodness; yet none ever exists without the other two. None of the transcendentals add something to being as none of the divine Persons add more to the Godhead. All is beauty.

If the threefold pattern is too complex, we can simplify it. The stages of purification, illumination and union are all aspects of one action. God loves, and we experience this variously depending where we are. To the beginner His love feels like purification, then comes growth, then union. But it is the same single action from God: love. To remove evil is a growth in holiness and this is (our ever-deepening) union with God. Consider the Psalm: *"Benedicat te Dominus ex Sion, qui fecit caelum et terram"* — *"May the Lord out of Sion bless thee, he that made heaven and earth"* (Ps 133:4). There is a threefold division here which is one: between God and us; between Sion and the world; between heaven and earth. They all explain each other. We are without God; then we are with God.

That God gives Himself to us flows from absolute sacrifices within the Trinity, though not quite like anything on earth.

- The Father giving all to the Son is a kind of Self-sacrifice, although the Father loses nothing thereby.
- The Son being nothing except what He receives from the Father, grasping nothing, is a kind of Self-sacrifice, although the Son loses nothing thereby.
- The Spirit's pure passivity in relation to both Father and Son is a kind of Self-sacrifice, albeit the Spirit gains everything thereby.

The immutable pattern is Self-sacrifice. Therefore it is the nature of history and of Holy Mass, the motor of civilisation. Whoever gives, does not grasp, accepts reality, grows.

We cannot change this any more than we can change Jesus. We should not wish to change this any more than we would wish to change Mary. It is the same truth running back to explain why Abel's sacrifice was pleasing (because it cost him) and why Cain's was not (it was self-centred, made for him rather than for God). The truth of the Trinity covers all generations.

What imperturbable contentedness we may have during the Prayers at the Foot of the Altar when it is prayed: *"Sicut erat in principio, et nunc, et semper, et in sæcula sæculorum. Amen"*. Sacred Scripture illustrates this congruence among the ages by both Testaments speaking alike of the beginning: *"In principio"* (Gen 1:1; Jn 1:1); by Isaiah and the Psalms telling of God recalling a past so old that men (except Jesus) did not even know it to forget while telling also of a future so far off that of it men (except Jesus) could not guess; and the very end of time is described by Daniel and the Apocalypse. Like the Bible, the Holy Trinity transcends all time and encompasses all, which may be inferred from the words: *"As it was in the beginning, is now, and ever shall be, world without end. Amen."*

The Mass belongs to eternity because it is from God, of God and for God. Our proper participation in no way dilutes this, but wilful neglect of Mass dilutes us. St John Eudes opined that, to say Mass well, one would need three eternities: the first in which to prepare, the second in which to celebrate, and the third in which to make a worthy thanksgiving. There is that much to it!

Truly, the Sacrifice of Christ is always — an eternal decree of God planned before the beginning of time, present throughout time, and rejoiced over forever in the hereafter.

γ) The One Perfect Actor of the Mass

Not according to our works, but according to His own purpose and grace, which was given us in Christ Jesus before the world began; but is now made manifest by the appearing of our Saviour (2 Tim 1:9-10). St Paul speaks of grace as given at a time when those to whom it was to be given were not yet in existence; for he looks upon that as already having been done in the arrangement and purpose of God, which was to take place in its own time, and St Paul speaks of it as now made manifest.

— St Augustine, *On Christian Doctrine*, III, 34

The immutable pattern is living. In Heaven souls literally *see* love. Eternal life is to know God and Jesus Christ Whom He sent. Real life is seeing God truly and seeing the saints in Him.

Jesus is among us in Holy Mass. To know Him there in Spirit is to see the Father. By baptism the Blessed Trinity enters our soul. By worshipping God we begin to enter eternal life. His glory is our life. We cannot have another lasting goal.

At Holy Mass we know Christ's Body, His Blood, His Priesthood. His love, expressed in the Mass for our imitation, is Self-sacrifice. Our conformity to Christ is a taste of Heaven. God desires to dress us in Christ, giving an idea of how with vestments which are exclusively for the sacred liturgy. If we see this at Mass, and understand Heaven, we will become like Him.

One Body

deliver me from the unjust and deceitful man
— Ps 42:1, Prayers at the Foot of the Altar

The eternal elements of Mass are several, yet they point to One Jesus: the Lamb, the Light, the Cross as His Altar. The immutable pattern appears intricate — how detailed is the tabernacle! — yet the *Logos* is perfectly simple (as one is the principle of all numbers). Similarly the traditional liturgy can strike newcomers as an impenetrable jungle instead of a well-kept garden. But once again it is Christ Who gives order to it all. By being present at Mass, seeking to understand and to live accordingly, we discover the only thing that can unite human beings for eternity: conformity to Christ, being members of His Body.

The Body of Christ has a unity like no other body, simultaneously extrinsic and intrinsic. Extrinsic unity is afforded to a body of persons by their sharing the same goal. A higher purpose gives a higher degree of unity. Invariably a body has a head: a captain for a sports team; a general for an army; a king for a people. Jesus Christ is Head of those who seek the salvation of souls. God's Son is Head because He is the One Redeemer Who has the substance, knowledge and power to achieve this goal.

Intrinsic unity belongs to a body which has one soul. An individual man has one soul which animates every member of his body. Expressing this single principle, his body has one head. The Body of Christ has this intrinsic unity too: not only Jesus' Body which once stood in Jerusalem's Temple, but His Body the Church. Each Christian in a state of grace is animated by Christ's Spirit. God lives in them, giving intrinsic unity to the whole Body. The same Jesus is Head.

Without Christ, we cannot live past death. United in Him, we have eternal life. Such is the message of creation and the liturgy.

Turned to One

The universe is one. Even at the natural level, creation is a perfect unity. There are changeless physical constants underlying the entire cosmos: from the gravitational constant (G) and speed of light (c) on the large scale, down to the sub-microscopic fine-structure constant (α) and reduced Planck's constant ($\hbar$). The whole universe is governed by the same laws. This unity was obvious to the Greeks with the word κόσμος (cosmos), meaning a single, orderly arrangement. The word *universe* derives from Latin terms for *turned-to-one* (*uni* as in one; *vertere*, to turn). The multitude of things are directed toward unity.

At a theological level, creation's unity is based on all of it being made through God's Word (Gen 1:3ss). *"All things were made by Him: and without Him was made nothing that was made"* (Jn 1:3). As all has one source, it necessarily has one purpose, the very reason for it coming into being. Every thing serves this end: Thou *"hast ordered all things in measure, and number, and weight"* (Wis 11:21). Nothing is overlooked by Him.

God established Jesus as Head over all so as to finally present all complete to the Godhead (1 Cor 15:28; Col 1:16-20), which work is underway as growth in Heaven. To this end, eternal Wisdom put down roots in Israel, in Jerusalem, in the Temple, in the souls of saints:

> *I came forth from the mouth of the Most High, and covered the earth like a mist... Alone I have made the circuit of the vault of heaven and have walked in the depths of the abyss... Then*

the Creator of all things... assigned a place for my tent. And he said, 'Make your dwelling in Jacob, and in Israel receive your inheritance.' From eternity, in the beginning, he created me, and for eternity I shall not cease to exist. In the holy tabernacle I ministered before him, and so I was established in Zion. In the beloved city likewise he gave me a resting place, and in Jerusalem was my dominion. So I took root in an honoured people, in the portion of the Lord, who is their inheritance. I grew tall like a cedar in Lebanon, and like a cypress on the heights of Hermon... Like a terebinth I spread out my branches, and my branches are glorious and graceful. Like a vine I caused loveliness to bud, and my blossoms became glorious and abundant fruit. (Sir 24:3-17 RSVCE)

From eternity, Wisdom, the Son of God, was due to enter Jerusalem and there vivify a dead tree — the Cross — which has grown tall like a cedar on a mountain, like a glorious terebinth offering shade across the whole earth. A budding vine is His Church, blossoming and bearing fruit in the saints.

The whole Church has grown from a seed promised verbally in Eden (Gen 3:15) and signified earlier by the design of *"trees bearing fruit in which is their seed"* (Gen 1:12). As the seed is tiny yet grows mighty, as the seed is first hidden but breaks out into the light, as it carries in itself the information (DNA) needed for the fulfilment of its being, so were Christ and His work encoded in the manner God first planted Paradise. The plan was written into nature before sin entered the world: for a seed to germinate and grow it must first fall to the earth and die. That is why Jesus came down from Heaven: to multiply life by dying.

To expound this mystery now unfolding, St Paul was graced

to preach among the Gentiles, the unsearchable riches of Christ, and to enlighten all men, that they may see what is the dispensation of the mystery which hath been hidden from eternity in God, who created all things. (Eph 3:8-9)

God's Purpose in Christ is served from the beginning. On every page of the OT, it seems we find His Life and Passion. If the Sacrifice of Christ were removed from the world, then creation would lose its foundation and goal. Indeed this may happen at the end, the removal of the Mass under the persecution of the Antichrist. Then the world will be wrapped up like a cloak, history will cease.

Meditating on creation's single purpose, finally it is not surprising that everything important was present in Eden — Adam's sleep as the Passion of Christ; Eve as the Church; the Tree as the Cross; its fruit the Holy Eucharist; God walking in the Garden, seeking man; God's Promise of redemption through the Seed of a Woman; God vesting man; friendship with God as origin and destination. The beginning would make no sense if it were not already aimed at the end.

By analogy, the opening seconds of Holy Mass efficiently summarise the whole of creation and history.

Our Sole Redeemer

Mass begins with the priest making a genuflection and signing himself with the Cross in the Name of the Blessed Trinity. In these few moments, the outline of God's plan from Eden to the Last Judgement is traced. The gestures declare that existence has one goal which gives creation unity. It is this purpose which literally all things serve. And though billions of souls participate in this labour, it all hangs on One Worker, One Mediator, One Saviour: Jesus Christ.

The genuflection, our bowing the knee to the ground and rising again, gives honour to the Divine Presence reserved in the tabernacle. This is Our Redeemer, the Son of God, Who according to the Creed "came down from Heaven... was made man... was buried... rose again... and ascended into Heaven". By our genuflection we confess the truth of this descent and rising, acknowledging it was accomplished by He Who is present in the tabernacle, God the Son.

The Son of God came down to redeem us by the Cross. As Mass commences, we make the Sign of the Cross on ourselves — the celebrant leading and laity following — to signify our willingness to take up our Cross and follow Him (Mt 26:24). Having fallen into sin and lost the earthly Paradise, our only way to attain to the heavenly Paradise is by the redemption won on Calvary. We have absolutely no way other than the Son. We must take up our cross as He commanded.

The purpose of all this — His descent and our crosses — is that we may worship the Living God for eternity. This worship begins here on earth, the seed of worship being planted when we are baptised "in the Name of the Father, and of the Son, and of the Holy Ghost". This sacrament is our mystical participation in the Death and Resurrection of Christ (Rom 6:3-5). By baptism we die and rise: God comes to live in us. With this entrance of God into our soul, we rightly reverence the Three divine Persons by name right at the outset of daily worship.

Thus the gestures and words of the first few seconds of Mass honour the Incarnation, the Passion and the Blessed Trinity. None could bring these to us but Jesus. That is the plan and purpose of creation: God with man, Self-sacrifice, Communion. In other words, adoring God through Him Who became incarnate to die on the Cross so that we can live in Heaven. The liturgy feeds us to understand this purpose and to act accordingly. To depart from this plan is futile: it is a rejection of reality; necessarily fails; ends in hell. Such a departure includes explaining away the Scriptures as if they are not true and rejecting tradition as if we can invent a new way. Holy Mass delivers us from this iniquitous deceit, teaching us that God's Plan cannot change. Everything is summed up in the beginning, in Mass as in creation.

Adam was required by God to *"dress"* and *"keep"* the garden (Gen 2:15). So for our redemption we cannot rely solely on the innocence re-won by baptism but upon reaching the age of reason, we must cooperate. Jesus brings God's power to our redemption and, by God's grace and on God's terms, we must contribute our own power, applying ourselves lifelong to grow in holiness and to fight against sin. Accordingly, after the opening antiphon of the Prayers at the Foot of the Altar, the priest prays the first line of Ps 42: *"Judica me, Deus..."* — *"Judge me, O*

God, and distinguish my cause from the nation that is not holy: deliver me from the unjust and deceitful man." Initially, we might think we are asking to be redeemed from unholy people, from the unjust, from the deceitful. On the Last Day we want to stand with the sheep on Jesus' right side, not the goats on His left (Mt 25:33). But we notice a problem. What if we are a goat, rather than a sheep? Is it not dangerous to ask, *"Judge me, O God"*?

The Doctor of Grace observes we struggle with temptation, with iniquity, causing our soul to *"go sorrowful whilst the enemy afflicteth me"* (Ps 42:2). He writes that we want to "admit [our] King, [and] shut the tyrant out".[158] This is entirely our choice. Nobody can take away our sovereign decision as to whether we seek God or reject Him. As this is completely down to us, then the sinful man, the *"homine iniquo et doloso"*, from whom we wish to be delivered, is in the first place ourself. If one asks, the Lord our Redeemer will do it.

Or, *"If we say that we have not sinned, we make Him a liar, and His word is not in us"* (1 Jn 1:10). All nature serves life (even the death of creatures feeds the life of others). So every human serves God's purpose, whether by way of doing good or evil. God only allows evil when He will draw a greater good from it, otherwise the finality of the universe would be shattered.

The entire OT testifies to a perennial longing for the Messiah, for God's Anointed to deliver His People from their enemies. Provided they worshipped truly and rejected sin, their enemies could not touch them. When they sinned, they fell under oppression, and needed to turn their hearts to God again, or indeed to Jerusalem, the Temple, and He would restore them. Likewise for us: in so far as Catholics adore God at Holy Mass, then so full of life and untouchable is the Church.

The supreme Way for our defeating the slightest sin, the most powerful means and motivation, is Jesus in the Blessed Sacrament. We become the Body of Christ by receiving the Body of Christ. Through the Holy Eucharist, God grants holiness,

---

[158] St Augustine, *Enarration on Psalm 42*, 3.

strengthening us to overcome our weakness for sin. But in order to receive, we need to hate sin, confess our sins. This might be hard work, but there is no greater prize to be had than Holy Communion.

Defeating sin necessarily heals divisions within the Body, because sins divide us. Holy Communion is the very sacrament of unity. Many grains, ground and baked, make one loaf. Many grapes, trodden and fermented, make one wine. Faith in the Real Presence and love thereof is the highest cause of unity on earth.

It might be objected that more people enjoy Coca-Cola than the Holy Eucharist. But what good can that achieve? It is a shallow commonality, hardly a unity. It is possible that more people put their hope in the United Nations than in the Blessed Sacrament. But what harmony among men does the UN really accomplish? Globalism abstracts from the particular in order to manage 'units' or data. Aspiring antichrists impose tyrannical uniformity by atomising men, destroying society. The Holy Eucharist has the capacity to unite all souls without reducing any one of them, rather by elevating them. Christ makes us to be more ourselves; our Redeemer leads us to be who we were made to be. Obviously no one can do this but Him.

But we must choose Him. Our wills are made one with each other only by being one in His, having His same purpose of pleasing the Father (*"not My will, but Thine be done"*, Lk 22:42). This is the highest conceivable unity of the many. This is the mystery, the dispensation, hidden in God for eternity and revealed by stages in Eden, in Moses' tabernacle, and in Jerusalem. In Christ we are one.

That They May Be One

One body, one Spirit, one hope, one Lord, one faith, one baptism (cf. Eph 4:4-5). This high unity is declared by creation, all of it. It is confirmed by history. It may overwhelm a soul in Holy Communion. Our body is to be God's temple; our soul to be His tabernacle; our life to be His Eden bearing fruit abundantly; He dwells in us, delights in our acts of charity. We are one with God.

Yet here is a mystery: to the non-believer this remains entirely hidden. They see without seeing, hear without hearing. They darken their hearts and understand nothing. For them the seed is still subterranean, invisible, ungerminated. Even the believer can make cold Communions, distracted, unmoved, caught in routine.

Or what other purpose has existence, except this union with God, this dwelling within each other as intimately as body and soul? Through His Son, God unites all generations through all millennia, whether Christians confessing His Name, OT saints anticipating His Advent, or the unevangelised submitting to the natural law (who by living reasonably give due homage to the *Logos* behind creation). Assuredly Jesus announced, *"many shall come from the east and the west, and shall sit down with Abraham, and Isaac, and Jacob in the kingdom of heaven"* (Mt 8:11), banqueting with the prophets at God's table (Lk 13:27-28). Holy Mass manifests this unity. Present are men and women of any age and class, of any level of wealth or intelligence, secret saints alongside serial sinners. They are joined in one apostolic faith and one apostolic worship.

At Babel the multiplication of languages meant divisions among men. Pentecost is the unity where the apostles "sang with one voice" (the Office of the Octave echoing this). Hence in our liturgy one language, Latin, is appropriate. This is not an absolute: the Orthodox and Copts have their sacral languages which express the same heavenly truths. Yet historically, Latin has proved itself to have the greatest reach. Precisely for this reason — its success — the Latin liturgy is most under attack.

Will saving the liturgy save the world? Yes. Besides worshipping well, we need to believe the Truth and live the Good. These are our paths to the transcendental fundamentals: the one, the true and the good. The three are Trinitarian: perfect liturgy, dogma, morality. There cannot be one without the others. To worship fully we need the faith, to believe the truth, to understand as best we can what is happening in Mass. To understand we need clear minds, which requires living purely, being directed by morality to our goal above. But there is no better means for living morally, nor a greater teacher of true faith, than traditional worship. The relations between the three are fully engaged like Father, Son and Spirit: *lex orandi, lex credendi, lex vivendi* — as we worship, so we believe, so we live. These three are inseparable. Together they rise or fall. In this sense of all things done in Christ, to save the liturgy is to save the world.

Our worship is through One Priest, One Redeemer, therefore the liturgy has one celebrant to show it. Nevertheless, to increase the bonds of love within the Church, God deigns to save each of His elect through the agency of many helpers. This the Mass shows in its constant calling upon the saints as intercessors and its reliance on servers. The same truth is manifested by the community which comes together to worship, for celebrating Mass is possible with a few, yet much more glorious with many. Observing the same rite across epochs and oceans, tradition achieves better than anything else that the many are made one Body in Christ. Our realisation that we are doing the same thing is a bond linking all generations.

All ought to assist at the liturgy. All ought to carry their crosses in life. But laity attempting to carry out tasks in Mass which are proper to a priest is as abortive as saying, "Who needs Christ on the Cross? I can do it instead of Him." Such achieves nothing for anyone. A lay-led Church, or women 'priests', is a climbing onto Calvary without receiving any grace. To worship, to unite, there is no other way but God's, the way Jesus established His Church.

Recall those simple gestures at the beginning of Mass. The genuflection offers adoration to the Head of the Body: Jesus Christ. The Sign of the Cross shows the singular way: Jesus' Sacrifice. Naming the Trinity shows our ultimate purpose: the beatific vision. One Lord, one way, one purpose: only this has the power to unite everyone — everyone who yearns for God to redeem them from sin, *"from the unjust and deceitful man"*.

So absolute is God's desire to do this, that for it He pours out His Most Precious Blood.

One Blood

to God who giveth joy to my youth
— Ps 42:4, Prayers at the Foot of the Altar

One Body lives by one Blood. When the Blood is God's, it follows that the Life of the Body is eternal. This is why the chalice in Mass, filled with Christ's Blood, is lauded as "the cup of eternal salvation". It wins for us eternal life.

God forbade men to shed their brothers' blood, *"for man was made to the image of God"* (Gen 9:6). Further, God forbade men to drink the blood of animals, *"for the life of all flesh is in the blood"* (Lev 17:14; cf. Gen 9:4-5). He had in mind a plan to proffer us a better Blood, shed from the best of brothers, Jesus Christ.

Under the Old Covenant, the blood of animals was offered for sin, to persuade God to forgive. It could not by itself wash away sin, for *"it is impossible that with the blood of oxen and goats sin should be taken away"* (Heb 10:4). Instead it was after the manner of the lamb's blood daubed on the lintels of Hebrew doors in Egypt, providing a notice so that the Angel of the Lord *"shall see the blood, and shall pass over you; and the plague shall not be upon you to destroy you, when I shall strike... Egypt"* (Ex 12:13,23). How did this work? It functioned as a sign of the Precious Blood to come:

Wouldest thou hear the power of the Blood of Christ? Then let us look at the figure thereof, let us call to mind the old type, and tell the story written in the ancient Scriptures... And could the blood of a sheep save a man? Yea, in good sooth, not because it was blood, but because it represented in a figure the Blood of the Lord... If the Angel let the type be, how shall not the enemy quail before the Reality?[159]

This victory is celebrated in the Litany of the Most Precious Blood: *Blood of Christ, victor over demons, R. save us.* It is God's own Blood, that of Jesus Christ, poured out in the New Covenant, that efficaciously delivers us from sin (Heb 10:19; 12:24; 13:20). In the OT it was anticipated with religious devotion.

The translation from shadow to substance, from the Old to a New Covenant in Christ, was prophesied by Jeremiah. In the heart of his book is written: *"Behold the days shall come, saith the Lord, and I will make a new covenant with the house of Israel, and with the house of Juda"* (Jer 31:31). This Covenant was cut on the Cross and is renewed in Holy Mass. In the heart of the Missal it stands written:

HIC EST ENIM CALIX SANGUINIS MEI, NOVI
ET ÆTERNI TESTAMENTI: MYSTERIUM FIDEI:
QUI PRO VOBIS ET PRO MULTIS EFFUNDETUR
IN REMISSIONEM PECCATORUM.

This New Covenant is Eternal. With God fulfilling both sides, it is total, cannot fail. We are invited to enter it too, allowing His pure Blood to wash us clean of sin. Christ's Blood changes everything. Its outpouring was made manifest by His material Blood, yet its form, its meaning, is spiritual. His Eternal Blood is rarefied like Spirit. There is no soul it cannot penetrate, no stain it cannot wash. It flows profusely. It is grace, and grace is Life, and Life is in the Blood.

---

[159] St John Chrysostom, *Homily LXXXIV in Johannes*, 19. Also Feast of the Most Precious Blood, Matins, *Lectiones* IV-VI.

The Sign of Wine

When Jesus touches our spirit, He is never contaminated by our sin, but we are made holy like Him. He desires to do this. The question is whether we are receptive. God does not force Himself upon us. Otherwise love is not love. Rather our will must decide to follow His Will. After Holy Communion, the Missal has the priest pray quietly:

> May Thy Body, O Lord, which I have received, and Thy Blood which I have drunk, cleave to my bowels; and grant that no stain of sin may remain in me, who have been fed with this pure and holy Sacrament...

The Body and Blood are given to "cleave to [our] bowels". By nature, the guts are where we assimilate food. The biological process is a figure for the spiritual, wherein the mind that ruminates on the Word of God, the heart that loves His Presence in the Sacrament, becomes like Him. The soul is nourished by Him, made strong and healthy. He deigns to enter the midst of us substantially so that we can enter into His Substance. By Holy Communion we are transformed in the bowels of Christ to become part of His Body.

Such graphic language helps us understand St Paul's formulation: *"I long after you all in the bowels of Jesus Christ"* (Phil 1:8).[160] The word σπλάγχνον connotes both "entrails" and "compassion". The connection is revealed in our speaking of "gut instincts" and "feeling in our guts", which expressions indicate a deep awareness even before the apparent engagement of intellect or will. God designed the body as a parable. The brain is the instrument of the intellect. The heart is the seat of the will. The bowels, or entrails, our deepest innards, represent the first act of our substance, that of being, of existing. Analogously, by the Holy Eucharist entering the deepest depths of our soul, God gives

---

[160] Zachary sings of *"the bowels of the mercy of our God"* (Lk 1:78). Inspired David asks: *"Create a clean heart in me, O God: and renew a right spirit within my bowels"* (Ps 50:12).

us supernatural substance, eternal being, His own divine Life. He not only forms our minds by faith; He not only lives in our hearts by charity; but He supplements our very being by the Sacrament. Jesus told us at the Last Supper: *"In that day you shall know that I am in My Father: and you in Me, and I in you"* (Jn 14:20). Now we see how St Paul can love the saints with the depths of Christ's love — because he himself lives in the depths of Christ.[161]

Jesus is whole. Whoever receives the Body also receives thereby the Blood, because by concomitance It is always present in the Host. Not recoiling from nature, in the natural body the bowels are where the blood picks up nutrients, distributing these to the whole body. So by Holy Communion Jesus' Blood circulates all manner of graces throughout the Mystical Body. In the depths of the soul each member can merit graces for other members. By the Blood there is one Life in the Body: we can suffer for each other, supply for each other, rejoice in each other.

Despite concomitance, the bread and wine are different signs. One way to understand the distinction would be to say that while the Host increases our being, the Precious Blood washes away non-being. Both mean life. The Body is life because it gives divine substance; the Blood is life because it takes away death (sin) forever. These happen together but are represented differently. The solid stands for increase; the fluid signifies washing away contaminants. The first is a gift and the second secures the gift for eternity, ensuring it cannot be lost. That is, the Blood overcomes every privation. It defeats disease, destroys evil, washes away sin. The Litany adores: *Blood of Christ, Eucharistic drink and bathing of souls, R. save us.*

To pour oneself out in imitation of Christ — in pain, in sacrifice, in peacefully bearing hatred or false accusations — is to bathe in the Blood of the Lamb, dressing our soul for Heaven:

---

[161] God enters our innards to show that we are to enter His. We need to see the human body with God's eyes. The soul is the metaphysical form of the body. Therefore the anatomy of the body reveals to us the virtual structure of the soul. We cannot see the will, intellect or act of being, but we can grasp a sense of them through the triad of heart, brain and guts. Being made in His image, we can associate hearts with the Spirit, brains with the Son, and innards with the Father.

186

Blessed are they that wash their robes in the blood of the Lamb: that they may have a right to the tree of life and may enter in by the gates into the city. (Apoc 22:14)

Besides our circumstantial sacrifices, this is also a description of Holy Mass, gateway to Heaven, where is *"a right to the tree of life"*. To be washed *"in the blood of the Lamb"*, as we have seen earlier, is the plea of the priest's prayer when putting on the alb prior to Mass. He covers himself from head to toe with an alb as our souls become dressed completely in Christ. Putting on the white alb is the physical sign of what will follow with receiving the Precious Blood: Christ dresses our soul in total purity. The vesting prayer witnesses that this is to "attain unto everlasting joys", which means to *"enter in by the gates into the city"*. Christ is *"the gate"* to Heaven.

We are meant to understand that the washing is unto joy, the Blood is unto bliss, and hence God chose wine for its sign. The chief effect of wine is to gladden us. Accordingly, it is with His eucharistic wine that God renews us: *"wine may cheer the heart of man. That he may make the face cheerful with oil: and that bread may strengthen man's heart"* (Ps 103:15). Three times in the Prayers at the Foot we acknowledge it is God Who "gives joy to my youth". Rejoicing is the sign of youth:

Rejoice therefore, O young man, in thy youth, and let thy heart be in that which is good in the days of thy youth, and walk in the ways of thy heart. (Eccl 11:9)

Youth is by nature a time of happiness. This fact was recalled very clearly by Job in his misery. He desired *"the days of my youth, when God was secretly in my tabernacle... When the Almighty was with me"* (Job 29:4-5). The Hebrew of Ps 42 speaks of *"joy joy"* (שִׂמְחַת גִּילִי), the concept being doubled translating as *"exceeding joy"*.[162] The Septuagint, like the Vulgate, and the Mass have *"God, Who giveth joy to my youth"*.

---

[162] Supporting the use of the word "youth" here, the second word for "joy" (גִּיל) is translated in Dan 1:10 as "youths [of your age]".

This is God *"Who satisfieth thy desire with good things: thy youth shall be renewed like the eagle's"* (Ps 102:5).[163] The Hebrew has *"Who satisfies your mouth with good things"*: *"satisfies"* as with the manna filling the Hebrews (Ex 16:8,12); and *"good"* as how God sees creation to be (Gen 1:4) and the fruit of the trees *"good to eat"* (Gen 2:9; 3:6). It is all eucharistic. We are made happiest — eternally happy — by that good fruit, the first Word from God's mouth, with which He fills the mouth of our soul, so we shall be renewed, made new, as in our youth.

The wine, the Blood, washes away sin, signs of age, restoring youth. Here it is licit to seek immortality. The point is summed up during the Office of *Corpus Christi*: *"Introibo ad altare Dei: sumam Christum, qui renovat juventutem meam."* — "I will go unto the altar of God, I will feed on Christ, Who renews my youth".[164] So says the dedicated Feast of the Holy Eucharist.

"Go then, and eat thy bread with joy, and drink thy wine with gladness: because thy works please God" (Eccl 9:7). There is One Life, ever young, no older than the present moment, knowing no past nor future, but touching all acts of charity ever done. This Life is in the Precious Blood. We all need to drink it and all can. The priest alone receives the Blood under the species of wine.

Nature carries an obvious warning to priests who might err here, and to laity who reach for the chalice: excess wine causes drunkenness, loss of the use of reason (by which we are in the image of God), or worse we pass out or even die. So an excess of the Precious Blood can cause death. That excess is to consume without discerning, without believing it is Christ's Blood, or without being in a state of grace through some mortal sin, or drinking distractedly, without devout attention. Then It is drunk unto our condemnation. Instead, the Precious Blood is given by concomitance to everyone who consumes the Host or in spiritual communions through our faith, hope and charity.

---

163 Scripture's first uses of *"renewed"* (חָדַשׁ) concern *"the kingdom"* (1 Sam 11:14); *"the altar"* (2 Chron 15:8); and *"the house of the Lord"* (2 Chron 24:4). The New Covenant renews God's house, altar and kingdom — that is, the souls of His Saints.

164 *Corpus Christi*, Matins, Antiphon VII.

The Bible gives lessons on the power and price of blood so that we consider it with profound reverence.[165] The first blood shed ritually was of the firstling lamb Abel offered (Gen 4:4). Next Abel's own blood was shed by his brother in fratricide, its voice *"crying out"* to Heaven (Gen 4:10). The blood of the innocent cannot stay hidden (Gen 37:26) but its price will be required (Gen 4:11; 42:22). Who could possibly pay the price? Cain could not.

Long in advance of the Messiah's sacrifice, Mount Moriah saw blood shed, a ram substituted for Isaac (Gen 22:13). Scaling up on Mount Sinai to commit to a covenant, Moses *"took the blood and sprinkled it upon the people"* (Ex 24:8). Sacrificial blood was daubed on the *"horns of the altar"* (Ex 29:12), *"drained out on the side of the altar"* (Lev 1:15 RSVCE), poured out *"round about the altar"* (Ex 29:16), as one day it would cover the Cross and colour the earth underneath. It was wiped on the right ears, right thumbs and right toes of Aaron and his sons the priests (Ex 29:20), a sign of grace perfecting nature. Blood consecrated their vestments (Ex 29:21). It was carried into the Holy Place and sprinkled *"seven times before the Lord, before the veil of the sanctuary"* (Lev 4:6) and decorated *"the altar of sweet incense most acceptable to the Lord"* (Lev 4:7), as Mary on Calvary was adorned with her Son's Blood. In the womb He had been content to be fed through her blood, but God's bigger plan is that we all be fed from His.

Annually under the Old Covenant, physical blood penetrated the Holy of Holies. On Yom Kippur, the High Priest alone was duty bound to bring:

> the blood... within the veil... And may expiate the sanctuary
> from the uncleanness of the children of Israel, and from their
> transgressions, and all their sins. According to this rite shall

---

[165] With wine as blood's sign, showing inebriations made holy in Christ, the first man to ferment wine was Noah, and his drunkenness prefigured Christ's Passion. Similarly, Boaz of Bethlehem, lying on his threshing floor, merry from drink, tasted Christ's bloody ecstasy.

he do to the tabernacle of the testimony, which is fixed among
them in the midst of the filth of their habitation. (Lev 16:15-16)

Jesus is not repulsed by the filth of our habitation. In Holy Mass,
He allows that, spiritually speaking, *"the priest shall pour the*
blood upon the altar of the Lord, at the door of the tabernacle"
(Lev 17:6).

Does this teach us of the purpose and copious power in
Christ's Precious Blood? We see only the accidents of wine in the
sacramental sign, and none would dare to pour out the chalice
contents anywhere, nor sprinkle nor daub it anywhere, save that
the celebrant drink it tenderly. But an image of the profusion of
graces poured out in Mass is given by the rivers of blood which
ran in the Temple, as at the time of its inauguration when
Solomon had 120,000 lambs slaughtered, plus tens of thousands
of other sacrificial beasts. The Levites must have been covered in
blood, the whole of Jerusalem full of its smell. May the same
atmosphere be sensed by us in Holy Mass! Moreover, the Temple
rituals were accompanied by brother Levites singing the Psalms,
as Mass is accompanied by angelic choirs.

A powerful image is conjured by Vespers of the Most Precious
Blood. The antiphons for Vespers are soaked in the blood of the
grape, the beautiful one made red from head to toe:

Who is this that cometh from Edom, with dyed garments from
Bosra, this beautiful one in his robe, walking in the greatness
of his strength. I, that speak justice, and am a defender to
save. Why then is thy apparel red, and thy garments like theirs
that tread in the winepress? I have trodden the winepress
alone, and of the Gentiles there is not a man with me: I have
trampled on them in my indignation, and have trodden them
down in my wrath, and their blood is sprinkled upon my
garments, and I have stained all my apparel. For the day of
vengeance is in my heart, the year of my redemption is come.
I looked about, and there was none to help: I sought, and
there was none to give aid: and my own arm hath saved for me
(Is 63:1-5)

This is Jesus, Who alone can save. Of Him Jacob prophesied:

> *The sceptre from Judah... will not be taken away, until he who will be sent arrives, and he will be the expectation of Gentiles. Tying his young colt to the vineyard, and his donkey, O my son, to the vine, he will wash his robe in wine, and his cloak in the blood of the grape. His eyes are more beautiful than wine, and his teeth whiter than milk.* (Gen 49:8-12)

The blood of the grape! God created grapes for this purpose, to give blood, or rather, wine which inebriates. The Verdun Altar, one of the most theologically intricate pieces of sacred art in the world, associates Christ crucified with the giant cluster of grapes 'thieved' from the Holy Land by the spies (Num 13:20-24). His abundance of Blood is shown by its staggering size; hanging heavily on a piece of wood, representing the Cross; positioned between two men on the same wood — the two thieves on their crosses.[166] Truly, Christ is the First-Fruit of the Promised Land (Num 13:26).

The Canticle sings of the Holy Eucharist, to award us far better than was once lost in Eden:

> *May my beloved enter into his garden, and eat the fruit of his apple trees. I have arrived in my garden, O my sister, my spouse. I have harvested my myrrh, with my aromatic oils. I have eaten the honeycomb with my honey. I have drunk my wine with my milk. Eat, O friends, and drink, and be inebriated, O most beloved. I sleep, yet my heart watches. The voice of my beloved knocking.* (Cant 5:1-3)

See the garden, fruit, tree, spouse, honey, wine, eating, inebriation, watching and the beloved. How profitable the sleep of the Cross!

---

[166] St Gregory of Nyssa, *Life of Moses*, II, 268 "What is the bunch of grapes suspended from the wood but that bunch suspended from the wood in the last days, whose blood becomes a saving drink for those who believe? Moses spoke to us of this ahead of time when he said in a figure: *They drank the blood of the grape.* By this he signifies the saving passion."

The Nature of Blood

Wine is a sign. How much richer is the signification of blood. To probe this further, instead of turning a page of the Bible we can look into God's other book: creation.

To discover what the Precious Blood achieves in the order of grace, we may investigate what our bodily blood achieves in the order of nature. Red blood cells carry oxygen and defeat certain pathogens and bacteria. Plasma carries nutrients, hormones and proteins. It also removes cellular waste. To donate plasma is called 'giving life'. White cells fight infection. Two per cent are eosinophil cells, thus are relatively few in number, but multiply when needed to attack parasites. Platelets clot to prevent bleeding by signalling to others of their kind, extending their tiny tentacles, binding to each other.

Now let us think of the Most Precious Blood as grace. It flows through the entire world and all history. It inspires the oxygen of prayer, carries nutrients for growth, it builds the Church, cleanses the Church, heals our souls. It overcomes temptation, washes away sin. To be a vehicle of grace for another is to give life. By grace are overcome error, falsehood and heresy; by it demons are repelled and defeated. Few might leap to be martyrs when persecution breaks out, as the eosinophil cells are few when infection begins. But others see their example, and imitate, and by their blood the Church is re-seeded a hundredfold. If the Church begin to haemorrhage, then let her little ones look to each other, and reach out to one another like platelets, so that where one cannot hold the line, many may do it together.

Our body has 25 trillion red blood cells (25,000,000,000,000). Each lasts about 100 days. That means we each produce some two million blood cells every second! What constant wonders are worked in your body. Could there possibly be less in Christ's Body, the Church? Are there not more than two million prayers going up every second? Are there not many more sacrifices being endured all the time? Are the acts of intercession of the Saints in Heaven or the deeds of charity of Christians on earth any less frequent than this, and are they not all fruitful for the good health of the whole?

The body has many members and the same blood goes to all of them. Blood shows the unity of life in the diverse organs. This unity also spans time, for although multiple generations of a family are not said to be one body, we do say they are of the same blood. While some social climbers desire to marry into aristocratic blood, how much more we should yearn to live by divine Blood.

Fr William Faber praised the Most Precious Blood for running through the entire cosmos, processing profusely, shaping human history, being adored everywhere by the angels, notably each drop He shed for our Salvation. St Thomas writes that each single drop thereof would be enough to redeem the whole world.[167] This is the price more precious than gold (1 Pet 1:18-19).

How goodly the vessel which holds His Blood. As the heart pumps blood round the body, so the chalice of Holy Mass is like His Sacred Heart, pouring His Blood for the life of the Body, His Bride, washing her spotless. We do not need to see it, only to see its sign and believe it. But for this we need His priests.

---

[167] St Thomas, *Adoro te devote*, *"Pie pellicane, Iesu Domine, me immundum munda tuo sanguine; cuius una stilla salvum facere totum mundum quit ab omni scelere"*.

One Priesthood

et tibi, pater... et te, pater[168]
— *Confiteor*, Prayers at the Foot of the Altar

The Son of God's Eternal Priesthood has always been with us and always will. The preparation and exterior marks of this One High Priesthood developed from Adam to the coming of Jesus Christ, Who fulfilled it. Ever since then it continues on earth by the Sacrament of Holy Orders.

All Christians are to participate in Jesus' Priesthood, but few are called to receive Holy Orders. The first kind, which is general and universal, is a spiritual priesthood. About this St Peter writes:

Be you also as living stones built up, a spiritual [πνευματικός] house, a holy priesthood, to offer up spiritual [πνευματικός] sacrifices, acceptable to God by Jesus Christ. (1 Pet 2:5)

Obviously St Peter is not asking people to be material *"stones"*, but to offer their soul to God for a *"spiritual house"* which is

---

[168] "and to you, Father... and you, Father".

achieved by offering up *"spiritual sacrifices"* through Jesus Christ. This does not require entering the sanctuary of the Church, or approaching the altar, or touching the sacred vessels, except spiritually — that is by intellect and will, which means by understanding and love, or faith and charity. This *"kingly priesthood"* is obtained by baptism, birthing a *"chosen generation"* (1 Pet 2:9).

Nobody saves themself. They must receive from Christ and cooperate. To make this clear, relatively few men minister at the altar. The laity are dependent upon them in crucial ways. This is to teach us that we are all absolutely dependent upon Christ as Priest. To reject His priests *per se* is to reject Him. Or to attempt to usurp the tasks of priests is a blasphemous attempt to be Christ.

The ministerial priesthood of the Latin Church is sacrificial, male, hierarchical, celibate and fruitful. These five marks do not constitute a definition of sacramental priesthood, but they are treated below because, though vital to it, they are under attack within the Church. Each of these five marks became increasingly obvious as the OT progressed, until Jesus came to perfect them, translating the Old into the New (Heb 7:11-12). Any attempt to recast the priesthood so that it no longer carries Christ's five marks should be unhesitatingly rejected.

Sacrificial

The chief purpose of the priesthood is to offer sacrifice. This is for the remission of sins. Scripture spells it out explicitly: *"every high priest taken from among men is ordained... [to] offer up gifts and sacrifices for sins"* (Heb 5:1; also 8:3). Atonement for the congregation was achieved through the priest's sacrificial offerings:

> *And Moses said to Aaron: 'Approach to the altar, and offer sacrifice for thy sin: offer the holocaust, and pray for thyself and for the people: and when thou hast slain the people's victim, pray for them, as the Lord hath commanded.'* (Lev 9:7)

Holy Mass is a sacrifice. Each Mass explicitly uses the word *sacrificium* nine times, besides other realities mentioned which are essential for sacrifice: offering, victim, priesthood, altar.[169] For those not following the text, that the action is a sacrifice to God is made clear by the altar, the orientation, the elevations, the solemnity, and ultimately by the priest consuming the separated Body and Blood.

That the OT was a preparation for Christ's Sacrifice is witnessed by the business of the Temple. One whole tribe of the twelve, Levi, existed to produce priests. Entered on a rota to serve one month per year in the Temple, their chief work was sacrifice.

Earlier the same was essential on a smaller scale in the tabernacle. God's very purpose in leading the Hebrews' escape into the desert, the Exodus, was explained by Moses and Aaron to Pharaoh: *"Thus saith the Lord God of Israel: Let my people go, that they may sacrifice to me in the desert"* (Ex 5:1; cf. 3:18; 5:3,817; 7:16; 8:1,8,20,25,27-29; 9:1,13; 10:3,7-8,11,24; 12:6*ff*). Evidently this was not an afterthought, for the day God first appeared to Moses He told him:

> *this thou shalt have for a sign that I have sent thee: When thou shalt have brought my people out of Egypt, thou shalt offer sacrifice to God upon this mountain.* (Ex 3:12)

The sign of being sent by the Living God is offering sacrifice on the mountain. Ultimately Jesus is meant here: His Sacrifice, His Mountain, His Mission from God, that is, His Eternal Generation from the Father — perfect Sonship, perfect filial love.

This is so momentous that the preparation was necessarily long. The tribe of Levi provided priests from the time of Aaron's High Priesthood through to that of Caiaphas. When Caiaphas illegally tore his robes at the illegal trial of Jesus, blasphemously accusing God of *"blasphemy"* (Mt 26:65), he fatally ruptured the

---

[169] *Sacrificium* is repeated in the Offertory and the Canon, both parts being essential to sacrifice: in the *In spiritu humilitatis*, the *Veni, sanctificator*, the *Orate fratres* and its response, the *Te igitur* [in the plural, *sacrificia*], the *Memento* for living, twice in the *Supra quæ*, and finally in summation at the close of Mass in the *Placeat*.

THE ONE PERFECT ACTOR OF THE MASS

OT type (Lev 21:10), while on the very same day, Jesus made His offering as eternal High Priest. Not a day was lost.

Even earlier than Aaron's day, Jesus' unique priesthood was foreshadowed by Melchisedech. His priesthood was also centred on sacrifice, who made of bread and wine a most pleasing offering to God (Gen 14:16-18). The Messiah is *"a priest for ever according to the order of Melchisedech"* (Ps 109:4). Altogether, Melchisedech points to Jesus inaugurating the sacramental priesthood while instituting Holy Mass at the Last Supper.[170]

Genesis does not waste a word, yet makes sure to convey that Abraham offered bloody sacrifices and Noah before him. Both cases were to mark a covenant with God, respectively for blessing the world and for delivering it. Undoubtedly both signify Jesus.

Abel pleased God in that he *"offered of the firstlings of his flock"* (Gen 4:4), even at the cost of his life. It is as if, in him, who belonged to the second generation, mankind was rushing to offer God a more pleasing sacrifice. It was not something to put off to a later time. Evidently sacrifice is essential to man. If sacrifice is removed, so is mankind.[171]

Scripture tells us that the Levitical High Priests, also Melchisedech, Abraham, Noah and Abel, all offered sacrifices, most all of them in Jerusalem. All anticipated Christ as best they could, sharing in His Sacrifice. It is unthinkable to have Christianity without sacrifice.

Male

The priesthood is properly male. Scripture shows this through all generations. Besides procuring innumerable practical advantages, and avoiding social difficulties, this has a vast theological significance. Below we probe the deep coherence in the meaning of priesthood and the meaning of male-female complementarity.

---

[170] St Thomas, *S.Th.* III Q.22 a.6 ad.2. Also Dom Anscar Vornier, *A Key to the Doctrine of the Eucharist*, pp.224-25.

[171] Even prior to the Fall, man owed God sacrifices of praise and thanksgiving. Now these are perfectly fulfilled by the Divine Office's perennial praise (*laus perennis*) and the Holy Eucharist (εὐχαριστία, thanksgiving).

Without question, the female is always present in Holy Mass. Mass is of the Church, who is Virgin, Mother and Bride. Likewise, Mass is always Marian. Mary was there on Calvary, spiritually engaged, willingly offering her Son. So Mary cannot be removed from the Mass, as she is part of it. The prayers of Holy Mass testify that Our Lady is there assisting before all other saints. Indeed the female aspect of our union with God — receptivity — is realised in every soul open to God, including the celebrant priest.

Meanwhile, maleness must be present too, and this primarily in the priesthood. This irrefutable truth emerges with sharp definition from the Scriptures.

Originally, in Eden, there was just Adam, one person, male. The spread of original sin to all of us is not because Eve ate of the apple but because Adam did (Rom 5:12-21). Had he refused, we would not inherit original sin. Some speculate that, in this case, Adam would have done much penance for the sake of his beloved Eve. As it is, he had to do plenty for himself — like priests today: we are not better than Adam. The point is, although Eve tempted Adam, she who had been given to him as a helper, it was entirely up to him whether he fell for the temptation or not. The Fall offers no pretext for misogyny. Rather we see there a relationship between man and woman, but also that man stands alone.

The profound significance of this is that although one man alone, Jesus Christ, can redeem us (because He is God), still He graciously chose to include His Mother Mary in the work of our redemption. To deny that Eve sinned in Eden is, effectively, to deny Mary's position as Co-redemptrix.

On the other hand, to claim women can be priests is, effectively, to assert that Eve's sin was as deleterious as Adam's, as if we could have all contracted original sin through her. This is theologically false. Its corollary would be to claim Mary is equal to Jesus, divine, our redeemer on the same level as Him. All such assertions are heresy.

If we deny the difference between Adam and Eve, we can hardly appreciate the redemptive roles of Jesus and Mary. Adam could have spared us hell by ignoring Eve but he did not. Jesus could have opened Heaven to us without Mary but He did not.

Proceeding from Adam to Noah, we recall the rabbi's description of a contemporary illustration, which

> depicts Noach about to light the fire under the sacrifice, as his three sons prepare the other animal and bird-offerings. The women of the family look on in the background, and pools of water remaining from the Flood can be seen in the distance.[172]

Noah himself offers the sacrifices, his sons prepare them, while their wives *"look on in the background"*. Deeply habituated in the *Torah*, orthodox Jews cannot think of sacrificial priesthood except as male. Christians who respect the *Torah* think likewise.

At the next great anticipation of Calvary, the *Akeidah*, the whole cast is male. There is Abraham and Isaac, both male; the ram, male; two servants at a distance, male. God did not call Sarah to be present. A midrash opines that when Sarah heard of the offering of her son, she died of shock. If so, how reverent we should be before the Mother of God, who freely offered her Son. Mary did this not as priest, but as daughter of God. For his part, "Abraham was a priest", as shown by the instruction he received to kill animals in sacrifice.[173]

In continuity with Abraham, Aaron's inauguration was a deep cultural preparation for Christian liturgy. Holy Mass is not something which could have been assembled from scratch in one generation, but required thousands of years of prior formation. Integral to this: all who served as Levites were male; all who ministered in the tabernacle were male; all who set it up, who took it down and who transported it, were male. All *Kohanim* (priests) were sons of Aaron, not daughters.

Setting this distinction in stone after Aaron, in Jerusalem the inner court of the Temple was the Priests' Court; outside this was the Women's Court. No woman was permitted to enter the

---

[172] TI article with illustration 4/11/2020.

[173] St Thomas, *S.Th.* III Q.31 a.2.

Temple vestibule, not to speak of the Holy Place. Although there were Hebrew queens of great power, prophetesses, female Judges who saved Israel, Hebrew heroines who did the same, prefiguring the defeat of the Antichrist, yet in this culture planted by God there were never female priests.

Of many OT sleeps which prefigure the Passion, such as Adam's, Noah's, Jacob's and Jonah's, the protagonist is always male. Where a female is involved in such a story, for example Sarah, Rebekah or Ruth, she represents the Blessed Virgin Mary, not Christ the Victim-Priest. Why? And why not?

This is all about understanding the post-Creation complementarity of the Divine and human and its corollary in the perfect complementarity of active and passive. God acts to create; and the world is created. When God created woman, taking her from man, Adam gave his rib and the woman was formed from it. Adam was asleep when this happened, not consciously active. Rather God was active through Adam, and Adam was passive in respect to God. But materially Adam gave, and Eve received.

All this is an image for the supernatural work of Christ on earth. The perfection of Divine-human complementarity came in Jesus Christ: True God and true man. He is the Truth Who gives growth to the being of all who receive Him. God's Word is the seed sown in the soil of our soul. Everyone receiving sanctifying grace lives with His life. God gives; we receive. Thereby the whole Church is built up as Bride of the Bridegroom as God *"filled up flesh"* around Adam's rib to create Eve (Gen 2:21). Christ and the Church do not have identical roles. Likewise, God acts through His priests to build up the Body of the Church.

The meaning of male and female, or the difference between man and woman, cannot be found in man and woman alone. They point to something much greater than themselves. The meaning is that difference between Divinity and humanity. Their union is analogous to the metaphysical marriages between form and matter, or any determining and determined principles.[174]

---

[174] The *causa finalis* (m) determines the *causa efficiens* (f) as the *causa formalis* (m) informs the *causa materialis* (f). Each case is a productive 'male-female' union.

The Son admits that all He is and has, He received from the Father (Mt 11:27; 28:18; Lk 22:29; Jn 3:35; 5:26; 6:39; 10:29; 13:3; 17:7,12). This giving and receiving in God is imaged, *secundum quid*, in male-female complementarity and in the relation of priesthood-laity. Accordingly, St Bonaventure teaches man and woman signify God and the soul, Christ and the Church, higher reason and lower.[175]

The best of the Greek philosophers already understood the male to represent the divine. Men are generally bigger, stronger and less emotional than women. These are little pointers to ways where God exceeds us all, Who is 'bigger' (omnipresent), 'stronger' (omnipotent) and 'less emotional' (entirely spiritual, perfect intellect: angels have no emotions because they have no bodies). The meaning of woman is not God, but God's beloved: we are not in competition.

So in the sanctuary of a Catholic church one should see only males (*bzw* clerics), to represent that this is the place of the divine. Obviously women have no call to be resentful. The role of the human in relation to God is to receive. Receptivity is accentuated in women in comparison with men, biologically, psychologically and spiritually.

The Virgin Mary is proof. The very height of a people, or the height of a creature, is its receptivity to God, to His grace. The highest creature is the Blessed Virgin Mary, for she is the most receptive to God. Mary superlatively illustrates that the dignity of matter is that it can unite with form, it can carry information, it can exhibit a trace of the *Logos*. In Mary's case, much more than a trace, for in mind and body she conceived Jesus.

To be envious of liturgical ministry misses the bigger point. We all remain human, we are all called to open our life to God. Every soul receiving Holy Communion receives more from the

---

[175] St Bonaventure, *II Sent.*, d.XVIII a.1 q.1 *"Per virum namque et mulierem signifcantur Deus et anima, Christus et et Ecclesia, superior portio rationis et inferior"*. Higher and lower reason refer to St Augustine's division between using our mind to contemplate the things of Heaven and using it to consider the things of this world. These two fields of knowledge connect as male and female in a fruitful union. Our existence on earth would be sterile if one or the other were missing.

altar than Aaron ever did. Every priest saying Mass may come closer to Heaven thereby than Zadok on the Day of Atonement, a holy High Priest who entered the Holy of Holies but did not encounter on earth God's substantial Presence. Does this mean Catholic priests are better than the saints of the OT? No, but we have been given a better office, better gifts, greater responsibility. Even so, as Jesus said: *"Rather blessed are those who hear and keep the word of God"* (Lk 11:28). So it brings us nothing to carry Christ in our belly or confect Him on the altar if we are not first obedient like Mary to God. And Mary knows no envy.

Any resentment that men should symbolise the Creator and women the created is a staggering petulance, as if God cannot put both signs before our eyes in order to help all reach Him in Heaven. Attempts at making men and women androgynous are part of the same effort as removing communion rails from churches. It is a misguided, even revolutionary attempt to blur the distinction between the divine and human, Heaven and earth, the sanctuary and the nave, clerics and laity, the active and passive. The result is disintegration. There is less and less left to unite.

But God cannot be pushed around by human insanity. Holy Orders cannot be conferred on a woman. That is divine law. No one can change it ever. It is sacrilegious futility to try.

Hierarchical

There are unmissable hierarchies in nature, in ancient Israel and in Holy Mass. They are intrinsic necessities of reality, all pointing to God. To reject hierarchy, or to wish to overturn it, is a prideful aversion to God.

Properly understood and loved, the existence of the Church hierarchy compels every honest soul to internalise that the main work of our salvation is done for us. There is someone greater than us above us. The layman cannot confect the Holy Eucharist. The priest cannot ordain himself. A bishop cannot appoint himself. No pope is greater than St Peter. And St Peter, obviously, is subordinate to Christ. Even Christ the Head subordinates Himself to the Divinity.

In nature the hierarchy of being is clear. The cosmos contains incalculably more mineral matter than organic, much more inanimate matter than animate. Think how outer space is full of dead rocks and balls of burning gas, and how life on Planet Earth inhabits only a thin layer at the surface. Among living beings, there is vastly more biomass of plants than animals. Among animals, the total weight of insects is far greater than that of all humans. It is impossible to imagine a biologically functioning universe without such a dramatically tapering hierarchy.

Furthermore, each organism is hierarchically made. Even a single-celled animal has a governing nucleus. Analogously, each animal with a head would be lost without it (or would be a monster if it had multiple heads, like the mythical Cerberus or Hydra). When the human body goes into shock, certain organs get priority: blood is withdrawn from the extremities to serve the core. This is necessary for survival.

Societies, also by necessity, have hierarchical structures. In every herd or flock of herbivores, the prime bull or ram will dominate for the good of the whole. Each pride of lions and troop of chimps needs its alpha. A hive of bees or army of ants has its queen, and will crown a new one if they lose her. And there has never been a group of humans who lasted long without a leader.

Importantly, hierarchy does not exclude equality. The Three Persons of the Blessed Trinity have a hierarchy of origin yet absolute equality of Majesty. The Father is Origin without Origin (innascibility); the Son is generated from the Father alone; the Holy Ghost proceeds from Father and Son. In this order of procession, there is a fixed hierarchy. But no one Person of the Trinity is any better in any conceivable regard than either of the others. Hierarchy is necessary for order, and order is necessary for peace. If there is not one single first principle, then harmony cannot be guaranteed.

For human society, while hierarchy of authority makes harmony possible, we find equality of dignity in terms of salvation. Each soul is made for God. A grandfather will not receive a lighter judgement than a teenager, a king not lighter than a tramp. Nobody disputes children may be holier than their parents, but they are not their equals in authority. God has placed a hierarchy within the family, the rejection of which is guaranteed to bring confusion and unhappiness: *"the husband is the head of the wife, as Christ is the head of the Church"* (Eph 5:23). Children are subject to their parents. The Holy Family is the perfect model of this. The divine Person, Jesus, was subject to His creatures. The highest creature, Mary the Immaculate Conception, was subject to St Joseph. For his part, the most chaste St Joseph, Shadow of the Father, subjected himself socially to the laws of pagan occupiers, the Romans. Prestige in the human hierarchy does not necessarily bear on one's dignity before God.

Modernity denies hierarchy as it denies much reality. The OT is not in denial. Hebrew families, society, civilisation, were founded by the great patriarchs. One's very identity was bound up in one's father, and his father, and his father's father *usw*.

Moses led the people. He first went alone up the mountain to encounter God. The people had to remain below, and were glad to do so. In due course, Moses brought Aaron and selected elders with him. Any unauthorised person would have died if they ventured to touch the mountain.

The Tribe of Levi were exclusively dedicated to the service of God for the benefit of all. Within the Levites, there was a hierarchy of families, named after three grandsons of Levi. In first place the sons of Kohath, then of Gershon, and then of Merari (Num 49).

Descended from Kohath were Moses and Aaron. Only Aaron's line produced legitimate High Priests. Inheritors of the High Priesthood were not permitted to make innovations to essentials. More than any others, they were absolutely bound in their duties. The higher that one is placed in the hierarchy, the stricter the necessity to serve — which Jesus taught indelibly by washing the feet of His apostles. That is a stunning overturning of the way of the world, where the leaders of the Gentiles *"lord it over"* their people (Mt 20:25).

Only the Kohathites produced priests, *Kohanim*, who could offer holocausts on the great altar. More generally, these sons of Kohath took care of the ministry in the Holy Place. *"And over them shall be Eleazar the son of Aaron the priest"* (Num 4:16). Respecting their place in the hierarchy was a matter of life and death:

> *And the Lord spoke to Moses and Aaron, saying: Destroy not the people of Caath [Kohath] from the midst of the Levites: But do this to them, that they may live, and not die, by touching the holies of holies. Aaron and his sons shall go in, and they shall appoint every man his work, and shall divide the burdens that every man is to carry. Let not others by any curiosity see the things that are in the sanctuary before they be wrapped up, otherwise they shall die.* (Num 4:17-20)

This is of God. Catholic clerics should have more reverence than this, not less, around our own tabernacles, for they house Christ.

Representing the middle of any hierarchy, the sons of Gershon were charged with caring for the outer part of the tabernacle:

> *The sons of Gerson shall carry, by the commandment of Aaron and his sons: and each man shall know to what burden he must be assigned, and they shall be under the hand of Ithamar the son of Aaron the priest.* (Num 4:27-28)

Hierarchy is a practical and metaphysical necessity for order.

At the hierarchical base, the sons of Merari, also *"under the hand of Ithamar"* (Num 4:33), transported boards, bars and pillars. These, too, are needful for perfection. Equality, misapplied, is a dangerous lie. Individuals underreaching or overreaching disfigure or endanger the whole.

Maintaining this orderly ranking, once the Temple was built, priests had a special place within its precincts:

> *the chamber which faces north is for the priests who have charge of the altar; these are the sons of Zadok, who alone among the sons of Levi may come near to the Lord to minister to him.* (Ezek 40:46)

Although accidentals may change, the Church is bound by the same essentials, that the entire arrangement came from Heaven, divine inspiration and through tradition:

> *[Solomon] appointed, in accord with the plan of his father David, the offices of the priests in their ministries; and those of the Levites, in their orders, so that they might praise and minister before the priests according to the ritual of each day; and the porters, in their divisions, from gate to gate. For so had David, the man of God, instructed.* (2 Chron 8:14)

Hierarchical systems serves harmony. The Bible shows us divisions which will never pass away. Porters and singers are essential for a peaceful society because they are needful for worship from whence peace comes. Holy Mass must be protected and is meant to be sung:

> *And the priests, and the Levites, and the porters, and the singing men, and the rest of the common people, and the Nathinites, and all Israel dwelt in their cities.* (2 Esdras 7:73)

That is a picture of peace.

Book-keeping of names and families was exact so as to keep the orders right, for example enrolment in genealogies from three years old for all destined for Temple service (2 Chron 31:16). Historically, no other people was so exact. It anticipates the care Catholic parishes take over baptismal registers with their annotations. This is very strictly regulated by Canon Law: avoiding doubts about the sacraments depends on it.[176]

Reading all this in the OT, it is hard not to think of the Church's hierarchy of bishops, priests, deacons; and within a Solemn Mass, the celebrant, deacon, sub-deacon. These divisions are ordered to the Holy Eucharist for the glory of God and salvation of souls. So also the minor orders of acolytes, exorcists, lectors and porters.

---

[176] Hebrew record-keeping ultimately serves all mankind. No other people ever dreamt of giving a genealogy going all the way back to the first man, Adam.

Ultimately all hierarchy points to our one Head, our one Mediator, our one Saviour, Jesus Christ. In all He points to the Father (Jn 14:9). He ministers to us from the heavenly courts, the invisible tabernacle:

> *Christ, being come an high Priest of the good things to come, by a greater and more perfect tabernacle, not made with hand, that is, not of this creation.* (Heb 9:11)

Within Christ lives a hierarchy of members. The hierarchies of the visible world, especially those of patriarchal genealogies, royalty and liturgical service described in the OT, along with the hierarchy of the Church Militant, all point to — though none of them replicate — the ultimate hierarchy of angels and saints in Heaven. This is the hierarchy of holiness, of closeness to God, the final hierarchy of being.

This order is outlined multiple times per Mass in the *Confiteor*. At the top is God, to Whom we pray. As intercessors above, we invoke first the Blessed Virgin Mary, then St Michael Archangel, then St John the Baptist, then SS Peter and Paul, then all the saints, then all present at Mass. This solidifies a picture in our understanding with God at the top of the hierarchy, Mary second, followed by the angels and saints. There are nine choirs of angels, the saints distributed among them. St John the Baptist has a privileged place, embodying the perfection of the OT in heralding the Messiah. SS Peter and Paul are pillars. The Church Triumphant is superior to the Church Militant (*"vos fratres"*).

The list of intercessors is given twice in each *Confiteor*. First they are honoured, addressed as holy. Then the list is repeated in an appeal to them as sympathetic helpers. Holiness is the source of power (a very important hierarchal note).

The priest prays the *Confiteor* first, bowing deeply, asking the servers to pray for him. Then the servers bow down and pray it themselves. There is hierarchy: priests first, then servers, while the faithful assisting are properly silent.

We find similar hierarchies given in the *Suscipe Sancta Trinitas, Communicantes, Nobis quoque* and *Libera nos*. Holy

Mass makes clear that — on earth as it is in Heaven — there must be hierarchy to keep order, harmony and unity.

From the *Orate Fratres* to *Ecce Agnus Dei* the priest does not turn to the people, for here, stationed on the predella, he enters the new Holy of Holies alone. Still, during this time there is a *Dominus vobiscum* before the Preface, a *Nobis quoque* in the Canon, and a *Pax Domini* after the *Pater Noster*, which show the priest remains united with the faithful through prayer, albeit not yet coming back out to them (facing them). The One Mediator Jesus Christ does not, from Heaven, forget His people.

Only ordained ministers may take their place on the predella. If servers are tasked to approach the altar, they must go the long way, and are permitted on the top step only if accompanying a sacred minister or in some sense fulfilling his task (as an MC might turn the pages of the Missal). Only the celebrant may touch the altar. The one exception is the deacon kissing the altar before the Pax, but he should not touch it with his hands. The priest touches the altar only at the times and in the reverent manner prescribed: either with his fingertips or flat palms, but never casually, never leaning his weight on it.

The hierarchical structure is much more striking in a Papal Mass, though this has not been seen in its right order for decades. Until the liturgical revolution, cardinals who were prefects of congregations, who had the highest positions in the Roman Curia, served as acolytes and thurifers for the pope. They had to work harmoniously together. Besides being a spectacular joy for the faithful, it reminds everyone that they have no higher work than the service of God. The mighty might imagine they have something better to do than long liturgies. This checks that temptation. Princes of the Church should set the greatest example. And any rivalry or disloyalty is quickly exposed, for it is unbearable to carry personal antagonisms into the sanctuary.

Again, all this points to Heaven. Will there be rivalries and disloyalty there? By no means. Everyone will be perfectly happy in their place. They would not want to be any higher or lower than they are. Our 'closeness' to God is existential rather than local, but for an image of Heaven we may think of a group assembled around a campfire, each finding their place of comfort, some closer to the flames, some further out, each taking as much heat as they want, and nobody among us able to bear it all. There is no jealousy.

Moreover, each rejoices over the place of every other. Our greatest happiness in Heaven, after seeing God as He is, will be in the honours shown to the Blessed Virgin Mary. That will give us such happiness, for we will see that she is worthy of it all. We will have a related joy over every single soul in Heaven, happy for them in perfect proportion to the reward God has awarded them. And we will be absolutely delighted by the least in the Kingdom of Heaven, overjoyed that God's Mercy brought them here and not to hell. It will be a special joy to be among them!

Those who on earth rebel against the ecclesial order established by God are set to discover very dark depths of the inverse hierarchy in hell.

Celibate

For reasons obvious and not so obvious, celibacy could not have been enjoined before Christ. It would have been absurd to require it of Adam and counterproductive in the days of the Patriarchs.

God's first words to Adam and Eve, before even forbidding the fruit, was: *"Be fruitful and multiply, and fill the earth and subdue it"* (Gen 1:28). God had already blessed the animals to *"increase and multiply"* (Gen 1:22). Man was to do so too, with the added task of dominating — being lord over them.

This imperative to procreate was not interrupted by the eruption of sin (Gen 3:16), nor by the Flood (Gen 8:17; 9:1,7). As to the number of offspring, God showed Abraham that the sky was the limit (Gen 16:10; 17:2). Similar promises were made to Ishmael, Isaac and Jacob. Generating descendants was a good and responsibility not only for couples, but for whole peoples.

He will love you, bless you, and multiply you; He will also bless the fruit of your body and the fruit of your ground, your

*grain and your wine and your oil, the increase of your cattle
and the young of your flock...* (Dt 7:13-14)

This duty in times of blessing persisted in times of punishment, as
when Judah was in exile for disobedience:

*Take wives and have sons and daughters; take wives for your
sons, and give your daughters in marriage, that they may bear
sons and daughters; multiply there, do not decrease.* (Jer 29:6)

Why? Because God loves life; God is Life; Subsistent Being
necessarily lives. God desires to show Himself on earth. A
preparatory step is to fill it with abundant life. While this was
underway, among the Hebrews new constraints were layered
upon procreation, not in order to hinder life, but to prepare for the
greatest increase in life the world has ever known: the
Incarnation. That is to say, divine Life entered in to dwell among
us. And He, Jesus, practised celibacy not to put the brakes on the
multiplication of life, but to accelerate it in a manner beyond all
men's dreams: *"I am come that they may have life, and may have
it more abundantly"* (Jn 10:10).

The abundant life Jesus came to give is eternal. This means far
more than everlasting. It means the whole, simultaneous and
perfect possession of boundless life; it is the fullness; it is to see
and know the Father. *"Lifting His eyes to Heaven"*, Jesus said:

*Thou hast given [Thy Son] power over all flesh, that He may
give eternal life to all whom Thou hast given Him. Now this is
eternal life: That they may know Thee, the only true God, and
Jesus Christ, Whom Thou hast sent.* (Jn 17:2-3)

God ordained that this goal — the Gift of life through His Son —
be achieved through celibacy. This is so counter-intuitive, that
Methodius (✝311) wrote Jesus had to be the first to practise it:

let us inquire for what reason it was that no one of the many
patriarchs and prophets and righteous men, who taught and
did many noble things, either praised or chose the state of
virginity. Because it was reserved for the Lord alone to be the

first to teach this doctrine, since He alone, coming down to us, taught man to draw near to God; for it was fitting that He who was first and chief of priests, of prophets, and of angels, should also be saluted as first and chief of virgins. For in old times man was not yet perfect, and for this reason was unable to receive perfection, which is virginity.[177]

Like pruning a vine, wise restrictions do not decrease life but channel it for superabundance. To understand how celibacy is so productive, we may consider its development through history.

As mentioned, Adam could not be called to continence nor Eve to virginity. Even so, both were definitely, like all of us, required to live chastely. The use of the generative faculty may never stray outside the design of nature. (We have warnings from Noah's contemporaries and Lot's neighbours in Sodom, as also from Onan's sudden death.) While God allowed the Patriarchs to take multiple wives, they did this with a holy temperance. It was not for the sake of pleasure that they had sexual intercourse, but for the sake of progeny.

St Augustine is very clear on this point: Abraham and Jacob with their multiple wives lived far more chastely and have a far greater reward than many clerics and virgins of the New Law who are perfectly continent.[178] The reason for the difference is that the Patriarchs did all for the purpose of God, whereas there are some who, mastering their concupiscence biologically, fail to master their ego, their pride, their elation at supposing themselves better than others. This, the Doctor of Grace explains, is a spiritual catastrophe, not leading to life but, if unchecked, to everlasting death.

The marital embraces of Abraham and Sarah, Isaac and Rebekah, Jacob and Rachel, were holy because of their goal. On the natural level, not gratification but "the begetting of sons... was formerly the only occasion of sexual intercourse to both holy

---

[177] Methodius, *Banquet of Ten Virgins*, Discourse 1, 4.

[178] St Augustine, *De bono coniugali*, 28-30; *De virginitate* 31-57; *De doctrina christiana* III, 18.

fathers and mothers".[179] Supernaturally, they were aiming at Christ. God promised them a Seed through Whom all nations would be blessed. It is above all because of their faith in the coming Messiah that the Patriarchs and Matriarchs bore children:

> [Although Christians differ in glory] according to their deserts, there is this great gift bestowed in common, to sit down in the kingdom of God with Abraham, and Isaac, and Jacob, who not for the sake of this world, but for the sake of Christ, were husbands, for the sake of Christ were fathers.[180]

This same aim — doing all for Christ — is enjoined on everyone: before and after Christ; single married and celibate. Some were ancestors of Christ in the direct line. So St Augustine praises Ruth for remarrying after the death of her first husband so that in due course Christ would be born of the house of Boaz, of the tribe of Judah, from whom David's house arose.[181] All Christians with children are to bring them up not only in good health, education and virtue, but in the faith, so after the Holy Trinity enters the little ones in baptism, there be an ever-expanding and more beautifully appointed dwelling for God in their soul, through the child's growth in sacramental life, prayers and works of charity. In this way, biological mothers and virgins may both become mothers of Christ.[182] Non-Christians all serve the same goal — if remotely — insofar as they pursue natural virtue and truth. They are building up souls to meet God.

In this great scheme, the Hebrew people were chosen for a supremely important role. Here emerged definite hints at celibacy.

---

[179] St Augustine, *De continentia,* 27.

[180] St Augustine, *De bono coniugali*, 35.

[181] St Augustine, *De bono viduitatis*, 10.

[182] St Augustine, *De virginitate,* 6 "Forsooth both faithful women who are married, and virgins dedicated to God, by holy manners, and charity out of a pure heart, and good conscience, and faith unfeigned, because they do the will of the Father, are after a spiritual sense mothers of Christ. But they who in married life give birth after the flesh, give birth not to Christ, but to Adam, and therefore run, that their offspring having been dyed in His Sacraments, may become members of Christ."

To maintain their identity, intermarriage with foreigners was forbidden to Hebrews, except in certain cases where the foreigner agreed to live by the Law of Moses (they had to assimilate to the cult). Nor was it proper for the various tribes of Israel to intermarry, for their calling until the time of the Messiah depended upon maintaining the twelve tribes, or at least Judah and Levi. (*Mutatis mutandis*, this holds for apostolic lines and Jesus' Second Coming).

Significantly, there were greater restrictions for Levites than for the other tribes. The higher the rank in the sacerdotal hierarchy, the greater the restrictions on marriage. Not any son of Levi could minister to the tabernacle, but he had to be chosen, had to be between thirty and fifty years of age (Num 4:3,23,30) and be unblemished (Lev 21:17-23). He had to be of proven lineage.[183] Levitical priests could only marry virgins, not harlots, nor a woman who had been defiled, nor even a woman divorced. Unconvinced Catholics should pay heed to the reasons God gives:

> *They shall be holy to their God, and shall not profane his name: for they offer the burnt offering of the Lord, and the bread of their God, and therefore they shall be holy. They shall not take to wife a harlot or a vile prostitute, nor one that has been put away from her husband: because they are consecrated to their God and offer the loaves of proposition.* (Lev 21:6-8)

Charity due to prostitutes is not the issue here. The point for celibacy is that the OT *"burnt offering of the Lord"* and the *"bread of their God"* anticipate the Crucifixion and Holy Mass. Given that the former sacrifices, the offering of *"the loaves of proposition"*, required a consecration and sexual restraint, it makes sense that restraint be enjoined in the New Law. With what proportion? Well the Levitical ministry lasted until he was fifty.

---

[183] See 3 Esdras 5:37-39 (*extra Vulgata*) for their not being able to serve as priests who could not demonstrate from the records their pure Levitical lineage. Even full Levites who had married foreign women, even under the stress of exile, were on return to Jerusalem ejected from the Temple service (see Esra and Nehemia).

Holy Orders is for eternity. 'Proportion' is the wrong word. The demands of the New Covenant are total, as the goods of the Gifts — the Holy Eucharist — are absolute. The level of sexual restraint enjoined is total: it is celibacy.

As an exception for *Kohanim* which proves the rule, a priest could wed the widow of another priest (in order to help a woman or family in need), but they could not wed any other widow. We might understand why from the sentences which follow the rule:

> *no priest... shall take to wife a widow, nor one that is divorced, but they shall take virgins of the seed of the house of Israel: but they may take a widow also, that is, the widow of a priest. And they shall teach my people the difference between holy and profane, and shew them how to discern between clean and unclean.* (Ezek 44:21-23)

The purpose of such restrictions, as God says, is that all His people learn to distinguish between what is holy and what is common. This is not primarily about us, about widowhood, divorce or prostitution. It is about God. Discerning holy and profane is infinitely more important now in the New Covenant where the *"bread of our God"* which is offered is nothing less than God Himself, the All Holy. Celibacy teaches this fact like nothing else can. So striking is celibacy that not seldom the first question non-Catholics ask priests, if encountering them by chance, is: *"Is it true you cannot marry?"* Clearly it gets people's attention. It provides an occasion for explaining the best that God wills to give us: His Real Presence. The priest is to teach about a whole new category: not just between profane and sacred, or natural and supernatural, but created substance and Uncreated substance. It is a new way to bring life into the world.

Vitally, celibacy is not against nature but above it. All states of life require grace, God's constant help. But continence requires also a specific calling: *"no one can be continent, unless God grant it"* (Wis 8:21 *non possem esse continens*). This is why Jesus said not everyone could receive the call to celibacy:

there are eunuchs who have made themselves eunuchs for the sake of the kingdom of heaven. He who is able to receive this, let him receive it. (Mt 19:12)

It is a gift with its own reward (Lk 18:28-30; Apoc 4:4). *"I wish that all were as I myself am. But each has his own special gift from God, one of one kind and one of another"* (1 Cor 7:7).

Clearly none should presume to become a priest who is not called and none who is called should neglect to pray. To fail here, or to fail to repent for falling, earns everlasting death, hell. This is prefigured among the Levites:

> *And thou shalt consecrate the hands of them all, and shalt sanctify them, that they may do the office of priesthood unto me. Thou shalt make also linen breeches, to cover the flesh of their nakedness from the reins to the thighs: And Aaron and his sons shall use them when they shall go in to the tabernacle of the testimony, or when they approach the altar to minister in the sanctuary, lest being guilty of iniquity they die. It shall be a law for ever to Aaron, and to his seed after him.* (Ex 28:41-43)

St Bede discerns a spiritual meaning to the linen breeches which are *"a law for ever to Aaron, and to his seed after him"*, that is, to Catholic priests:

> these undergarments, which are commanded to be made to cover the indecency of the flesh, designate that part of chastity which holds one back from desiring the bond of marriage. Without it, no one can assume the priesthood or be consecrated for the ministry of the altar... that is, unless he will either remain a virgin or dissolve the covenant of union that he has contracted with his wife...[184]

Here it is worth clarifying that although no priest is ever permitted to marry, in the early Church it did happen that some married men were ordained to the priesthood subsequent to their marriage. Because this required practising continence (no sexual

---

[184] St Bede, *On the Tabernacle*, III, 9.

relations permitted), then, as a matter of justice, ordinations of married men were only possible by mutual agreement of the spouses, due to their prior claims to the marital debt. Over time it became simpler to cease ordaining married men.

Continuing to hear from St Bede:

> They themselves should cover the nakedness of their flesh. *'You shall make linen undergarments for the high priest and his sons'*; you shall teach them the rule of chastity; you shall tell those who are to serve in the priesthood that they must abstain from the embrace of a wife. However, you shall not impose the yoke of this sort of continence upon any of them by force, but if any wish to be priests and to serve at the ministry of the altar, let them of their own free will cease to be servants of wives... For if anyone who is living wantonly presumes to usurp the priestly office for himself, his soul shall surely incur most certain death.[185]

Our holy Benedictine, always mild, understands priestly celibacy as a matter of Heaven and hell.

If we struggle to understand that the *"linen breeches"* of the Levites signify celibacy for Catholic priests, then we might consider the whole programme of ritual purity in the OT which was designed to teach all generations about holiness.

Ritual purity awakens our sense of moral purity. What other system could optimally prefigure the holiness offered by Christ alone? Hence the priests' washing themselves when they entered the tabernacle signifies the examination of conscience and confession all Catholics are called to make before approaching Holy Communion. A *"great sea"* was made to demonstrate this, a massive bronze bowl on the back of twelve bronze oxen. We recall it by the use of holy water on entering a church.

---

[185] In AD 866, Pope St Nicholas I gave a like interpretation in his *Responses to the Questions of the Bulgars*, Letter 99: "Of course, because we have said that trousers [*femoralia*] are ordered to be made, it should be noted that we put on 'trousers' spiritually, when we restrain the lust of the flesh through abstinence... This is why the first humans, when they felt illicit motions in their members after sin, ran into the leaves of a fig tree and wove loin cloths for themselves (Gen. 3:7)."

Under the OT, priests were tasked to judge whether someone or even their house was suffering from leprosy (Lev 14:34*ff*), discerning whether they were *"clean"* or *"unclean"*. This signifies, *inter alia*, the priest judging whether someone's sins exclude them from Holy Communion or not. In the worst case, they must remain outside the camp until they are clean. So the Catholic must give up attachment to mortal sins and do penance before receiving the Blessed Sacrament.

Those charged to judge regarding purity are surely obliged to uphold it themselves. Not merely ritual purity, but holiness was necessary for ministering to God: *"he shall be holy to you; for I the Lord, who sanctify you, am holy"* (Lev 21:8). If the priest is not holy, how can he give holiness to the people? If the Catholic priest is not celibate, how can he expect heroic chastity from those plagued by impure temptations? Some homosexuals ask if their seemingly unquenchable same-sex attraction is meant to condemn them to a life without love. Celibate priests prove God makes no exclusion between continence and a life full of love. A sexually active priest could hardly be convincing to these souls, requiring of others a level of temperance which he does not himself attempt. Among many other reasons, God wants His priests celibate for the sake of those who struggle the most.

Significantly, the burden of OT restrictions is increased higher up the hierarchy. God commanded Levite priests to not defile themselves by touching a dead body, except for the closest family members (Lev 21:1-3). However, the restrictions regarding touching the dead and marriage were far heavier on the High Priest, for he was called to anticipate Christ even more closely:

> *The priest who is chief among his brethren... shall not go in to any dead body, nor defile himself, even for his father or for his mother... And he shall take a wife in her virginity. A widow, or one divorced, or a woman who has been defiled, or a harlot, these he shall not marry; but he shall take to wife a virgin of his own people, that he may not profane his children among his people; for I am the Lord who sanctify him.* (Lev 21:10-15)

All this was so that Israel could be trained for the coming of Christ. Once arrived, He would teach the whole world through a new, apostolic hierarchy.

Objectors to celibacy point out that in Eastern Churches married men can be ordained priests. They can continue to beget children. But it is the common understanding that a priest refrain from embracing his wife for a number of days before offering the Divine Liturgy.[186] Moreover, married priests may not be consecrated as bishops. Again, the higher the position in the hierarchy the more closely it must be conformed to Christ.

Another key to understanding priestly continence is the holiness of the objects handled by the minister. We have an instructive example about continence and holy bread from King David's men, with an unusual use of the word *"vessels"*:

> *And the priest, responding to David, said to him: 'I have no common bread at hand, but only holy bread. Are the young men clean, especially from women?' And David responded to the priest, and said to him: 'Indeed, as concerns being with women, we have abstained since yesterday and the day before, when we departed, and so the vessels of the young men have been holy. And although this journey has been defiled, it will also be sanctified today as concerns the vessels.' Therefore, the priest gave to him sanctified bread. For there was no bread there, but only the bread of the Presence, which had been taken away from before the face of the Lord, so that fresh loaves might be set up.* (1 Sam 21:4-6 SB)

What was the condition for non-Levites to eat the bread of the Presence? Even old loaves which had finished their week of service and gone cold? Even men who were on the brink of starvation? Even men risking their lives to protect the Lord's Anointed? It was not permitted for them to consume this bread except that they had for several days *"kept themselves from women"*. So vital was temporary abstinence. How much more for

---

[186] Eastern liturgies, typically being of much longer duration than Holy Mass, are not usually offered daily by any given priest, making periodic abstinence workable.

priests who offer and consecrate and handle the Holy Eucharist, the Real Presence, should there be perfect continence.

In the passage quoted above, the purity of the men's *"vessels"* (*vas*, σκεῦος, כְּלִי) somehow depends upon their use of the generative faculty. The term is most often employed for the *"vessels"* and utensils fit for use in the Temple. Such items are exclusively for use in the sacred services and may not be used for anything else. Nor may anything else be used in the sacred services. These signs communicate that God is a jealous God: He wants souls for Himself. Therefore, also deacons should be continent who at the altar in Mass handle the sacred vessels — paten, chalice, ciborium — which touch the sacred species. If we wonder why, it helps to make a comparison with marriage.

Why are married people encouraged both to have children and at the proper time to come to Holy Communion? Bringing life into the world does not exclude one from receiving the Sacrament. The pertinent point is that they are not permitted to commit adultery and consume the Host. They must be true to their spouse. Likewise the sacred minister. His spouse is the Church. The mother of the priest's spiritual children is Holy Mother Church. He should not marry because he should not make another become a mother. As priest he is to refrain from bringing life into the world by begetting biological children because he is already committed to bringing substantial life into the world through the Holy Sacrifice of the Mass.

To grasp this, it helps to see the difference between accidental and substantial life. We are all called to increase life. First we increase our own life by proper growth, including in virtue and grace. We can increase the life of others by feeding the hungry, housing the homeless, tending to the sick, visiting prisoners. All of these works of mercy increase the vitality of others. People who establish or teach at schools, who found or toil in hospitals, are demonstratively serving life. All who preach or catechise or evangelise, or who serve Sacraments or offer sacrifices and rosaries for others, they also bring an increase of life into this world: supernatural life, grace.

But all this, including grace, is accidental life. It increases life for souls which already exist. In order to bring substantial life into this world, substantial rational life, there are only two legitimate ways. Either generate a baby, biologically, within marriage, or confect the Holy Eucharist in an apostolic liturgy.

A human embryo is a new person, a rational substance, a hypostasis. God creates their soul; the mother cooperates by providing the material for the baby's body plus, like the father, providing half the information for the baby's genes. The Holy Eucharist is also substantial life, Jesus Christ. He is not a new Person when He becomes present on the altar, but it is new substantial supernatural life generated by God in this world with the cooperation of the Church (mother) and a priest (father). These two acts of generation are so life-giving, so important, so holy, that God wants us to be highly aware of what we are doing. We may do one or the other. One cannot appreciate how sublime it is to forego children unless one has an idea of the immense good of children as the first end of marriage. What is the good of giving up progeny, if progeny are not regarded as good?

The married person has one spouse. The priest has one Church. Marital fidelity is part of nature, for it is best for the spouses, best for the children, best for society. A true marriage also evangelises: the exclusive nuptial bond points to the devoted, indissoluble bond between Christ and the Church (Eph 5:31-33).

Priests and consecrated virgins, meanwhile, do not enter a sign (Sacrament) of this bond but enter the reality. St Augustine says:

> They who have made a vow of their virginity to God and have thereby attained to an higher degree of honour and holiness in the Church, are not unmarried, for they are a special part of the marriage of the whole Church, the Bride of Christ.[187]

---

[187] St Augustine, *Tractatus 9 in Joannem*, 2. See also *De virginitate,* 5 "There is, therefore, no reason why the virgins of God be sad, because themselves cannot, keeping their virginity, be mothers of the flesh... that Birth of the Holy Virgin is the ornament of all holy virgins; and themselves together with Mary are mothers of Christ, if they do the will of His Father... Mary doing the will of God, after the flesh, is only the mother of Christ, but after the Spirit she is both His sister and mother."

There is a much bigger picture than the merely temporal scene (Mt 22:1-14). Those who oppose celibacy fail to offer an adequate theology of Jesus' marriage with the Church and the priestly imitation of Christ. One's own struggles or failings in celibacy are no reason to deny the truth of the teaching.

Mankind's long preparation for this sublime revelation neared completion in the souls of St Jospeh and St John the Baptist, both so perfectly continent that they were suitable saints for nurturing and heralding Christ. Greater than these men is the Blessed Virgin Mary, so immaculate she was fit to bear Jesus as her Son. As we contemplate the Virgin Mary, her most chaste Spouse St Joseph and the friend of the Bridegroom St John the Baptist, it is evident that their lives are responses to God's call. Only by ignoring the surpassing significance of these saints can modernists discount the fecundity of continence.

Worse are those who dismiss God's prerogative to call, who see nothing divine in the priesthood, grasping the office for themselves:

> So if you should now see someone purifying himself to some degree of the disease of pleasure and with great zeal considering himself above others as he thrusts himself into the priesthood, realise that this man whom you see is someone who is falling to earth by his lofty arrogance. For in what follows the Law teaches that the priesthood is something divine and not human.[188]

To underscore divine election, St Gregory continues by relating the miracle of Aaron's rod budding (Num 17). At the altar:

> one rod became a testimony to the heavenly ordination, for it was distinguished over the others by a divine miracle... The rod of the priest took root by itself (not through any extraneous moisture but through the power which was placed in it by God), and brought forth branches and fruit, and the fruit ripened. The fruit was a nut.

---

[188] St Gregory of Nyssa, *Life of Moses*, II, 283-85.

Against the laws of nature, God's priesthood is fruitful.

> By this event all the people were instructed in discipline. In the fruit that Aaron's rod produced it is fitting to perceive the kind of life that must characterise the priesthood — namely, a life self-controlled, tough and dried in appearance, but containing on the inside (hidden and invisible) what can be eaten. It becomes visible when the food ripens and the hard shell is stripped off and the wood-like covering of the meat is removed.

We do not want this quality in women: this hardness, dryness. A queen may be an exception because of her office. Still, we do not say she is hard, but stately. In men gravity is always becoming.

All these considerations of nature, of religion, of revelation in the OT and NT, are to raise our minds and hearts to God. Within the Holy Trinity, the Father is a single principle from Whom is generated the Son. And it is as a single principle that Father and Son breathe out the Holy Ghost. In God we discern this celibacy: processions from one principle. Then solely by His sovereign choice, God created creation unassisted. There is no duality, no demiurge. He needed no other to create the world, to bless it and give increase. Perhaps this is the ultimate meaning of celibacy: that though marriage be fruitful, celibacy is more so, for marriage is human, while celibacy is divine.

Fruitful

Catholic priests are ubiquitously called 'Father'. In the *Confiteor* he is addressed as *"tibi, pater... et te, pater"* — "to you, Father... and you, Father". This one word sums up our five marks.

"Father" confirms the priest is *male* by definition. Further, he is the head of a local *hierarchy*, the pastor of a flock. By nature his work is *sacrificial*, in order to provide and defend. The title "father" means he has children, but not biological, for he is *celibate*, rather it is in the spiritual field that he is *fruitful*.

The Church's *doctor gratiæ* extols the proper fruitfulness of marriage: children brought up in Christ. He notes that fertility of the flesh is a thing of this earth but not of Heaven, whereas the fruitfulness of the spirit is everlasting:

> virginal chastity and freedom through pious continence from all sexual intercourse is the portion of angels, and a practice, in corruptible flesh, of perpetual incorruption. To this let all fruitfulness of the flesh yield, all chastity of married life; the one is not in (man's) power, the other is not in eternity; free choice has not fruitfulness of the flesh, heaven has not chastity of married life. Assuredly they will have something great beyond others in that common immortality, who have something already not of the flesh in the flesh.[189]

St Augustine assures that generating fruits for eternity begins here on earth. St Clement reads the OT to identify the fruits of the NT:

> The blessed Moses... said to them: *'Brethren, God has chosen for His priestly service that tribe the rod of which will bud.'* When day broke... it was found that the rod of Aaron had not only put forth buds but also borne fruit... Happy the presbyters who have before now completed life's journey and taken their departure in mature age and laden with fruit![190]

This "fruit" is life in Heaven — for themselves and for others. Everyone is called to contribute, but leading others to salvation is essential for priests. The hierarchy exists to deliver supernatural goods, not to manage social workers. The Church is the ark of eternal salvation, not an NGO. The fruitfulness of priesthood has its root in sacrifice. God calls, appoints and equips men for this. It is not easy. Undoubtedly, the laity live lives of sacrifice, especially when children come their way. And there are priests who fail — God help us:

> If you should discover the life of the priest we are discussing to be quince-like, fragrant and rose-coloured, like the lives of many who are adorned with linen and purple and who fatten

---

[189] St Augustine, *De virginitate,* 12.

[190] Pope St Clement, *First Letter to the Corinthians*, 43-44.

themselves at rich tables and who drink pure wine and anoint themselves with the best myrrh and who make use of whatever seems pleasant to those who have a taste for a life of luxury, then you would with good cause apply to this situation the word of the Gospel: When I look at your fruit, I do not recognise the priestly tree by it.[191]

Good fruits were always intended. God instructed Adam to *"tend and keep"* the garden (Gen 2:15). St Ephraim notes this word *"tend"* (עָבַד) is also used for due *"service"*, as in worship meant for God alone (Ex 3:12; 12:31; Dt 6:13).[192] It is used specifically for liturgical service (Ex 13:5), including in the tabernacle (Num 3:7-8). Yet in parallel it is used for slave labour (Ex 14:12) and worse still, for serving false gods (Dt 28:64; 29:18; 2 Kngs 10:19). We get to choose our service. One way or another we will certainly serve: either serve the Living God, which is freedom; or serve as slave to totalitarians and demons. Evidently, we want to follow the right priesthood.

The second term, שָׁמַר, is also for *"keeping"* (looking out for) one's brother (Gen 4:9) in the way God *"keeps"* (guards) His elect (Gen 8:15); for our *"keeping"* (observing) the Covenant (Gen 17:9) and Commandments (Ex 16:28); for *"keeping"* (shepherding) the flock (Gen 30:31); for *"keeping"* (celebrating) God's salvific feasts (Ex 12:17). Again this pastoral, moral and liturgical term speaks to the necessity of the priesthood.

God taught Adam to be purposeful in his service of the Garden, respecting the immortal fruitfulness of priestly labours. Dioceses which refashion the priesthood will wither and die.

Priesthood Summarised in Heaven

If the priesthood is present in Adam, and inaugurated sacramentally at the Last Supper, it is also discernible after the Last Day. The Prophet Ezekiel tells of a future Temple, greater than Solomon's, to be established once the Messiah has visited

---

[191] St Gregory of Nyssa, *Life of Moses*, II, 286.

[192] St Ephraim, *Commentary on Genesis*, 7.

(Ezek 44:1-3). This is nothing less than the Church. She is one in Heaven and on earth. The priesthood, along with the five characteristics considered above, are all discernible in the same single chapter of Ezekiel's vision (Ch 44).

God's prerogative to call to the priesthood is given in two stages. The first figures baptism: *"No stranger uncircumcised in heart, and uncircumcised in flesh, shall enter into my sanctuary"* (Ezek 44:9). And second, only Levites may minister: *"the Levites... shall be officers in my sanctuary, and doorkeepers of the gates of the house, and ministers to the house"* (Ezek 44:11).

Having a figure here for the ministerial priesthood (Holy Orders), there follows the first of the five marks examined above, that the purpose of priesthood is to offer sacrifices:

> *the priests, and Levites, the sons of Sadoc, who kept the ceremonies of my sanctuary... they shall come near to me, to minister to me: and they shall stand before me, to offer me the fat, and the blood, saith the Lord God.* (Ezek 44:15)

The second mark, that priests are male, is given in the phrase *"the sons of Sadoc"* (Ezek 44:15).

The third mark, hierarchy, is manifest within the Levites' ranks (Ezek 44:14-15) and in setting priests to make judgements concerning the laity: *"when there shall be a controversy, they shall stand in my judgments, and shall judge"* (Ezek 44:24).

Celibacy, the fourth mark, is hinted at in symbols of purity (Ezek 44:17-19,25-26,31) and in certain restrictions on marriage which we have already examined (Ezek 44:22).

Finally first-fruits are given to the priest as a suitable sign to acknowledge the immortal benefits he bestows on the people, that is the fifth mark, his spiritual fruitfulness:

> *And the firstfruits of all the firstborn, and all the libations of all things that are offered, shall be the priest's: and you shall give the firstfruits of your meats to the priest, that he may return a blessing upon thy house.* (Ezek 44:30)

The Sacrament of Holy Orders imposes an indelible character on the soul of the ordinand. Therefore whatever was essential to his service on earth, will be recalled with joy for ever in Heaven. This is what Ezekiel saw: Christ's ministerial priesthood.

The best fruit of Holy Orders is souls brought to Heaven. Each priest is, by his ministry, not only to save his own soul, but to help beget and bring up many children to God. That is why although many are called to the priesthood, few are chosen: so that it is necessary they bear much fruit. This serves as a sign for everybody that while all are called to cooperate, there is only One Who brings in the harvest: the Christ.

Vested in Christ

May the almighty and merciful Lord grant us
pardon, absolution, and remission of our sins.

— Prayers at the Foot of the Altar, after the *Confiteor*

Ever since the Fall, God has provided man with clothes as a sign of how He intends to dress our souls with grace upon grace. Clothes have meaning. They are much more than practical, achieving more than keeping us warm and protecting our modesty. Clothing communicates our state in life and can signify deep truths about the soul. Their highest expression is in the vestments for Holy Mass, which announce Jesus Christ.

What Clothing Reveals

Describing Levite ministers, St Gregory speaks of their clothing as practical, serving modesty and teaching conformity to Christ:

> There was a girdle which held together the loose folds of the garment, as well as an adornment for the hidden parts of the body, and the other articles of clothing which symbolically instruct concerning priestly virtue…[193]

Clothing communicates. Uniforms are an obvious example of it conveying information for the benefit of society. It helps us to

---

[193] St Gregory of Nyssa, *Life of Moses*, I, 55.

know who is a policeman, who is a qualified nurse, an appointed judge, a professed religious. More generally, the clothes which dress the body tell us something about the person wearing them.

At a deeper level, the virtues which 'dress' a particular soul tell us about the person who possesses, or 'wears', these virtues. Qualities like courage, humility and kindness perfect the being of one who practises them, making his soul admirable and even resplendent. Virtues of science, art and prudence perfect the intellective faculty of the soul. The virtue of justice perfects the will. Virtues of temperance and fortitude perfect the concupiscible and irascible appetites. The theological virtue of charity adorns the soul in saving grace.

Why do we say virtues 'dress' the soul? Because we are born naked, and need to put on clothes. Similarly the soul is born naked, without virtues, and needs to put them on.[194] We must learn to act well and repeat these good acts in order to build up good habits. It is no coincidence that the clothes of a monk are called his habit: he puts on and practises simplicity and poverty which identify him as a follower of Christ. The external practice of wearing particular clothes speaks of a more vital internal practice of wearing goodness. The Angelic Doctor gives the following definition: "human virtue which is an operative habit, is a good habit, productive of good works."[195]

After the Fall, Adam and Eve stitched up some inadequate clothes: *"when they perceived themselves to be naked, they sewed together fig leaves, and made themselves aprons"* (Gen 3:7). After discovering we are *"naked"*, we likely recognise our natural efforts to put on virtue are unsatisfactory. We need God's help, God Who clothed our first parents worthily: *"And the Lord*

---

[194] Similarly, strong muscles or good skin tone are accidental to a body, but real. The body develops them through good living. Virtues adorn us as accidents, but again are real. They are qualities developed in the soul. The relation of accidents to substance (where the former inhere in the latter) shows how close virtues are to the soul: closer than your garments to your body.

[195] St Thomas, *S.Th.* II-I Q.55, a.3 adds precision to the insight of Aristotle who taught virtue is that which makes its possessor good and his work good likewise (*Nicomachean Ethics*, II, 6).

God made for Adam and his wife garments of skins, and clothed them" (Gen 3:21).[196] To appreciate what God does for our souls here, for sinners ashamed of themselves, we will inspect the three terms used: *"garments"*, *"skins"* and *"clothed"*.

The word for *"garments"*, כְּתֹנֶת, or *"tunics"*, next appears for what Jacob made for Jospeh, because he *"loved Joseph above all his sons..."* (phraseology which alerts us to Christ) *"...because he had conceived him in his old age. And he made him a tunic, woven of many colours"* (Gen 37:3 SB). After this came Aaron's priestly *"tunic"* (Ex 28:4) of chequered work. These are meaningful clothes with which God dresses His favourite and elect children, symbolising putting on Christ (Rom 13:14).

It was in *"skins"* (עוֹר) that God clothed our first parents. This necessarily involved the death of animals, a hint at sacrifice.[197] The tabernacle being covered in dyed skins (Ex 25:5) represents Jesus' total sacrifice with red dye for His Blood. *"Skins"*, or עוֹר, is pronounced like 'light', אוֹר, as if a divine pun anticipating our being clothed in Christ's Light by the mystical death of baptism. This is putting on the white *"wedding garment"* which we do not want to lose (Mt 22:11-14) — as intimated in Eden.

Finally, the next usage of *"clothed"* (לָבַשׁ) is Jacob being *"clothed"* in animal skins hunted by Esau (Gen 27:15). Jacob putting on another's kills is an image of Christ: *"God sent His own Son in the likeness of sinful flesh"* (Rom 8:3). Then pharaoh *"clothed"* Joseph royally (Gen 41:42), imaging the glorification of the Saviour of the World. We are called to be *"clothed"* in *"justice"* (Ps 131:9) and *"salvation"* (2 Chron 6:41), which latter in Hebrew sounds like being clothed in יֵשׁוּעַ, Jesus. Significantly, *"clothed"* is the word used when Moses *"vested"* Aaron as High Priest and *"vested"* his sons as priests (Ex 28:41; 29:5), a shade of sacerdotal meaning already entailed in Eden.

---

[196] Sister Lucia: "God did not give us clothing as an adornment in order to feed our human vanity and frivolity. No! He gave it to us as a protection against sin, as a sign of penance for sin committed." *Calls from the Message of Fatima*, 18th June 2005.

[197] The fact that *"Adam"* is singled out by name in contrast to *"his wife"* may point to the man's calling for a particular sacrifice, that is Holy Orders for offering Mass.

The Meaning of Vestments

As clothes have meaning, vestments for Mass have a high meaning. While a priest's cassock and collar express his underlying clerical state, the vestments pertain to his sacerdotal powers in operation. This is a proper meaning: nobody else should ever wear these vestments and the priest should never wear them outside of liturgical service (Sir 45:8-16). This exclusiveness signifies the unique work of our Redeemer.

The first thing the priest puts on, after washing his hands before saying Mass, is the amice. It is a rectangle of white cloth which he kisses, touches on the top of his head, then uses to cover his neck and shoulders. Originally the amice was a hood. It signifies the protection of a helmet (Eph 6:17). Donning it the priest prays: "Place, O Lord, upon my head the helmet of salvation, that I may repel the assaults of the enemy."

After the amice the priest puts on the alb, also white, which signifies being washed by the blood of the lamb. By now completely covered from neck to ankles by amice and alb, the priest has largely disappeared, as his personality ought to do for the Mass. He must decrease so Christ may increase. Neither should his shoes be personalised. Black shoes, possibly the best ones he owns, are fitting.

The girdle, or cincture, is then wrapped around the waist with an oration to God for the gift of chastity.

The enemy had first attacked in Eden, momentarily gaining our head, Adam. But now, wearing the protective helmet of salvation, having been washed in the blood of the lamb, being girded with chastity, the priest arms himself with the maniple (to which we will return) then takes up the stole, asking God:

> Restore to me, O Lord, the stole of immortality, which I lost by the collusion of our first parents. And although I am unworthy to approach Thy sacred mysteries, may I yet gain eternal joy.

Before Mass begins, the priest is thinking of our first parents, of their fall and our common predicament, and imploring the Lord that we be restored to immortality through the sacred mysteries.

The chasuble signifies the yoke of Christ. After putting this on, most priests look the same. The athletic do not stand out, priests with weak frames look broad, priests who are out of shape look dignified under a chasuble or cope.[198] The priest disappears, except for his face, which is his identity, for the Mass is always personal. But it is not about his personality, so his expression should be calm and grave. Most of the time it is only the back of his head that the faithful can see. When he turns to them, his eyes should be lowered, so from the beginning of Mass to the end he might well see nobody but the servers.

For a solemn Mass, the sub-deacon puts on his tunicle, praying: "May the Lord clothe me in the tunicle of delight and the garment of rejoicing" while the deacon dons his dalmatic with the words: "Clothe me, O Lord, with the garment of salvation and the vestment of gladness, and encompass me always with the dalmatic of justice". Putting on these vestments expresses our desire — the clerics on behalf of the faithful — to be clothed again by God. We want not to be left naked, stripped of grace; nor left to our own inadequate designs in flimsy fig leaves; nor to be clothed only in animal skins, left in penance (Gen 3:7-21). Rather to be clothed by God in salvation, joy and justice — exceeding the precarious immortality granted before the Fall with an immortality that cannot be lost, exceeding paradisal pleasures with celestial beatitude. Heavenly rest would not be true rest if there were even a possibility of losing it.

With the first Psalm of the Mass (Ps 42), we are asking God to save us from the old Adam in ourselves, *"the unjust and deceitful man"*, for we wish to put on the New Adam, to be clothed in Christ (cf. Eph 4:22-24; Col 3:9-10; Rom 6:6; 13:14). The vesting of the priest for each Holy Mass expresses in ritual what is to be achieved spiritually by all. The whole transformation is conveyed especially well by the maniple.

The maniple symbolises work. Originally it was a cloth worn on the arm of the farm labourer to wipe away the sweat of his

---

[198] This effect is not granted to women who dress as priests. Either they seem to be wearing a sack, or if tailored for femininity, the impact is out of place, as are they.

brow, and stylised by the officers of the Greek state, called liturgists, to identify their civil appointment while remaining practical for swabbing sweat. Some say, disparagingly, that Roman Mass vestments are just a holdover from pagan dress of antiquity. In fact their roots are much older than that, the greater input being Hebrew. But so what? The Church can 'baptise' pagan festivals. There is good in nature. The Church elevates it, purifies it. Greek and Roman dress had meaning. If officers of the Greek state wore maniples to announce the directives of the king, why should not priests do so for their liturgical service in the name of Christ? Before a Solemn Mass the deacon and sub-deacon wait until the priest has his maniple on before they put on their own. None can do the work of Christ until He is ready.

Vestments adapt over time to become perfect for Mass. The maniple should not be so long as to be an incumbrance; nor so short that it carries the danger of wiping away precious particles from the corporal. Further, the priest is aware of its presence on his arm. It has a good effect like a veil on the head of a woman, which helps her keep still, her posture poised, her movements graceful, looking directly ahead or looking down. It is all about decorum, a part of the virtue of modesty. So the maniple helps the priest to maintain movements with decorum, a certain slowness to his actions, because you do not want the maniple flapping about in a comical way (or the chasuble flailing out when you turn). The priest is conscious of something hanging on his arm, which impels him to do things with care, avoiding extraneous movement, keeping his arms still except for deliberate action.

In their origin, maniples are everything to do with sweat, toil and penance. We recall for his sin Adam was told:

> *with labour and toil shalt thou eat... Thorns and thistles shall [the earth] bring forth to thee... In the sweat of thy face shalt thou eat bread till thou return to the earth... (Gen 3:17-19)*

A digression here on the theme of thorns might help us understand the meaning of the maniple. What is the meaning of *"thorns"* (קוֹץ)? Biblically, if not botanically, they represent failed fruit. That is to say, plants were created to bring forth fruits, but since the advent of sin, many have brought forth thorns. So we read: *"They have sown wheat, and reaped thorns… you shall be ashamed of your fruits, because of the fierce wrath of the Lord"* (Jer 12:13). We may think also of the vine, the House of Israel (today the Church) planted by God. Despite all His care and favours bestowed, *"he looked that it should bring forth grapes, and it brought forth wild grapes"* (Is 5:2). With this sense in mind, St Augustine notes:

> when Jesus saith: *'I am the true vine'* (Jn 15:1), doth He not make distinction between Himself, and that which indeed seemed to be a vine, but to which it is said: *'How art thou turned into the degenerate plant of a strange vine unto Me?'* (Jer 2:21). For by what title shall that plant be called other than a false vine, whereto they looked that she should bring forth grapes, and she brought forth thorns?[199]

Good, sweet fruits represent holy souls harvested by God. Thorns represent the reprobate who are cast into hell to burn:

> *transgressors shall all of them be plucked up as thorns: which are not taken away with hands. And if a man will touch them, he must be armed with iron and with the staff of a lance: but they shall be set on fire and burnt to nothing.* (2 Sam 23:6-7; cf. Is 33:12)[200]

The thorns which appeared after the sentencing in Eden are noticeable later on Mount Moriah (same place) troubling the ram with its head stuck in briers, as Jesus on Calvary (same place) wearing the crown of thorns. Is anything more agonising? Adam had been sentenced to the torment of thorns (Gen 3:17-18) and Jesus in the Passion took the most extreme infliction of this punishment on Himself. In Eden God had decreed pains for the

---

[199] St Augustine, *Tractatus 80 in Joannem*; Matins, *Lectio* VIII, Common of Martyrs.

[200] Gideon warned the men of Soccoth that if they did not give him bread he would whip them with thorns and briers, which he did (Jdg 8:5-17). If we do not offer the Lord the Eucharist as He wills, we will suffer subjugation to the punishments of sin.

woman in childbirth (Gen 3:16). On Calvary Mary bore the pain of Eve's punishment a billion-fold in our spiritual birth. Finally Jesus took on the punishment of death of Adam and Eve. He took on our sins, He bore our stripes. He always meant to. Thereby He redeemed the world, turning pain into everlasting glory.

Acacia wood was selected for the Ark, altar and tabernacle. Once worked upon, stripped of thorns, smoothed out and covered in gold, it is fit for the Ark and altar in the tabernacle and Temple. These are works without thorns. But thorns grow to cover and smother the idolatrous altar (Hos 10:8), symbolising sin.

The work then conducted in Holy Mass, the liturgy, is the same work as Calvary: our Salvation. The thorns of sin are to be removed. The maniple accords with this laborious farm work, this toilsome gardening. Fittingly, in a Pontifical Mass, the sub-deacon hands the maniple to the bishop for him to kiss and then wear just as these words are prayed: "May the almighty and merciful Lord grant us pardon, absolution, and remission of our sins". This is the labour of Holy Mass: our redemption. The celebrant kisses the cross on his maniple as Jesus kissed the Cross. Is the maniple the least of the vestments? What a disaster if it is discarded.

Pontifical vestments have a long history. They go back to Moses' day. And they were God's idea:

> After his descent from the mountain Moses, employing workmen, constructed these things according to the pattern shown to him. While he was in that sanctuary not made with hands, he was commanded how the priest should be adorned when he entered the sanctuary. The law prescribed the details of the under and outer garments... There was an ephod embroidered of different colours with gold thread predominating... Clasps held the ephod together on both sides and provided a setting of gold for emeralds. The beauty of these stones was due partly to their natural radiance... and partly to the marvellous skill of the engraving.[201]

---

[201] St Gregory of Nyssa, *Life of Moses*, I, 51-52.

Man, inspired by God, made the best of nature. The High Priest's vestments were so precious, so costly, they were handed down for generations. The ephod was so unique one would hope that it were never lost or damaged through all the centuries of its use.

To produce these items which we might call the early model for pontifical vestments, God informs Moses:

> the wise of heart, whom I have filled with the spirit of wisdom ... shall make the holy vestments for thy brother Aaron and his sons, that they may do the office of priesthood unto me. (Ex 28:3-4)

This is a high aspiration. For Catholics, the bishop's liturgical dress should be the best that craftsmanship, devotion and generosity can produce. God reciprocates love. The TI writes that not only the makers of vestments but every generation can invest themselves in the High Priest though thought of his vestments and that this is a powerful part of the fight against sin *for all*. The breastplate worked heartfelt repentance, the tunic atoned for sins of bloodshed, the breeches pacified sexual disturbance, the turban tamed haughtiness, the ephod countered idolatry. Yet these:

> were not super powers invested within the very fabric of the High Priest's garments. On the contrary, the potential for repentance and the perfecting of ourselves was granted to the priestly garments via the *'honor and glory'* that we, ourselves, invested in these garments. When we dress our brother with the very best of who we are, the very best of who we can be, we are granting to him the privilege and responsibility to stand before G-d on our behalf. When G-d fashioned garments for *Adam* He did so, not merely to escort *Adam* out of Eden, but also to pave the way for *Adam's* eventual return to the place of Eden. When the *Kohen Gadol* enters the Holy of Holies on Yom Kippur, the place of the cherubim who guard the Tree of Life, he does so by virtue of the honor and glory that we, his brothers and sisters, have invested in him.[202]

---

[202] TI 6/3/2020.

This is the honour with which orthodox Jews esteem the clothing of a High Priesthood which they have not seen for 2,000 years. Of the bishop's vestments today, we can trace back to Aaron the *"straight linen garment"* (the alb), the *"girdle"*, the *"tunic"* (chasuble), the *"mitre"* (μίτραν, turban) all *"as the Lord had commanded"* Moses (Lev 8:7-9). Analogously, the sons of Aaron wore *"tunics... girdles... caps* (χιτῶνας)*"* (Lev 8:13) as priests have their albs, cinctures and birettas.

Shall the Temple Institute recall the reverence of the OT while the Church forgets it? Shall anyone be seen in the sanctuary who is not a cleric, and not vested? The Hebrews would never have tolerated such irreverent incoherence:

> *And when the priests shall have entered in, they shall not go out of the holy places into the outward court: but there they shall lay their vestments, wherein they minister, for they are holy: and they shall put on other garments, and so they shall go forth to the people...* (Ezek 42:14)

The Levites' linens — their breeches, tunics and turbans — were set aside and burned after their month's service. For some these would have been fairly soiled with animal blood, or soot, certainly sweat. But though in former times people knew how to conserve (repair, recycle, reuse), it was clear that clothes once worn in the Court of Priests for divine service could have no use apart from the sacred. Hence they were not washed but burned.

Replacing such reverence with rebellion, Catholic clerics have, in living memory, burned vestments intending that the like never be seen again. If we do not repent and return to God's ways, we will find ourselves cast out of the Garden, withered from the vine, choked with thorns. And others, who long ago were severed from the olive tree, although they belong by nature to it, filling their reverence with tears, will be grafted back in.

δ) The Greatest Wonder
of the Mass

Father, I will that where I am, they
also whom Thou hast given Me may be with Me;
that they may see My glory which Thou hast given Me,
because Thou hast loved Me before the creation of the world.

— Jn 17:24

Even if we cannot see the invisible, we can know it. The Holy Eucharist teaches us a truth about the entirety of creation: beyond appearances, there is God. In the Eucharist, Jesus is present substantially, as He is now in Heaven. How shall we believe that the invisible fullness lies under a veil of visible poverty?

If a tree can turn inorganic matter into organic (which it can), if a man can turn inanimate matter into animate (which he can), can God not turn man into gods? Yes He can. And does. Exercising this power, God — He Who called beings out of non-existence, creatures out of the void, that which is from that which was not, stars from the darkness by naming them — this same God, every single day on earth, turns inanimate substances into Himself. At Holy Mass. By transubstantiation.

To taste a related transformation in ourselves, we attend the liturgy. We assist, contemplate, receive, give thanks. Assist, in this context, does not mean to help but to be present, to stand. Our soul must be awake, attentive. Then we are changed.

Transubstantiation

Thou wilt turn, O God, and bring us to life
— Versicle during the Prayers at the Foot of the Altar

The greatest wonder of the Mass, the greatest occurrence on earth today, is transubstantiation. It is defined infallibly that:

by the consecration of the bread and of the wine, a conversion is made of the whole substance of the bread into the substance of the Body of Christ our Lord, and of the whole substance of the wine into the substance of His Blood; which conversion is, by the holy Catholic Church, suitably and properly called Transubstantiation.[203]

Here God works in one instant the wonder which otherwise takes a lifetime in the soul of each of the saved, or even takes the whole course of history for the life of the Church. That is to say, there is a slow process in nature, with which man collaborates, and then God transforms, in order that what was once dust may be raised up to share in divine life. By nature stalks of wheat draw from the dust of the earth to produce grain. Next man toils to harvest this grain, to mill it and bake it to produce bread. Then, in Holy Mass, God turns this bread into His own Body, united with His Blood, Soul and Divinity. It used to be dust; now it is God.

---

[203] Council of Trent, Session XIII, 4.

All this shows the long journey of man. He is taken from the dust of the earth, fed with water (grace) and sunlight (truth from Christ) to produce grain (good works). He is milled and baked by the trials and furnaces of this world. If he offers these to the Triune God as sacrifice, he is conformed to Christ, is ratified as a member of Christ's Body, and rejoices in Heaven, living by God's own Life.

This analogy works even better for the Church considered as a whole, who began in Adam taken from the dust, is fed on the sacramental Body of Christ to be herself the mystical Body of Christ, and rejoices in Heaven, living as one with God.

Therefore transubstantiation is the meaning of life, of creation, the main theme of history, God with man to bring about man with God. There are hundreds of thousands of priests who offer Mass daily. That means transubstantiation is being effected multiple times every second — or constantly. This entire wonder may be brought to mind by the versicle in the Prayers at the Foot of the Altar: *"Deus tu conversus vivificabis nos..."* — *"Thou wilt turn, O God, and bring us to life..."* (Ps 84:7).[204]

God's action of *turning* is, in Latin, *"conversus"*, from which comes 'conversion'. In Greek, ἐπιστρέφω is used elsewhere to mean 'to be converted' or 'to turn to oneself'. In Hebrew the term is שׁוּב, first used to describe Adam's return to dust when he dies

> *In the sweat of thy face shalt thou eat bread till thou return to the earth, out of which thou wast taken: for dust thou art, and into dust thou shalt return.* (Gen 3:19)

So man turns to dust, but God turns the turning around. By turning Himself to our food, God turns dust — man — into *"gods"* (Ps 81:6; Jn 10:34)! For this tremendous converting we must cooperate by the conversion of our hearts.

---

[204] The Psalm involves the eucharistic theme of our conversion to God through His turning to us: *"Lord, thou hast blessed thy land... Convert us, O God our saviour... Thou wilt turn, O God, and bring us to life... Truth is sprung out of the earth... earth shall yield her fruit"* (Ps 84:1-13).

"conversus vivificabis nos" — *"Thou wilt turn... and bring us to life"*. Thou wilt quicken us. In the Holy Eucharist God gives us life everlasting. The priest, before receiving, prays that the Body of Christ preserve his soul unto eternal life. He prays similarly for each of the faithful as they receive the Host: *"Corpus Domini nostri Jesu Christi custodiat animam tuam in vitam æternam. Amen"*.[205] The "eternal life" requested during the Prayers at the Foot of the Altar (*perducat vos ad vitam æternam* and *Deus, tu conversus vivificabis nos*) is granted in our receiving the Body of Christ, where God has turned Himself to meet us.

More literally, *"conversus"* means God turns to face us. But precisely this, at its deepest level, is transubstantiation. In Heaven when we shall see God as He is, when God fully reveals His Face to us, and we see Him immediately, then we become like Him. The sight of Him is a sharing in His divine substance. On earth this is most fully played out in the Mass when He turns to us in transubstantiation, so that we might be united with Him, becoming like Him.

Here on earth we see not by vision but by faith. Faith is radical, a deep root for a deep life. St Thomas teaches that faith is "whereby eternal life is begun in us".[206]

Preparation in the Law and the Prophets

The OT feeds our faith. The Shewbread in the tabernacle was a precursor to the Holy Eucharist. God instructed Moses to set upon the sacred table twelve *"loaves of proposition in my sight always"* (Ex 25:30). This word *"proposition"* derives from the same as for the Mercy Seat on the Ark which the cherubim covered: *propitiatorium*, a place of atonement, of reconciliation, of soothing. Behind the visible bread is the invisible mercy of God. In Greek the *"loaves of propostion"* are called the "ἄρτους ἐνωπίους", meaning *"Bread of the Face"*, as in *"face to face"*,

---

[205] "The Body of our Lord Jesus Christ preserve thy soul unto life everlasting. Amen."

[206] St Thomas, *S.Th.* II-II, Q.1 a.4 "faith is a habit of the mind, whereby eternal life is begun in us, making the intellect assent to what is non-apparent."

Bread of a Personal Encounter (cf. LXX Gen 16:13; Ex 33:11; Prov 8:9). In Hebrew we have לֶחֶם פָּנִים לְפָנַי תָּמִיד, *"the Bread of the Presence before My Face always"* (Ex 25:30). The OT guides us to where God's Face is to be sought: in the Holy Place, in church sanctuaries, in tabernacles.

The Shewbread was not merely a permanent presence in the Temple, but was always to be fresh, even warm, precisely because the Real Presence of Jesus is alive, we can say warm-blooded (1 Sam 21:6). Likewise, that the liturgy of Temple and tabernacle involved daily offerings of flour and flesh, of wine and blood, can only be fully understood in light of the Holy Eucharist. All these elements are central to worship, then and now. Moses commanded:

> *This is what thou shalt sacrifice upon the altar: Two lambs of a year old every day continually... With one lamb a tenth part of flour... and wine for libation of the same measure... It is a sacrifice to the Lord, by perpetual oblation unto your generations...* (Ex 29:38-45)

The sacrifice is to be *"every day continually"* a *"perpetual oblation"*, offered through all generations. It is fulfilled only in the Church where the elements from the OT (lamb, altar, flour, flesh, wine, blood) are all at play in transubstantiation. The Holy Eucharist is not a late invention but is the goal toward which these precursors ran. Ezekiel prophesies the same essential ordinance in reference to the Church:

> *Daily he shall offer, as a holocaust to the Lord, an immaculate lamb... mixed with the fine flour, as a sacrifice to the Lord, by a continual and everlasting ordinance... morning after morning, as an everlasting holocaust.* (Ezek 46:13-15 SB)

If this were not fulfilled in the Holy Eucharist, then the *"everlasting ordinance"* would have been impossible to keep without the Temple. The *"everlasting holocaust"* would have failed in AD 70. But God's plan is sure.

241

God's plan is so sure that even those who oppose Him end up serving it. His enemies have no chance. They think they will kill the prophet with poisonous *"wood"*, but in the Holy Eucharist this becomes nothing less than the source of life:

> *And I was as a meek lamb, that is carried to be a victim: and I knew not that they had devised counsels against me, saying: Let us put wood on his bread, and cut him off from the land of the living, and let his name be remembered no more.* (Jer 11:19)[207]

The sacrificial victim is like a *"meek lamb"* (we think of Jesus). In *"his bread"* (we think of the Holy Eucharist) we find deadly *"wood"* put there by enemies (we think of the Cross, meaning the Passion is figured in the Eucharist for the separation of the species means death). But as Jeremiah's enemies miscalculated, so did those of Jesus. By the Cross, He was not eradicated *"from the land of the living"*, but entered into it! His Name has not been forgotten, but is *"remembered"* every day at the altar. Death is turned to life.

Aptly the versicle at the Foot of the Altar continues with its response: *"Thou wilt turn, O God, and bring us to life: and thy people shall rejoice in thee"* (Ps 84:7). However true this is on earth, it is infinitely more true in Heaven. Such an ending — rejoicing in God — and such a work to bring us there — transubstantiation — has unsurprisingly been prepared from the foundation of the world. It lies hidden to be discovered, announced in a way which is, for those who have converted, impossible not to hear and see and understand (Is 6:10). We will look at various examples.

The Book of Leviticus, all about the priesthood, repeatedly makes the point that the victim is to be laid *"on the wood which is on the fire which is on the altar"* (Lev 1:12 cf. 1:7,17; 3:5). Why repeat this, except that we should notice the dead victim on the wood figures Christ on the Cross while the fire on the altar

---

[207] Prayed at Maundy Thursday, Matins, *Responsorium* VII, in reference to Jesus.

anticipates the operation of the Holy Spirit, Who is invoked before transubstantiation occurs, so that the victim, or Host, is utterly consumed. In this way, the Levitical rites announce the unity of the Sacrifice of Calvary with the Sacrifice of the Mass.

If one is unsure of this interpretation, it becomes more convincing when used as a key to unlock the following strange story about Gideon which then becomes perfectly coherent. From previous chapters we may take the *"oak"*, *"rod"* and *"wood"* to stand for the Cross, and the *"rock"* to mean Christ or the altar. The perfect submission of Gideon to the Angel of the Lord represents Jesus' utter obedience to the Godhead:

> *And an angel of the Lord came, and sat under an oak... And when Gedeon... was threshing and cleansing wheat by the winepress... The angel of the Lord appeared to him, and said: The Lord is with thee... And Gedeon said to him: I beseech thee, my lord, if the Lord be with us... Where are his miracles...? ...And the Lord looked upon him, and said: Go in this thy strength... I will be with thee...*

> *So Gedeon went in, and boiled a kid, and made unleavened loaves of a measure of flour: and putting the flesh in a basket, and the broth of the flesh into a pot, he carried all under the oak, and presented to him. And the angel of the Lord said to him: Take the flesh and the unleavened loaves, and lay them upon that rock, and pour out the broth thereon. And when he had done so, the angel of the Lord put forth the tip of the rod, which he held in his hand, and touched the flesh and the unleavened loaves: and there arose a fire from the rock, and consumed the flesh and the unleavened loaves: and the angel of the Lord vanished out of his sight. And Gedeon seeing that it was the angel of the Lord, said: Alas, my Lord God: for I have seen the angel of the Lord face to face. And the Lord said to him: Peace be with thee: fear not, thou shalt not die. And Gedeon built there an altar to the Lord, and called it the Lord's peace, until this present day...*

That night the Lord said to him... thou shalt build an altar to the Lord thy God in the top of this rock, whereupon thou didst lay the sacrifice before: and thou shalt... offer a holocaust upon a pile of the wood... (Jdg 6:11-26)

The early mention of *"cleansing wheat by the winepress"* alerts us to a possible eucharistic story while *"the Lord is with thee"* primes us to see if Gideon might represent the Incarnate Christ. Then the Angel of the Lord, perhaps the Holy Ghost, orders a sacrifice be made which involves *"unleavened bread"*, *"flesh"* and the *"broth of the flesh"*. These foretell the Body and Blood of Christ under accidents of food and drink. They are laid on the *"rock"* (Christ, the altar), and when the angel *"put forth... his hand"* are consumed by *"fire from the rock"*, both aspects showing the operation of the divinity.

If the vanishing of the angel of the Lord upon the loaves being consumed pre-echoes Jesus in Emmaus (Lk 24:31), then seeing *"face to face"* alludes to the Real Presence. Gideon feared this might cause him to die, but God preserved him, as Jesus was not held by death. For future partakers in the sacrifice it is a warning that receiving this meal is coming into contact with God, *"face to face"*, so those who eat the loaves unworthily face hell, but those whom the Lord favours will live.[208] The *"peace"*, *pax*, given to Gideon and the life promised to him both speak of the Mass, for Gideon next builds an altar for a holocaust which continues the work of the original sacrifice.

Obviously I cannot insist on every detail of interpretation. But as I find this eucharistic key opens more and more locked doors in the Bible, then I am more and more confident that the key is given by God. For example, a vivification through bread is seen also in a story of David.

And they found an Egyptian in the field, and brought him to David: and they gave him bread to eat, and water to drink [and] raisins. And when he had eaten them his spirit returned,

---

[208] In this context, "unworthily" basically means those who do not believe in the Real Presence or those who have unconfessed mortal sins.

*and he was refreshed: for he had not eaten bread, nor drunk
water three days, and three nights.* (1 Sam 30:11-12)

If the Egyptian, who is so exhausted as to be near death,
represents fallen man, we see he is revived by *"bread"* and a
"drink" (*"raisins"* remotely signifying wine). So man is given
life by the Holy Eucharist. That *"his spirit* (רוּחַ) *returned* (שׁוּב)*"*
to him after three days and nights connects the man's recovery
with the Resurrection, as our being quickened by Holy
Communion depends upon Christ Risen.

Some might object that bread and wine were ordinary staples,
inevitably appearing often in the Scriptures, and that it is not
appropriate to read the Holy Eucharist into every reference. But
these are everyday items precisely because God created them to
be so with the knowledge of what they would signify. God can
scarcely lay them in the Scriptures, in meaningful contexts,
without awareness of compelling eucharistic interpretations,
especially when their inclusion would otherwise seem
superfluous.

Every Book of the *Torah* and all the major prophets mention
both *"bread"* and *"wine"*. Numerous such references by the
minor prophets are best explained by the Holy Eucharist.

Hosea says that the corn and wine shall *"hear"* Jezrahel: *"And
the earth shall hear the corn, and the wine, and the oil, and these
shall hear Jezrahel"* (Hos 2:22). What does this mean ultimately
but that the elements of bread and wine obey the Word of God,
"This is My Body" and "This is My Blood"? The elements react
obediently. *Jezrahel* means "God shall sow" or "seed of God".
God sows His Word as a seed in the soil (*"earth"*) of our souls,
thereby making Himself a people (Hos 2:23) when we hear Him,
are attentive to Him, in the *"corn and the wine"*.

Joel cries that *"The country is destroyed, the ground hath
mourned: for the corn is wasted, the wine is confounded, the oil
hath languished"* (Joel 1:10; cf. Hag 1:11). Still, he declares
God's promise that, at a future point:

Behold I will send you corn, and wine, and oil, and you shall be filled with them: and I will no more make you a reproach among the nations (Joel 2:19; cf. 24).

Can anyone think God's whole plan for our well-being and satisfaction is about bread and wine and oil, rather than about His Body and His Life and His Spirit? Has God allowed all the misery we see in the world, only to repay those who endure with mere bread? Can bread fill us? The Prophet Zachariah makes such low thinking impossible to maintain by asking: *"For what is the good thing of him, and what is his beautiful thing, but the corn of the elect, and wine springing forth virgins?"* (Zec 9:17)

The Old Covenant is pregnant with the New. This is something we cannot discern until our Mother, the Church, tells us. Then, like a pregnancy, looking at the OT the inner life becomes more and more noticeable, indeed unmissable.

As the king of Israel was passing by the wall, a certain woman cried out to him, saying: Save me, my lord O king. And he said: If the Lord doth not save thee, how can I save thee? out of the barnfloor, or out of the winepress? (2 Kngs 6:26-27)

The King of Israel responds to a plea for salvation by saying that he cannot achieve it from the threshing floor and winepress, but the Lord Himself must do it. Which God in very deed does — He gives His bread and wine, from the places of division and trials, for salvation — as requested!

The first Psalm of Sunday Compline (Ps 4) is echoed on the Feast of *Corpus Christi*: "His faithful ones which are increased by the fruit of His corn and His wine do lay them down in peace and sleep in Christ."[209] The Holy Eucharist is our growth, our security against death, our pledge of everlasting life, our eternal rest with God.

That we can trust this divine food to overcome death is taught to us daily by the basic meaning of food and drink. They are consumed to give life. So the sacrifice is consumed to be a source

---

[209] *Corpus Christi*, Matins, Antiphon II. Cf. Ps 4:8-9.

of divine life (grace). The OT offerings are edible: lambs, goats, bulls, rams, birds, flour, cakes, bread, wine, oil, honey, salt. Or if they are not eaten, they are consumed by fire as holocausts, as also incense is burned. Everything is to be consumed, as ultimately is Jesus. He is the life-giving holocaust, consumed in Holy Communion.

This is why flesh and bread are so often mentioned together, because in Holy Communion they belong together:

> *Boil the flesh before the door of the tabernacle, and there eat it. Eat ye also the loaves of consecration, that are laid in the basket, as the Lord commanded me, saying: Aaron and his sons shall eat them: and whatsoever shall be left of the flesh and the loaves, shall be consumed with fire.* (Lev 8:31-32)

The victim is to be killed and eaten. Nothing *"of the flesh and the loaves"* is to be left over. It is *"holy of holies"* (Lev 6:25-26). This was the life of Levitical priests, and remains so in Holy Orders:

> *Know you not, that they who work in the holy place, eat the things that are of the holy place; and they that serve the altar, partake with the altar? So also the Lord ordained that they who preach the gospel, should live by the gospel.* (1 Cor 9:13-14)

The life given from serving at the altar and preaching the Word means much more than stipends, wages, payment. When we receive Holy Communion, when we ruminate on the Word of God, they are not assimilated to us, but we are assimilated to Him. The higher assimilates the lower. We are surrounded by examples of this and find no counter-examples. If a bucket of water is thrown on a flame, the water does not become hot, but the flame is extinguished. If a drop of water falls into a furnace, the furnace does not become wet, but the water is vaporised. When two forms meet, the outcome depends on which is the stronger. All agents strive to pass on their form in so far as they have power and another is receptive.[210] Jesus is the Most powerful; His form is love; whoever is open to Him, receives Him; and is made like Him, receives His form.

The process is illustrated for us in digestion. If a man eats an apple, the apple becomes part of him. But the reverse happens for those who receive Holy Communion. If they hear the Word of God, and believe, they become partially conformed to Christ; then if they desire Him in Holy Communion, and are open to Him, their souls receive the full form of Jesus, the *anima* Christi. As His form is stronger than ours, He assimilates us, making us holy, making us members of His Body. Unlike an apple, which becomes part of us when we eat it, we eat the Body of Christ to become part of Him.

We cannot see this. But then we cannot even see ourselves digest an apple. We know it happens and we know we become healthy. Likewise, if we receive Holy Communion with love then we see spiritual growth — or at least our superiors will. The opposite happens for those defiled by sin which they refuse to repent. Just as part of an apple is assimilated to become our body and part is passed out as waste, so of all who eat Holy Communion, some are assimilated as members of Christ's Body and others pass through.

> *If any one that is defiled shall eat of the flesh of the sacrifice of peace offerings, which is offered to the Lord, he shall be cut off from his people. And he that hath touched the uncleanness of man, or of beast, or of any thing that can defile, and shall eat of such kind of flesh, shall be cut off from his people.* (Lev 7:20-21; cf. 1 Cor 10:15-22; 11:27-32)

Is God's teaching too hard for us to receive? Jesus said:

> *I am the bread of life. Your fathers did eat manna in the desert, and are dead... I am the living bread which came down*

---

[210] St Thomas, *S.Th.*, I, Q.4 a.3 "Since every agent reproduces itself so far as it is an agent, and everything acts according to the manner of its form, the effect must in some way resemble the form of the agent." See also *Commentary on Aristotle's Metaphysics*, X, 11, 2134; *Commentary on Physics*, II, 11, 242.

from heaven. If any man eat of this bread, he shall live for ever; and the bread that I will give, is My Flesh, for the life of the world. (Jn 6:48-52)[211]

To this divine teaching many responded: *"This saying is hard, and who can hear it?"* (Jn 6:61). They *"murmured"* against Him (Jn 6:41,43,62). In all three instances, St John uses the same word which the Septuagint uses for the murmuring and grumbling of the Hebrews against God in the desert when they complained (LXX γογγύζουσιν; Vulgate *murmurare*) He would not feed them:

> *I have heard the murmuring of the children of Israel: say to them: In the evening you shall eat flesh, and in the morning you shall have your fill of bread: and you shall know that I am the Lord your God...* (Ex 16:12-13)

Here is indicated that the proper lesson from the flesh and the bread is that you shall know *"Ego sum"* — *"I am"*, He is Present, *HaShem*. It is the very Name of *"the Lord your God"*. This is our lesson for Holy Communion. How can our hard-heartedness be explained, our slowness to believe? How can Protestants, who say they believe every word Jesus speaks, deny the Real Presence? Even worse are Catholics — even clerics, bishops like Judas — who eat without discerning, despite God laying out a pedagogy for thousands of years in advance.

That God prepares in advance is proved by the Last Supper. It shows Jesus certainly knew He would die on the morrow: He erected the sacramental memorial to His death the night before it

---

[211] *Feria III infra Octavam Corpus Christi,* Matins, *Lectio VI,* provides a commentary on this Scripture from St Augustine, *Tractatus 26 in Joannem:* "But the death whereof the Lord doth sound the alarm, the death that their fathers died, is another death than that which is outward and bodily. Moses ate manna, Aaron ate manna, Phineas ate manna, many ate manna in whom the Lord was well pleased and these are not dead. Wherefore because they understood spiritually that outward bread, spiritually hungered thereafter, spiritually tasted thereof, and spiritually were satisfied therewith. So also do we this day feed on a visible food, but the Sacrament is one thing, and the grace of the Sacrament is another."

happened.[212] Looking closely, we see that the Last Supper is the culmination of four thousand years of preparation, all leading to the Crucifixion. Prefigurations of His Passion from the first days of creation, from Eden, Abel, Abraham, from the Law of Moses and all the Prophets, from tabernacle and Temple, increased in expressive perfection until Jesus was ready to sum up the meaning of it all at the Last Supper. Jesus could have celebrated the first Mass after His Resurrection, but He chose to do so before His Crucifixion, reinforcing the lesson that God's way is to anticipate as only He can.

If God did not wish to signal the Mass long in advance, why is it that of all the things he could have done, of every possibility in the world, the High Priest Melchisedech, King of Peace, offered bread and wine in Jerusalem?

The same eternal offering may be traced back to Eden. What did Adam sacrifice there? We are not sure if he offered animals. Perhaps he did after the Fall when death had entered the world, after God had made aprons for Adam and his wife from animal skins. But before learning to do this, did Adam first offer fruits? If so, how fitting. Certain fruits are said to have 'flesh'. If the juice be squeezed out to produce a drink, which juice in the case of grapes is even called 'blood', we have flesh and blood, a hidden allusion to the Eucharist. It is sweet, refreshing, desirable, nutritious and abounds in Paradise.

Still more hidden, in the description of Eden's environs we read: *"And the gold of that land is very good: there is found bdellium, and the onyx stone"* (Gen 2:12). There are hints here of what is to come. By mentioning the precious bdellium, בְּדֹלַח, Eden is pointing early to the Holy Eucharist, for the only other use of this word in the OT is to describe the manna from Heaven: *"Now the manna was like coriander seed, but with the colour of bdellium"* (Num 11:7). This manna figures the Holy Eucharist. The paradoxical *"onyx"* by its blackness which shines, tells of

---

[212] The sacraments transcend time. They can be instituted before the Crucifixion, as the Holy Eucharist and priesthood on Maundy Thursday, and even earlier as with baptism — see St Thomas, *S.Th.* III Q.66 a.2.

life defeating death, the resurrection. Therefore for the saints the glory or *"the gold of that land is very good"*.

Before man was created, the essence of God's plan with the Cross and Holy Eucharist was written into nature and recounted by multiple references to the *"seed"*. For the repetitious insistence of Gen 1-2 that living creatures bear *"seeds"* and that they bring forth according to *"their kind"* is not only a safeguard against the godless and metaphysically impossible theory of macro-evolution, it is an announcement that Jesus (the *"Seed"* Gen 3:15) plans to generate countless sons of God, not only made in God's *"image and likeness"* (Gen 1:26), but receiving live substance from Him. In Genesis not one word is wasted. God's use of repetition here is not redundant but interpreted properly allows the passage to be heard like the Gospel:

> *God said: Let the earth bring forth the green herb, and such as may seed, and the fruit tree yielding fruit after its kind, which may have seed in itself upon the earth. And it was so done. And the earth brought forth the green herb, and such as yieldeth seed according to its kind, and the tree that beareth fruit, having seed each one according to its kind. And God saw that it was good. And the evening and the morning were the third day.* (Gen 1:11-13)

The *"seed"* is Christ and the *"fruit tree"* is the Cross and the *"fruit"* is the Eucharist which gives its *"seed"*, Christ, for the multiplication of Christians — souls *"according to [the] kind"* of Christ — for Christ's Cross is *"the tree that beareth fruit"*. The *"third day"* indeed, evening followed by morning!

This is the plan of the Passion and Resurrection, of overcoming the darkness. Immediately there follows the descriptions of the *"great lights"* to rule the heavens *"and to give light upon the earth"* (Gen 1:15-16). This is the sun and moon which regulate our liturgical calendar with its days, weeks, months and years (Gen 1:14) along with *"the stars"* to stand for the saints, a Sanctoral cycle.

This all prepared, God made man and told him:

Behold I have given you every herb bearing seed upon the earth, and all trees that have in themselves seed of their own kind, to be your meat. (Gen 1:29)

That last word, *"meat"*, is no mistranslation:

- In Latin, it is *esca*, the food God gives to those who fear him in the memorial He made to His eternal Covenant: *"Escam dedit timentibus se..."* — *"He hath given food to them that fear him. He will be mindful for ever of his covenant"* (Ps 110:5). Mass or memorial meat.

- In Hebrew, it is אָכְלָה, the same as used for the miraculous manna from heaven (Ex 16:15) of which the Jews boasted to Jesus (Jn 6:31), but which He unambiguously clarified meant Himself (Jn 6:32-35). Flesh from Heaven.

- In Greek, it is βρῶσις, which Jesus offers to supplant the penitential toil imposed after Eden with life everlasting. Our Lord said: *"Labour not for the meat which perisheth, but for that which endureth unto life everlasting, which the Son of man will give you"* (Jn 6:27). He leaves no doubt this is the Holy Eucharist by clarifying: *"For My Flesh is meat indeed: and My Blood is drink indeed"* (Jn 6:56). Incorruptible flesh.

All this was promised in Eden. According to Gen 1:29, this food, this *"meat"* (*esca*, βρῶσις, אָכְלָה), should come from a tree — meat for a memorial, meat from heaven, meat for redemption. The only tree that can provide such meat is the Cross.

When Adam saw the tree, he yearned to eat the fruit thereof, at least after Eve prompted him to do so. When Jesus saw His Cross looming, He yearned for it: *"with desire I have desired to eat this Pasch"* (Lk 22:15). He longed to suffer for us, to give Himself to us. Mary covers even Eve in glory by explaining her life. As our first mother prompted the first Adam to fall, it was Mary our ultimate Mother whose observation at Cana (Jn 2:3) set her Lord's public ministry, that is our redemption, in train.

Without the Gospel, Genesis cannot make sense. Ergo, without the Gospel, nothing makes sense.

Arbor dignissima

A tree is a perfect metaphor for the Cross. The very nature of a tree, as created by God, is to change dirt into fruit. That is to say the Cross, the wood planted in the earth, turns sinners into saints. It reaches down into the soil from which man was made, which is all dark and so packed together it seems nothing can move, except the worms and grubs which signify corruption and demons. So may this world seem to us. And yet roots can grow in it, water can penetrate it, as truth and grace can reach every soul. And the tree draws the dirt upwards, heavenward, finally transforming it into luscious fruit. Is this not what the Cross achieves with souls, raising them from the darkness of the underworld to the sweetness above?

The life history of one nourished by the Holy Eucharist — going from sinner to saint, from earth to Heaven, from the dirt to the divine — is a slow unfolding in the soul mirroring the event of transubstantiation which takes but an instant in the sacred species. This process is figured by the achievement of each tree. Or why should God not sketch out His great plan for us into nature, into every fruit-bearing tree?

This insight underscores that the Crucifixion informs all time. It shapes all history, not only *post factum* until the end times, but even God's planting the Garden in Genesis. All that was purposefully done as a parable to tell the power of the Cross.

Making this connection with beautiful solemnity, on the Feasts of the Invention and Exaltation of the Cross it is sung that the *"Crux"* is the *"arbor dignissima, in paradisi medio situata"*:

> This is that most noble tree [*arbor dignissima*], planted in the midst of the garden... Even the Cross... whereon the Author of our salvation did by His Own death openly triumph over the death of all men. Alleluia, Alleluia.[213]

Jesus died on the Cross to offer us a better fruit than that which was denied Adam and Eve from the Tree of Life after they

---

[213] Exaltation of the Cross, Matins, *Responsorium* III.

stole fruit from the Tree of Knowledge. The fruit of that first tree would have bestowed immortality, but not the beatific vision, and it would not have taken away the possibility of sin. With sin but no death, life on earth would become an inescapable hell. Or it might have meant immortality for a tyrant, a globalist, an antichrist, with the murderous exploitation of everyone else. The remedy given by God is the fruit from the Cross, the true Tree of Life. This Holy Eucharist bestows on the well-disposed who receive it eternal life which necessarily excludes any possibility of sin: the beatific vision. How much more there is to trees than meets the eye! They all like to sing of their relation to the Cross:

> I was exalted [the Cross] like a cedar in Libanus [towering], and as a cypress tree on mount Sion [mountain of Jerusalem]. I was exalted like a palm tree [martyrdom, victory] in Cades, and as a rose plant [virginity] in Jericho: As a fair olive tree [sacraments] in the plains, and as a plane tree [helps sinners] by the water in the streets, was I exalted [the Cross]. I gave a sweet smell [virtues, grace] like... aromatical balm: I yielded a sweet odour like the best myrrh [anointing in death]: And I perfumed my dwelling as storax [wounds]... onyx, and aloes, and as the frankincense [priesthood] not cut, and my odour is as the purest balm [healing]. I have stretched out my branches as the turpentine tree [shade, protection], and my branches [churches] are of honour and grace. As the vine [Jesus] I have brought forth a pleasant odour: and my flowers [saints] are the fruit of honour and riches [heavenly glory]. (Sir 24:17-23)

Flowers, too, tell the Gospel in their nature. Tertullian comments:

> there shall be born a rod from the root of Jesse — which is Mary — and a flower shall rise up from his root. And the Spirit of God shall rest upon him... (Is 11:1-2). Indeed, the totality of spiritual gifts was befitting to no man but to Christ, who was compared to a flower because of His grace, linked to the root of Jesse because He should come from it through Mary.[214]

---

214 Tertullian, *Adversus Judaeos*, IX.

Jesus is the 'flower', Mary the 'stem'. Pre-Fall flowers preached Jesus from Mary, for the Incarnation was always the plan.

Saints have asked, would Jesus have become incarnate amongst us if Adam had not sinned?[215] Some say He would have dwelt among us but He would not have been crucified. Instead, He would have been welcomed as King, Lord, God. But I think the planting of Paradise before the making of man already anticipates sin and promises the Crucifixion. For the ultimate meaning of "fruit" is Jesus. Preparing us for the Incarnation, the OT speaks of various fruits: *"Blessed will be the fruit of your body, and the fruit of your ground, and the fruit of your beasts..."* (Dt 28:4). Men's descendants are explicitly likened to seeds and fruit, to be blessed or cursed by God (Dt 7:13; Ps 20:11). And the ultimate man is Jesus Christ. We pray to His Mother: *"blessed is the fruit of thy womb, Jesus"*. Where were fruits to be found first, but hanging on trees? And where was the best fruit, promising immortality, but on *"the tree of life... in the midst of paradise"* (Gen 2:9; see also 3:22). How could seeds germinate without dying? So it was written into nature and Scripture that Jesus would hang on the wood to give everlasting life when we eat Him, becoming like God.[216]

A world without sin was never expected. The variety of animals before the Fall anticipates numerous classes of saints (lambs as victims; rams as kings; bulls, eagles, oxen and lions as evangelists) but also the reprobate (foxes for Herod; vipers as poisonous hypocrites). The separation of land from waters on the third day speaks of the Church arising from death (Gen 1:9-10). The dividing of light from the darkness indicates from the inception that the devil must fail, that being would be loosened of all privation, that good would emerge unharmed from evil, all in a day's work (Gen 1:4-5). That day was the evening of Holy Thursday through to the going down of the sun on Good Friday.

---

[215] St Anselm (✝1098), *Cur Deus homo.*

[216] St Thomas, *Commentary on the Gospel of St John* (7:44) "those who are good, who believe, want to seize Christ to enjoy Him: *'I will go up into the palm tree and seize its fruit'* (Cant 7:8)."

God's certainty that Adam would sin in no way diminishes Adam's free will, otherwise there would not be sin. Rather it underscores for us the greater certainty God had in Mary's *Fiat*. This too must have been an act of free will on Mary's part, otherwise there would not be love. The use of any faculty of nature is greater than and logically prior to its abuse. The fixation of the will on God is a more comprehensible choice than rejecting Him. Though God knows all things in advance, He was more sure of Mary's "yes" than Adam's "no" — not because there is any uncertainty in God's knowledge, but because there is more to be certain about in Mary *Fiat* than in Adam's fall; there is more substance to her yes than his no. God permitted us to risk death because He was certain of offering Salvation unto better Life through the fruit of Mary's womb, Jesus. In wonder the Church sings to Mary: "Daughter, thou art blessed of the Lord: for by thee we have partaken of the fruit of life [*fructum vitæ*]".[217]

The very beginning, Gen 1 speaking repeatedly of *"seeds"* bringing forth according to their own kind, is a pre-Fall assurance of God's plan of the Passion and Resurrection of Christ. He always intended to bring forth a Seed from Eve, that is through the Blessed Virgin Mary, which Seed must fall and die in order to bring forth abundant fruit: saints who are members of His Body. This is the reason we are made in the *"image and likeness of God"*: so that we are capax to receive God's substance too. The human body is created to house not merely a rational soul, but even Divine persons, to be a temple for God. What is so proportioned to effect the building of this temple as transubstantiation? Is there anything greater on earth?

---

[217] Maternity of Our Lady, Vespers, Antiphon IV *"Benedicta filia tu a Domino, quia per te fructum vitæ communicavimus."*

II: Tearing out Ancient Roots

And we charge you, brethren, in the name of
our Lord Jesus Christ, that you withdraw yourselves
from every brother walking disorderly, and not according
to the tradition which they have received of us.

— 2 Thes 3:6

Holy Mass gives us the structure of reality: threefold; self-sacrificial; God with man. To distort the Mass is to lie about God and is tantamount to murdering souls. This was the aim of the serpent in Eden: to lie to murder. He continues, through all generations, trying to separate men from God.

The devil hates that we can now eat from the Tree. He hates that God gives Himself to us as the Fruit. The devil hates that he actually helped plant this Tree, the Cross, when he instigated the Crucifixion. Ceaselessly satan seeks to tear this Tree up from the roots, to destroy Holy Mass. His apparent success over the past seventy years signals not a near victory for him, rather that soon his head will be crushed.

The Opening Assault on Holy Week

In the 1950s, seduced by the world, the Catholic hierarchy began systematically dismantling the Church's liturgical traditions. The 1951-55 changes to the ceremonies of Holy Week amounted to hacking at ancient roots and pouring in poison, resulting in the now obvious devastation of the vineyard of the Lord.[218]

For Palm Sunday and the Easter Vigil, tables were introduced into the sanctuary so that the celebrant could face the people. Now almost everywhere high altars are abandoned while priests 'perform' man-centred Masses, a fatal spiritual narcissism.

The vernacular was introduced to the Easter Vigil. Now the Church is divided like Babel with a profusion of languages. For Good Friday, all were told to recite the priest's *Pater noster* and also a vernacular version inserted into the Vigil rites. Ever since there has been a deepening confusion of roles, of who can do what. Laity have been groomed to say the *Our Father* aloud in daily Mass in the way the serpent talked Eve into tasting the fruit: "you will be like gods priests". Irresponsible, grasping vanity.

By the resentful demotion of His minister, Christ is demoted in hearts. Priests sit while laity distribute Holy Communion. Also catastrophic is the abolishment of duplicated readings. Traditionally in a Solemn Mass the priest would quietly read the Scriptures at the altar while another minister chanted them for all to hear. This is profoundly Christo-centric.[219] But beginning in 1951 with an option for Holy Saturday and achieving devastation within a decade through a universal norm, priests were told to abandon their duty, to read no Epistle or Gospel at all, but leave this to a subordinate minister.[220] When the *novus* erupted a decade later, it became usual to even let laity read these from an ambo.

---

[218] The deformation was launched with the decrees *Ordo Sabbati Sancti instaurati* (1st March 1951), and *Maxima redemptionis nostræ mysteria* (16th Nov 1955).

[219] After the deacon chants the Gospel, it is not he that is incensed but the priest who whispered it at the altar. This signifies that it is not God's ministers active on earth to whom the glory goes, but to Christ Himself, the High Priest acting 'unheard' from His high station in Heaven, He Who really gives the Gospel power.

[220] *Rubricarum instructum* §473; 513f (25th July 1960).

This reveals a retarded view of the purpose of the readings, to Whom they are directed, and their power. They are a sacrifice, to be performed at the altar by a minister, offered to God for His glory and for the redemption of the living and dead.

The solemn readings of the Passion through Holy Week had the Last Supper expurgated, erasing the most expressive lesson in the liturgical year that the Last Supper, like every single Holy Mass, is a sign united to the greater reality, the Crucifixion. Delusion now reigns, with Catholics imagining Mass is mainly a meal. They are unaware it is primarily a sacrifice.

Deepening this confusion, from 1955 Holy Communion was distributed on Good Friday, the one day of the year It really ought not be received. Withholding the Sacrament on Good Friday was a striking way to prompt people to ponder the original: the Passion. The new way makes it harder to apprehend the reality behind the sign, to understand the substance standing under the sacred species, that every Communion is rooted in the Crucifixion, that His Body is the fruit of the tree.

For Maundy Thursday's stripping of the altars, traditionally the crucifix and candles were left in place. These all belonged together in an inseparable unity, even after the moving ceremony of stripping. But in 1955 a heedless innovation instructed that crucifix and candles be removed too. The proper inseparability of these symbols having been severed on this day, there are now everywhere Catholics whose minds make no connection between daily Mass (at the altar) and Christ's death on Calvary (portrayed by the crucifix) and the saving truth this propagates (symbolised by the candles). Congruently their churches obscure such connections in architecture and furnishings.

Did the architects of these changes want to overturn everything? Yes. Fr Annibale Bugnini, later Archbishop, saw the changes to the Easter Vigil as "the first step to a general liturgical renewal".[221] Fr Carlo Braga boasted of their work as "the head of the battering-ram which pierced the fortress of our hitherto static

---

[221] Bugnini, Braga, *Ordo Hebdomadæ Sanctæ Instauratus Commentarium* (1956), 5.

liturgy".[222] They knew full well their changes would revolutionise the liturgy utterly, eventually making it unrecognisable. Whether or not they understood that this would lead to a collapse in faith and morals is unclear. But this was understood by the satanists whom they served and who operate today.[223]

In 1968 the rite for the consecration of bishops underwent a reordering so savage as to spurn many graces and even to make its very validity questionable. The purpose for the changes, explained by Dom Bernhard Botte, principal author of the consecratory formula for the 1968 rite, was to shift the Church's understanding of the bishop from one who sanctifies to one who rules.[224] Lust for power replaces a heart for service. The new thinking, which claims to be a return to the ancient ways, was that the bishop be directed not explicitly by the Holy Spirit, but by the ominous-sounding "governing Spirit", the *hegemonicos*.[225]

If the 1950s changes to Holy Week seem slight to some, if the 1968 gutting of episcopal consecrations is too remote from most, then the 1969 promulgation of the *novus ordo missæ* has been an earthquake resulting in uncounted millions of souls falling away from the Church. The new ordering of the Mass follows the principle *solve et coagula*, meaning to dissolve in order to rejoin, that is, *if such evil were possible*, to dissolve the Body of Christ and subject its members to a vaunting spirit. Altogether the changes are a demonic delirium.

---

[222] Braga, *Maxima Redemptionis Nostræ Mysteria, 50 anni dopo (1955-2005)*, p.33.

[223] In 2019, Braga was declared a Servant of God by the pornocratic Vatican.

[224] As prophet, priest and king, the bishop teaches, sanctifies and rules. But the chief among these is sanctification, as this is our goal. Teaching and governing are to serve holiness, our union with God. The bishop is a key instrument in this plan.

[225] Dom Bernard Botte, *Spiritus Principalis (formule de l'ordination episcopale)*, *Notitiae*, 10 (1974), 410-11: "it is clear that *principalis* must be correlated with the specific functions of the bishop... The bishop is both leader who must govern the new people, and the high priest of the new sanctuary which has been established in every place. The bishop is the ruler of the Church. Hence the choice of the term *hegemonicos* is understandable: it is the gift of the Spirit apt for a leader. The best translation in French would perhaps be 'the Spirit of authority.' But whatever the translation adopted, the meaning seems certain."

There follows a survey of the seismic damage, indeed devastation, caused by the *novus ordo*, which is detaching men from reality.

Tabernacle, Altar and Crucifix

The modernist aversion to Christ is seen in the degradation of altar, crucifix and tabernacle. Tradition had solidly established a practical inseparability of altar, crucifix and tabernacle. This is an inspired combination so full of meaning that it serves salvation. How? For man, the three reinforce reality.

There is no place holier nor more important than the tabernacle of Catholic churches. God dwells here substantially. Its most obvious prefiguration is the tabernacle built by Moses in the desert. The rabbis say this was God's plan since before even the creation of the world: the tabernacle accommodates the very purpose of the universe, for it is the place of God's encounter with man. The saints are in broad agreement with the rabbis on this, except Christians, crucially, understand Moses' tabernacle to be an image of the Sacred Humanity taken on by the Son of God in the Incarnation.

An altar for sacrifice has been vital to man since the generation of Abel, or even earlier with Adam himself. Noah and Abraham built altars to God. It is the place where we make a return to God for all that He has given to us. Sacrifice, being the chief obligation of religion, when made through Jesus Christ, re-binds us to God. It makes perfect sense that altar and tabernacle belong together.

With these two must stand a crucifix. On the Cross the Flesh of the Son of God, His tabernacle, was put to death. The Cross itself is the altar of His Sacrifice, it is the meaning of the altar at which Mass is offered. Therefore the crucifix joins tabernacle and altar formally. The Cross is so central to all reality that it is glimpsed in the Tree of Life with the best fruit hanging on it; it is traced across the cosmos in the first verses of Genesis; it is actually encoded in the first word of the Bible. The Cross joins Heaven and Earth; as does the altar; as does the tabernacle with

His Real Presence. Here is a threefold visual rhyme of 'God with man' at the place of His Self-sacrifice. Outside Heaven, it cannot get more real than here.

Understanding this, ever since the Church had the freedom to build altars and the craft to produce crucifixes, it has been proper to associate them together. Once tabernacles developed, despite experimentation with suspended pyxes, and the challenge of free-standing altars in many cathedrals, it became a much-loved norm to have altar, tabernacle and crucifix together, if possible backed by a breathtaking reredos pointing magnificently heavenward.

Then came the 1970s. Tabernacles have been separated from altars, even moved out of the sanctuary and out of sight. In many churches they are removed to a side chapel where few faithful ever visit. The countless adoring angels who crowd round every tabernacle are there with Christ, but no longer with the people.

Altars have been abandoned and tables introduced. Instead of sacrifice modernists want a meal, hoping to appease heretics who hate the Mass. What was once fixed and immovable might now be carried or even wheeled away. What consisted ideally of stone may now be made from glass or ugly cement. By church law altars should contain the relics of saints. Who knows how many are without relics today? Beautiful, sacred high altars have been literally torn out of churches.

The purpose is an heretical shift away from a priest offering to God a sacrifice on an altar. Instead we have a president addressing the assembly before a meal on a table. Traditionally, only in a secondary way may the altar be thought of as a meal table, acknowledging divine food and drink are indeed served there as a pledge of the heavenly banquet. But we are not there yet. We are in a vale of tears fit for sacrifice, redeemed from sin only by the Crucifixion. Without this, not one of us will taste the banquet in Heaven. Whosoever imagines the altar is primarily a table, or nothing more than a table, as if we commemorate Holy Thursday's Last Supper rather than Good Friday's Passion and Death, such persons think with the heretics of whom the Welsh martyr Richard Gywn (+1584) wrote:

Instead of altar, a sorry trestle; instead of Christ, mere bread. Instead of holy things, a miserable tinker making a boast of knavery. Instead of images, empty niches.

In German these tables are called *Volksaltäre*, "people's altars", as if the changes are all done for the people. This has been the slogan of every demonic revolution from the French to the Bolshevik to BLM. It is all done to separate us from God's order.

Degrading and moving the altar becomes a pretext for degrading and removing the crucifix. In some churches it is no longer close to the altar or even central to it. A deep aversion to Christ's sacrifice has seen crucifixes replaced with empty crosses: His Body, His Sacred Flesh, His tabernacle, is gone, and I do not know where they have put Him. Others illegitimately mix mysteries, affixing a likeness of the Risen Jesus to the Cross. Although there has been no thing on earth more excellent than the Risen Jesus, the Cross is neither the time nor the place for Him.

The 1969 rubrical changes follow the serpent's aspirations concerning tabernacle, altar and crucifix. In a traditional Mass the priest genuflects to the Real Presence sixteen times; in the *novus ordo* only five. Traditionally the priest kisses the altar nine times; in the *novus* twice. Traditionally during the Canon he makes twenty-five crosses over the gifts; in the *novus* it is just one.

These gestures matter. They form and express the disposition of the soul. The loss of genuflections manifests and causes a loss of reverence; the drastic reduction of kisses manifests and causes affection to grow cold; the abandonment of the crosses manifests and causes a failure in understanding. Aggregated it all renders the new Mass formless and threatens to do the same to our souls.

Orientation and Architecture

This dissolving and turning away from the tabernacle, the crucifix and the altar all facilitates a turning away from God and toward each other. The priest now faces the faithful. Or rather, the presider engages his audience. This detachment from the highest reality leaves man to gaze upon man. Spiritual sterility.

What does modern man think? We do not need our Redeemer because we are excellent anyway. We do not need a Redeemer because now we celebrate our sins. We do not need a Redeemer because nobody goes to hell. And if we do not need a Redeemer, the One Mediator Jesus Çhrist, then we do not need His priest ministering at Mass. Proliferating concelebrations deliberately obscures the singular role of the celebrant. Services of the Word run by deacons or women obliterate it altogether.

It used to be obvious the Mass was offered to God. The most important part, the Canon, is explicitly addressed to the Father. It is manifestly not addressed to men, for it is whispered such that the people cannot hear, in sacral language which few understand, all to Him Whom we can access only through the Son. The people, seeing only the priest's back, know he is talking to God.

But in the new Mass he faces the faithful, and calls out the Canon in a loud voice from which no one can hide, in everyday language carrying worldly associations precluding contemplation. He even makes eye contact and sometimes strains to entertain. He might improvise, forgetting the Father. Symbolically the people are the centre of his attention, even as he makes himself the centre of theirs. The *novus ordo* is anthropocentric.

In the traditional Mass the *Pax* — the peace of Christ — comes from the altar, strictly through the hierarchy, in an expressive and orderly ritual. In the new Mass it is chaotic, participants spontaneously greeting each other with whatever 'peace' they can give from themselves, not that of Christ from the altar, which is a peace the world cannot give (Jn 14:27).

Traditionally, the first words the priest speaks aloud are of the Blessed Trinity in making the Sign of the Cross. He does not greet the people. The *novus* often begins with "Good morning!" Maybe it is a good morning. Maybe it is not. It is not relevant. But this disorientation entraps many who are well-meaning. They want to be friendly, to show they care. But its origin is diabolical, from the soft-spoken serpent seeking to turn us from Heaven.

Church architecture is meant to teach us the structure of reality, to direct us to God. As in Eden, tabernacle and Temple, traditionally churches too distinguished world (nave), Holy Place (sanctuary) and Holy of Holies (altar). It is disastrous to remove boundaries, like altar rails or steps, for we must see the distinctions in order to understand. Otherwise we are lost.

Now churches are wrecked or newly built so there are no steps at all up to the altar, which might even sit in a pit, lower than the seating as in an amphitheatre, a place of entertainment. There is no mountain, no spiritual ascent. Life, supposedly, is easy, not Calvary. Now there is wheelchair access to the altar. The Holy Place is not exclusively for the service of God, but the sanctuary is invaded by important women or by children to hold hands. With barriers and steps gone it becomes a safe space for liturgical dancers to prance around without tripping.

Violating the sanctuary

What is all this for? It is not an accident. It is to reject Heaven in favour of hell. Having removed Christ, having diverted attention from the divine, the next step is to destroy the sacred space so no one will yearn for God's *place*, *HaMakom*.

In Abraham's tent, in Moses' tabernacle, in Solomon's Temple, the *"door"*, the gateway to the Holy Place, represents Jesus Christ as the only Way. Physically this was accompanied by a screen, a fence — because if there is no kind of wall, then what is a door? Similarly, without a boundary there is no sanctuary. This preference of the *novus* signifies a loss of Heaven. To remove the tabernacle from its central place at the altar is to reject God's heavenly throne on Earth. To have no steps to the altar or no communion rail is to dissolve the distinction between Holy of Holies and Holy Place, that is the Temple's inner and outer courts. This renders the liturgy mute on the *Our Father*'s petition, that as it is in Heaven so it be on earth. It is replaced with the reverse, that as it is on earth so it be in Heaven — for we see the world invading the sanctuary: girl servers, women lectors, clown Masses, liturgical dancers, pagan ceremonies. If the sanctuaries of our churches are not distinct from the nave, then this hellish world is likely the closest we will ever get to Heaven.

No one could approve this who has reverently read Ezek 44, which chapter repeatedly hammers into us that the sanctuary is exclusively for appointed clerics carrying out the service of God (Ezek 44:5,6-7,8,9,11,13,15-17,19). Forcefully God insists on *"a separation between the sanctuary and the place of the people"* (Ezek 42:20). Moses insists on separation at the mountain of God (Ex 19:21). The same is accentuated by the High Priest entering the Holy of Holies alone (Heb 9:7). On pain of death he had to prepare properly (Lev 16:2), not a light thing. God ordered:

> *Let no man be in the tabernacle when the high priest goeth into the sanctuary, to pray for himself and his house, and for the whole congregation of Israel, until he come out.* (Lev 16:17)

Wherefore in Holy Mass only the celebrant should stand for the consecration, this signifying his agency, while all others kneel as a sign of their receptive assistance. It is the unique work of the Passion. This is why Abraham left his two servants at a distance while he took his dear victim son up the mountain (Gen 22:5,19). This is why Elijah *"was afraid"* and *"dismissed his servant there [and] continued on [to pray] that he might die"* (1 Kngs 19:3-4). Alone Christ made His journey down to hell. And now for some diabolical reason, perfidious liturgists forbid the faithful to kneel during the Canon, insisting they stand, as if we are the equals of Christ. That was the ambition of the serpent.

God is the just judge. He will weigh the souls of those who have engineered these changes, of those who have colluded, of those caught up in it, of those who lament and resist. But if the changes are not from hell, how is it they are so comprehensive?

A Dark Rebellion

Traditionally, the altar is backed by the Big Six and a crucifix. That is, standing on the gradines there are six tall candlesticks with six tall candles and in the middle of them a beautiful crucifix. They are evenly spaced, perfectly parallel. Their symmetry speaks of order, their wonderful verticality carries our souls, even subconsciously, up toward Heaven. The six lights plus a crucifix give continuity to the Menorah, the seven-branched candlestick. By this arrangement we see in Mass that the central light, promulgating eternal truth, is Christ on the Cross.

What is found in many churches now? The crucifix is often missing from the altar and the candles are not six. So we can forget the Menorah. Rarely are the candles so tall and slender as formerly, so we lose verticality, the pointing to Heaven. Instead candles might be squat, holding the mind down; if they are not symmetrical, balance is gone; if not white, the sense of purity is lost; if different colours, harmony is dispelled. There can literally be two differently sized, differently coloured, fat, squat candles sitting on the same corner of the altar with a pot plant or worse at the opposite end. (Nothing should be on an altar except items being used during Mass or else a cover outside of Mass.)

Is such ruination deliberate? Some of the above might be womanly home-making, which is fine in its place (the home). But how is it permitted in churches, in the terrible, awesome place of sacrifice? Adam is becoming effeminate.

Where is the seven-branched candlestick now? As it is being lost from Catholic sanctuaries, it has been recast at the turn of the Millennium and erected in Jerusalem, a half-ton Menorah plated with pure gold. At the same time that we are losing Christ, the Old Covenant seeks to reassert itself.

What has the *novus* done for stability, for continuity, for the flock's sense of security? In every church Mass is different. Travellers who visit have no idea what they might face. This disintegration is symbolised by the new Missal. Previously a parish was fine with a missal over a hundred years old. But with the *novus*, at least six books are required to cover the new multi-year cycle (a missal, two books for the readings, three for the Gospels). In an international shrine, to cover just ten languages that means sixty books instead of one. And because Rome cannot resist changing the text they will need to be regularly replaced with the latest versions, a painful expense for poor parishes.

Further, arguments over translations are divisive of the laity and a waste of clerical energy, of priests who should be teaching the faith, not tinkering with liturgical books. Who thought of all this when it was decided to abandon Latin? Maybe none but the devil knew what was coming. We humans act in enthusiasm, we love our own ideas without understanding their consequences. We may carry a contempt for past generations and think it time to try something new. Then we learn that some things cannot change.

How deep can man's rebellion go? Churchmen have obscured the pattern of reality. The threefold distinction is obliterated in church architecture and spiritual sensibility. The 'worship space' is homogenised so no pattern remains: the court, the place of priestly work and sacrifice, is invaded by the laity and the altar is removed to be replaced by a table; the Holy of Holies, the tabernacle, is literally gone. And then the Trinity must go. First from the Missal, the number of reverences in each Mass to the Blessed Trinity is reduced from over forty to a thin few in the *novus ordo*. Not caring for the Trinity, we see projects for collaboration in worship between Catholics, Jews and Muslims; we see the House of Abraham being promoted; we see imams singing their prayers in churches and popes looking lost in synagogues. Having let go of the true, we chase after the false. It is not the first time this has happened in the history of salvation:

> *King Achaz went to Damascus to meet Theglathphalasar, king of the Assyrians, and when he had seen the altar of Damascus, king Achaz sent to Urias, the priest, a pattern of it, and its likeness, according to all the work thereof.* (2 Kngs 16:10)

Achaz had a new altar built in the Temple after the pattern of the godless. His apostasy is a close image of what we suffer today:

> *In the time of his distress he became yet more faithless to the Lord — this same King Ahaz. For he sacrificed to the gods of Damascus which had defeated him, and said, 'Because the gods of the kings of Syria helped them, I will sacrifice to them that they may help me.' But they were the ruin of him, and of all Israel. And Ahaz gathered together the vessels of the house of God and cut [them in] pieces... and he shut up the doors of the house of the Lord... In every city of Judah he made high*

*places to burn incense to other gods, provoking to anger the
Lord, the God of his fathers.* (2 Chron 28:22-25 RSVCE)

By adopting a religion of the world, by cutting up vessels of true
worship, by provoking *"the God of his fathers"*, King Achaz
became *"the ruin of him, and of all Israel"*. The whole people
suffers when the leader is idolatrous. Since October 2019, the
whole world has suffered demonic scourges after Francis
honoured Pachamama in the Vatican, idols in St Peter's Basilica.

Sacrilegious Disorder

Holy Orders are called "orders" because they are ordered to the
principal of all order on Earth, the Holy Eucharist. The minor
orders, too, serve this hierarchy. On the lowest step is the porter
who guards the gates of the church. Then the lector performs his
ministry close to, but not in, the sanctuary. Exorcists, like porters,
are to protect the holy ceremonies from hostile persons, but for
the exorcist the spiritual rather than human, which office they can
perform in the choir. Ascending a step further, the acolytes in
their proper ministry accompany the Gospel with lights from the
foot of the altar and at the Offertory approach right up to the altar,
bearing water and wine for the sacrifice.

Entering major orders, the sub-deacon accompanies the priest
on his left to the altar; he touches the chalice and paten before and
after they bear Christ. The deacon, sacramentally ordained, is at
the right hand of the celebrant. He touches the chalice as it is
being offered and holds the patten during Communion. He opens
the ciborium. The priest alone consecrates, the priest alone gives
himself Holy Communion, the priest alone drinks from the
chalice. He exists to offer this sacrifice.

Summarising: the celebrant handles the sacred species; the
deacon touches vessels containing sacred species; the sub-deacon
touches the vessels without the sacred species. Those in minor
orders or servers never touch these vessels during Mass, and if
they have to outside of Mass then it should be wearing gloves or
equivalent. What reverence all this inculcates and exhibits.

Above the priest is the bishop: his speciality is that he can ordain men to be priests. At the top of the earthly hierarchy is the reigning pope. He approves bishops and unifies them so the Church lives on through the generations to offer the One Sacrifice. Everything is for this. God redeems; we praise.

What do we have now? Paul VI's *Ministeria Quaedam* (1972), his attempt to abolish minor orders, though they are of the early Church; laity have been groomed to touch the chalice; women stand at the altar and pronounce words of consecration. They have no fear, although touching the holy items without being authorised by rank and mission is a matter of spiritual death. Whatever the guilt of the laity, the heavier damnation belongs to clerics for allowing it. The Most Precious Blood is mishandled. It is spiritual torture to see it. The abusers do not care.

Comprehensive Rejection of the Divine

Why bury minor orders? In order to bury major orders. The same worldly spirit that murdered Abel, murdered the prophets, and murdered Jesus, is now trying to murder the Catholic priesthood. At the cutting edge is Germany's *Synodale Weg*, a fourfold attack on the sacramental priesthood as male, celibate, hierarchical and fruitful. Thus it attacks the highest goods in Heaven and on earth.

On earth because by calling for women priests it would make the Sacrifice of the Mass invalid; by calling for sexually active priests it would make the offering of the Sacrifice unworthy; by overturning the hierarchy which is entirely ordered to the Holy Eucharist it would make the Sacrifice a pointless, human affair; by inviting those in mortal sin to receive Holy Communion it negates the fruitfulness of the Sacrifice, bringing condemnation instead of grace and life. In these four ways the Synodal Way attacks the greatest good on Earth: Christ's Sacrifice.

It is also an attack on the first Truth of Heaven: God the Father. A female priesthood (which is impossible) obscures the paternity in spiritual paternity; sexually active priests obscure with biology the spiritual aspect of paternity; rejecting God's hierarchy is done on the grounds that Patriarchy is oppressive, whereas in truth Fatherhood is the source of order and peace; inviting those in mortal sin to receive Holy Communion is designed to rob God the Father of children.

The Mother of God defeats all these attacks on the Sacrifice of her Son and the worship due the Father. Our Lady's defences are unassailable. We may always be grateful that Mary triumphs.

Though Queen of Apostles and Angels, Mary never sought the sacramental priesthood for herself. As perpetual Virgin and Mother of the divine, the Theotokos confirms the measureless fecundity of continence. Ceaselessly Mary points to her Son as the Head and source of order. And being immaculately conceived, Mary shows the relation between holiness and closeness to Christ. In these four ways, the attacks on Christ's Sacrifice fail.

Defending against the assaults on the heights of Heaven, as Mary is only human, her Motherhood of God indicates the divine involvement is Fatherhood. Her being Virgin necessitates that ultimate Fatherhood is spiritual. Though the greatest of creatures, Mary gladly submitted to God's hierarchy, recognising St Joseph as head of the Holy Family and later by being received into the home of St John. As Mother of God's children, Mary assiduously raises and rescues souls for God, with guaranteed success despite all the attacks of the devil, who is a spiritual abortionist.

The Virgin Mary, Mother of God, comprehensively defeats the *Synodale Weg*. The German disease is metastasising globally, and hopelessly, in Bergoglio's Synod on Synodality. Why is there such a hatred of celibacy?[226] Many objectors like to raise the case of Eastern priests, who if married may be sexually active. Most often this is mentioned not in an attempt to understand celibacy, but to bring it down. Celibacy is a fact of Christianity. It comes from Christ. Why? That is a crucial question. To interject that the East is more lax than the West is fine as a matter of record; but we should not let that distract us from probing for deep answers.

---

[226] Canon Law prohibits sexual activity for Latin rite priests. "Clerics are obliged to observe perfect and perpetual continence for the sake of the kingdom of heaven and therefore are bound to celibacy which is a special gift of God" (Canon 277 §1). Bishops cannot dispense from this obligation. Rather the law is ignored.

For the sake of the Kingdom, Jesus calls certain men to celibacy. But what connects them? How does this work? The chapter above, *One Priesthood*, addresses aspects of this in detail but here we simply listen to Moses making clear that the question matters. Moses warned that any unauthorised human or beast who touched the holy mountain would be stoned to death. After this:

> *Moses came down from the mount to the people, and sanctified them... when they had washed their garments, he said to them: Be ready against the third day, and come not near your wives.* (Ex 19:14-15)

If it were proper for the men of the Old Covenant to refrain from embracing their wives for three days before God manifested His power on the mountain, how much more necessary is continence for Catholic priests who handle the Holy Eucharist — a substantial divine Presence even more real than that Presence on Sinai. A priest who fails has confession and external forum discipline. A priest who refuses to confess damns himself.

Why is there no fear from these modern theologians though they have Numbers to read? Do they not recognise themselves as followers of Core, Dathan and Abiron? Do they not know they will be swallowed up by hell just as these were with all their household — that is the fools who willingly follow them: *"And they went down alive into hell the ground closing upon them, and they perished from among the people"* (Num 16:33). Using true hierarchy, God then commanded Moses to command Eleazar to make a memorial so that

> the children of Israel might have for the time to come wherewith they should be admonished, that no stranger or any one that is not of seed of Aaron should come near to offer incense to the Lord, lest he should suffer as Core suffered, and all his congregation, according as the Lord spoke to Moses. (Num 16:40)

Lamentably — and tragic to admit — today many nominal Catholics are as godless as the multitude in the desert who witnessed all this, because instead of being corrected and repenting, the very next day *"the multitude of the children of Israel murmured against Moses and Aaron, saying: You have killed the people of the Lord"* (Num 16:41). God slew 14,700 before Aaron's intercession with holy incense placated Him to spare the rest. Here we have a preview of the spiritual effects of the Synod on Synodality, the death this rebellion will cause.

Do those who want to reinvent the priesthood not read the Bible? Do they not know it warns them from spiritual suicide? Are they not terrified of hell? Are any so blinded by pride as to say the OT no longer has anything to teach? Or what do we read: departing from God's order, it was in Bethel and Dan instead of Jerusalem that Jeroboam established worship; he did this with golden calves, abominations, and attributed to idols Israel's deliverance from Egypt. Congruent to this blasphemy, he initiated a false, non-Levitical priesthood (1 Kngs 12:28-29), satanic losers (2 Chron 11:14-15). In hubris they went to war against Judah, God's chosen, and lost badly. The speech whereby Judah's good King Abijah admonished the rebels before the battle shows the necessity of true priesthood to this day:

> *And you have cast out the priests of the Lord, the sons of Aaron, and the Levites: and you have made you priests, like all the nations of the earth: whosoever cometh and consecrateth his hand with a bullock of the herd, and with seven rams, is made a priest of those who are no gods...* (2 Chron 13:9-10)

The record continues by praising continuity in essentials and fidelity to what was passed down from God's elect. We might recognise this Scripture passage points to the traditional Mass:

> *But the Lord is our God, whom we forsake not, and the priests who minister to the Lord are the sons of Aaron, and the Levites are in their order. And they offer holocausts to the Lord, every day, morning and evening, and incense made according to the ordinance of the law, and the loaves are set forth on a most clean table, and there is with us the golden candlestick, and the lamps thereof, to be lighted always in the*

evening: for we keep the precepts of the Lord our God, whom you have forsaken. (2 Chron 13:10-11)

Here we see requisite elements of worship made by genuine priests. They *"are in their proper order"* and act *"according to the precept of the law"* — tradition. They offer both outer and inner oblations, that is *"holocausts"* and *"incense"*, respectively signifying the external rites and the true heart. They offer daily, *"morning and evening"*, as kept ideally by Holy Mass and Vespers. The *"bread of presence on a very pure table"* anticipates the Holy Eucharist on an unadulterated altar. The *"gold lampstand [burning] continually"* indicates continuity of the seven Sacraments or preserving use of the Gifts. The false priests, like rebels today, cannot bear the lamb's meek silence. Everything in the chapter is about those who love or hate the lamb. We are all found in Abel or in Cain. We will each follow the one or the other into the next life.

Cain was cheap. He would not give the best. So the *novus ordo* is inherently cheap (though valiant souls may attain holiness despite it). It is designed for man's convenience. It is meant to be so easy as to be effortless. Formerly, the richness of vestments spoke to the high ministries in Heaven and Gregorian chant to the singing of angels. Now what do we have? Folded chasubles were folded away and thrown out. The maniple was neglected then abandoned. The loss of dalmatics is a loss of meaning. In countless places the chalice veil has disappeared along with the burse; the amice is forgotten; the cincture deemed unnecessary and priests wear their alb like a bag. If chasubles are kept they are tacky, polyester, suited to a cheap ceremony. The only vestment thought essential is the stole. Often these, too, appear cheap (though paradoxically costing a fortune). They might be coloured with a rainbow to taunt God, or dispensed with altogether. The same degradation has happened to music — unthinkable a century ago, for it belongs to the Mass to be integrally sung.

If one looks for the male priesthood in the OT it is easy to find. It is hierarchical, sacrificial, tending toward celibacy. How, though, do those who happily inhabit the *novus* world or are

274

enthusiasts for the Synod find their scheme in the OT? They struggle, they cannot. Letting women come up to do readings is only slightly more ignorant than allowing any laity to do it, for this erases the boundary between profane and holy, nave and sanctuary, earth and heaven; it makes the liturgy like a children's game where total dedication is not required.

Do bishops who allow this think it an easy matter to read the reading? Is it just like reading a story, such that you do not have to be trained for it, formed for it, ordained for it? Yet it is an act of liturgical service, therefore one must be ordained. It is a cleric's job because it is primarily worship. It is meant to be chanted in Latin. Perfectly. It is worship before it is education. It is meant to be offered first of all to God, then for the living and the dead. It is not directed chiefly at the people present. Failure to recognise all this allows the execrable idiocy of attempting vernacular readings even in the traditional Mass. The best education which worship can give us is to see God properly prioritised always.

The *novus ordo* dreams up women ministers. Vainly it spurns old vestments. Shamelessly it replaces angelic choirs with embarrassments, timeless chant with dated banality. Perfidiously it omits most references to the Holy Trinity. Deluded it does away with ancient Books. That the altar is much, much more than a table used to be made obvious in every church. The reredos or ornate decoration with saints and artwork would show this. Today architectural symbols are wrecked, barriers broken down, reverences removed, linens reduced. Where is it all going? It all serves a denial of the greatest wonder on earth: transubstantiation.

How many Catholics believe in the Real Presence? Has It not been hated from beginning to end, from the first prefigurations in Eden until Catholic cathedrals today? This is satanic; nothing else explains the desperate thoroughness.

An example which churchmen treat with indifference: the removal of the Last Gospel is as hellish as the removal of the Prayers at the Foot of the Altar. The latter contains everything in seed that is about to come in the Mass. The former recalls everything that happened at the altar in the light of the new creation. They show the eternity of God's plan, His action. The Mass which runs between them is like the course of history which flashes as a spark. The Prayers at the Foot and the Last Gospel mirror each other conceptually. The one prepares us for Mass like nothing else can; the other sums it all up like nothing else could.

The enemy rages

The enemy is desperate. The *Synodale Weg* is the *novus ordo* even further degenerated. It is unable to attract or edify souls with its worldly novelties. The *novus* is sterile, unfruitful, poor at drawing men to the priesthood. In a futile effort to break the spear that will slay it, the enemy has had *Traditionis custodes* issued, an attempt to deny that the traditional Mass is the Roman Rite at all. The document is illegal in its premises (which are deceits), illegal in its goal (seeking to abolish the old Mass) and internally incoherent. In a diabolical inversion, it attempts to ban tradition in the name of the chief custodian of tradition, the pope. If their cause were advanced with misguided goodwill, why would they still be using lies, injustice and cruelty to achieve it? Rather, as such attacks on Truth intensify, we should depend all the more upon the unwreckable pedagogy of the OT.

As the abominable Jeroboam was defeated in battle by King Abijah, so the appalling apostasy of Achaz was overcome in the restoration by King Josiah (2 Chron 34:11-12). Giving us hope for the widespread re-introduction of minor orders, porters were assigned and armed to literally kill 'non-clerics' who sought to enter the Temple after an OT apostasy:

> And let no one come into the house of the Lord, but the priests, and they that minister of the Levites: let them only come in, because they are sanctified... and if any other come into the temple, let him be slain. (2 Chron 23:6-7)

Now in the New Covenant we do not shed the blood of those who profane the sanctuary, but angels mark them for damnation, eternal death if they do not repent. They who want to bring women into the sanctuary — altar girls, readers, extraordinary ministers of the Eucharist — should pay heed to the fate of Queen Athalia. Forgetting her place, she trespassed into the Temple and within three short verses was dead (2 Chron 23:12-15). The political-religious restoration undoing her evil saw the priests of Baal killed (v.17), the appointment of porters to keep out the unclean (v.19) and the revival of traditional music (v.13).

The Levitical priesthood was male, chaste, consecrated. It was a matter of death for priests to disobey rubrics (Lev 8:35; 10:5). The Holy Place was death to the impure (Lev 10:9-11). How much more, spiritually speaking, is the Mass. Not even the king could burn incense at the altar. For thinking to try it, King Ozias was turned leprous, lost his kingship and was cut off from the house of the Lord:

> *immediately Azarias the priest going in after him, and with him fourscore priests of the Lord, most valiant men, withstood the king and said: It doth not belong to thee, Ozias, to burn incense to the Lord, but to the priests, that is, to the sons of Aaron, who are consecrated for this ministry: go out of the sanctuary, do not despise: for this thing shall not be accounted to thy glory by the Lord God.* (2 Chron 26:17-18)

Why are we seeing these attacks in the Church? This hatred of priesthood, of the altar, the Cross, the Holy Place? It is all basically an attack on Christ. It is a plague in the Church. The hatred of Tradition is born of the same envy through which Cain murdered Abel. We see it in Esau's resentment of Jacob, in the murderous jealousy of Joseph's brothers against him, and in the doomed rebellion of ambitious families against Aaron. It reached its lowest pitch in the Sanhedrin against Jesus, but continues today in those who wish to end the Traditional Latin Mass. This thread of envy runs through all history ever since the serpent targeted Eve. It is the corollary of the prior good which God has always desired to lavish upon man. The good comes first; envy is a twisted reaction to it.[227]

---

[227] Wis 2:24; 1 Jn 3:12; Acts 7:9; Sir 45:16-18; Mk 15:10.

satanic revolt

So rich, strong and healthy has the Church organism been that it has taken seventy years from breaching Holy Week and fifty years of *novus ordo* hegemony before modernist infiltrators have been able to make their mortal threats with the Synod on Synodality. They will lose, but there will be a period of pain to endure: once again we have false altars and idols erected in churches even by God's People, while roundabout sorcery and child sacrifice are practised as they were in the days of King Manasses (2 Chron 33:5-7). The two abominations belong together: the purpose of a false altar is satanic sacrifice.

Today, babies are killed to serve the cosmetic industry, the vain who want to look young. Stealing another's youth, stealing their life, is the insane dream of satanists and billionaires who destroy myriads of embryos in the impossible hunt to gain immortality by ourselves — just as the devil deceived Eve. Embryos are also killed to produce vaccines, promoted by churchmen and administered in cathedrals.

Those responsible for all this, unless they repent, God will drag by hooks like Leviathan. He will bind them in the eternal fetters of hell (2 Chron 33:11). Which side do you wish to be on when this happens? Thanks be to God, in the historical scenario referenced above, King Manasses did repent.

Worldliness in its latest synodal expression seeks to overturn everything good since Eden. When we see the earliest revealed truths attacked, we know the enemy is close to completing his rebellion and that his defeat is exceedingly near. The first chapters of Genesis reinforce inerrantly nature's revelation of male-female complementarity, of the indissolubility of marriage, of the purpose of marriage as procreation (Gen 1:27; 2:24; 1:28). That these three primordial truths are fanatically despised is proven by the widespread promotion of transgenderism even for children, the ubiquity of divorce and the universality of abortion.

These three show the extent not only of godlessness in the world, but mindlessness, mental disease. It is a complete rejection of nature, the created order. The spiritual equivalents of these rebellions within the Church, her deliberate sterilisation, discloses enemy infiltration. These crucify creation.

Ezekiel compared Assyria to an exalted tree of Lebanon and Egypt's empire to a tree in the Garden of Eden (Ezek 31:1-18). All nations find shelter there. Somehow Eden signifies the world rightly ordered. So it would be if all nations of the world were ordered to the Cross, to the reign of Christ the King, His sceptre the Tree of Life. If Holy Mass were everywhere honoured:

> the desolate land shall be tilled, which before was waste in the sight of all that passed by. They shall say: This land that was untilled is become as a garden of pleasure [Eden]: and the cities that were abandoned, and desolate, and destroyed, are peopled and fenced. And the nations, that shall be left round about you, shall know that I the Lord have built up what was destroyed, and planted what was desolate, that I the Lord have spoken and done it. (Ezek 36:35-36)

Pope St Clement, the third pope after St Peter, drew timeless lessons from the OT on how vital it is for Christians to maintain the liturgical order first given by the Lord. In writing he maintained: "Those, therefore, that do anything contrary to what conforms to His will, suffer death as the penalty."[228] The holy pope uses the OT teachings to explain this.

---

[228] Pope St Clement, *First Letter to the Corinthians*, XL-XLI "we are obliged to carry out in fullest detail what the Master has commanded us to do at stated times. He has ordered the sacrifices to be offered and the services to be held, and this not in a random and irregular fashion, but at definite times and seasons. He has, moreover, Himself, by His sovereign will determined where and by whom He wants them to be carried out. Thus all things are done religiously, acceptable to His good pleasure, dependent on His will. Those, therefore, that make their offerings at the prescribed times are acceptable and blessed; for, since they comply with the ordinances of the Master, they do not sin... Each of us, brethren, must in his own place endeavour to please God with a good conscience, reverently taking care not to deviate from the established rule of service. Not everywhere, brethren, are sacrifices offered... but at Jerusalem only; and there offerings are not made in every place, but in front of the sanctuary, where the gift to be offered is inspected for blemishes by the High Priest and the aforesaid ministers. Those, therefore, that do anything contrary to what conforms to His will suffer death as the penalty. You see, brethren, that the greater the knowledge vouchsafed to us, the greater the risk we incur."

The justice of God's Judgement is that He need not execute those who reject Him, for precisely in doing it, they have committed spiritual suicide themselves (Jn 12:48). They refuse to enter eternal life so inevitably hell is what follows. Those who hold others from entering will die a deeper death (Mt 23:13). Our entrance into Heaven is aided by contemplation on earth. The *novus ordo*'s regimentation of the faithful in responses and posture makes contemplation near impossible. It is a death trap.

God will have mercy on sheep who bleat, but not on wolves who scatter, who actively oppose tradition. Fidelity to the form of the Mass is as fidelity once was in Eden and in Jerusalem, a matter of life and death. Choose life.

III: Homecoming
to Paradise

*This blessed Annunciation, when the angel showed the conception of
our Lord to the glorious Virgin Mary, happened the twentyfifth day
of March... On that same day Adam, the first man, was created
and fell into original sin by inobedience, and was put out of
paradise terrestrial... Also that same day of the month Cain
slew Abel his brother. Also Melchisedech made offering to God
of bread and wine in the presence of Abraham. Also on the same
day Abraham offered Isaac his son. That same day St John Baptist
was beheaded, and St Peter was that day delivered out of prison, and
St James the More that day beheaded of Herod. Our Lord Jesu Christ
was on that day crucified, wherefore that is a day of great reverence.*

— *Legenda aurea* III, On the Salutation
of the Angel Gabriel to Our Lady

T he inspired account of Adam and Eve in Eden could not be
more truthful. In the first few chapters of Genesis, Moses
describes man's fall into sin and death. Deeper than its
literal sense, this is a parable about the Crucifixion. Adverting to
this, the cover of this book depicts Jesus taking Eve from Adam's

side and presenting her to him as spouse. By showing Jesus in Eden looking like Adam, the artist, Hieronymus Bosch (✝1516), conveys important theological facts: God was working through Adam and Eve to instruct us about His Son's Passion and our redemption. Adam's *"deep sleep"* means the Passion of Christ. His Bride is the Church. The promise that *"a woman"* would crush the serpent's head speaks of Mary, Mother of the Church, defeating the designs of the devil and Antichrist. Thanks to Jesus and Mary, that which was lost by Adam and Eve is restored with infinite gain. The pledge of their success — the fruit of the tree which overcomes death — is offered to us unambiguously in the traditional Mass, which is why the devil wants it destroyed, desperate now to achieve this before Jews notice and convert.

This final chapter is not a programme on how to restore the liturgy. It is the conclusion that the traditional Mass, because it retells the immutable pattern of reality, cannot be eradicated. It takes more energy to suppress than the enemy can summon or sustain. Sanctifying grace is the strongest life force on earth. God's love is infinitely stronger than satan's hatred. Our desire to honour God with a worthy liturgy, according to His Will, can always grow stronger than the ceaseless efforts of satanists to destroy it. But we need to choose.

Few seem to value God's liturgy. But all are called, for all have a sense of Paradise. How so? Most adults recall childhood as a time of innocence. They might long for a return to that ease of life, or at least lament the evil they have discovered since. But no one really wants to be a child again. What is the meaning of this little tension within us?

Before being born, St John the Baptist apprehended the goodness of his Saviour. His mother testified: *"behold as soon as the voice of thy salutation sounded in my ears, the infant in my womb leaped for joy"* (Lk 1:44). Before he died, St John, recognising the same source as his first joy, witnessed:

> the friend of the Bridegroom, who standeth and heareth Him, rejoiceth with joy because of the Bridegroom's voice. This my joy therefore is fulfilled. (Jn 1:29)

If we recognise Jesus anywhere, for example, in the liturgy, Who is the same Word of God by Whom Paradise was created in the beginning, then we have a joy worth dying for. Jesus fulfils and exceeds everything else which life ever promised. This is why many discovering the old Mass are overwhelmed by the sense of having found "home". It is familiar because it is the place of truly human culture. It is where we belong. The Mass is literally the foretaste of Heaven. We have no other way on earth to connect so fully with Adam and Eve, with Abel and Seth, with Shem and Abraham. If we do not care to take this chance, how can we enter conversation with them in Heaven? What will we have in common?

Instead let us ask, how do we follow the Baptist in regaining our original joy? God has so arranged human existence that we come into this world tiny and helpless. If a mother is devoted to her little one with cuddles and kisses then how blissful that baby's beginning. If the child's father is generous with his time for play, and if later he is fair and merciful in discipline, then how secure that child's sense of being. The mother gives experiences which dispose the child to understand God as immanent, attentive and tender, and the father similarly helps the child know God as transcendent, just and powerful.

Even when the parents are not loving, as babies everything is done for us: we are fed, washed, clothed, carried. Most babies experience that when they cry out, sooner or later help comes. This also is training to know God. Although this connection with the divine is obscured for children who are neglected or hurt by adults, there is a joy in general discovery which every human experiences in their early years. We know how excited six-year-olds are by Christmas or a pending visit to the zoo. They cannot contain themselves. They are full of questions, amazed by new sights, delighted to play for hours on end. A baby is full of happiness to see a ball or a face appear, disappear and appear again. We cannot remember how amazed we were in our first months simply to see light, to discern objects and noises and begin recognising faces and voices. Aristotle said the beginning of philosophy is to wonder at the world. All babies do this and love it. The Philosopher said the eye never tires of seeing. Children know it well. We begin happy.

After this we realise that something has gone wrong, something is missing. Though we cannot recall the details, at some stage we discover pain, alarm, horror at evil. At first we recoil from the wrong which others do, injured by their selfishness, lies, injustice. Some end up bitter, trusting no one. Healthier, though still shocking, is to recognise the evil in one's own heart, to discover the depths of one's own sinfulness. What happened to childhood, to innocence? Was it an illusion, a folly?

God is giving every one of us access to Eden. We have a memory of man's earliest trajectory. Everything began good. Later we learnt good and evil. And we realised we had broken the commandments. The world is scourged by corruption and death. We lost innocence, it seems, forever. But our longing for paradise is not futile. God intends to restore us to a much better place than Eden. If we seek Him, and love Him, and repent our sins, then, like our first parents, we will come to a Paradise that can never be lost. The way all this happens is through the Cross of Christ.

The Son's Sacrifice on Calvary was known even prior to Eden, before the beginning of time. Eternally God thought of it. He signalled it from the first moments of creation. After many detailed prefigurations through history, the Crucifixion was memorialised perfectly at the Last Supper, the first Mass. It will continue to be memorialised until the end of the age and will be unforgettable at the heavenly Banquet. Our confidence, our unconquerable hope, grows as we grasp its importance to God's Plan.

Christ's Sacrifice was anticipated in the design and activity of Solomon's Temple; before that in Moses' tabernacle; still earlier in Isaac's *Akeidah*; earlier again in Eden; and before God said *"Let there be light"* the Cross was present in His eternal decree. Being perfectly anticipated, which can only be the work of God, so Christ's Sacrifice is remembered perfectly, also a work of God. The Holy Ghost has guided the Church across centuries to let the liturgy unfold to its fullness. Thereby the Mystery of Faith informs the whole world: divine love is sacrifice. The Self-gift of God, the inner Life of the Blessed Trinity, is the truth of eternity filling up time, from beginning to end, impossible to eradicate. Woe to those who try, who impose their own ideas on the liturgy, dropping what was received to introduce incongruities.

Are the enemies of Christ to be feared? No! They are to be fought. A spark is enough. See the restoration of the sanctuary undertaken by the Maccabees (1 Macc 4:36-51): from a single spark comes fire for the holocaust, hot coals to burn incense, flames for the lamps and perhaps for the oven to bake bread:

> *They purified the sanctuary, and made another altar of sacrifice; then, striking fire out of flint, they offered sacrifices, after a lapse of two years, and they burned incense and lighted lamps and set out the bread of the Presence.* (2 Macc 10:3)

What does this single spark symbolise, this *"fire out of flint"*? Jesus rising from the pitch black tomb. It symbolises the Easter Triduum which is memorialised in each Holy Mass. So long as there is one Triduum celebrated according to the venerable rites, then the fire has not gone out from the first Easter, the light has not been overcome by the darkness. So long as on any given day there is a Mass celebrated according to the immemorial rites, then the gates of hell have not prevailed and hope remains alive. Because from this seed Christ's Cross can reconquer.

To recognise this in the Mass is to have that latter joy of the Baptist. Though he faced death, his beatitude in the Lord abounded. He could easily part with passing life who had tasted eternal. And we, if we have once been properly present at Mass, would welcome death as a carriage to the banquet eternal.

For those in exile, from whom the traditional Mass is taken away, it is enough for God that we yearn for it:

> *Daniel... opening the windows in his upper chamber towards Jerusalem, he knelt down three times a day, and adored and gave thanks before his God...* (Dan 6:10)[229]

---

[229] The offering God desires of us is primarily spiritual (Ps 39:7; 49:8-14; 50:18-21).

In Holy Mass we face *ad orientem*, looking for Christ's coming, He Who is *"the Orient"* (Lk 1:78):

> *Behold a man, the Orient is his name: and under [Jesus] shall he spring up, and shall build a temple to the Lord. Yea, he shall build a temple to the Lord: and he shall bear the glory, and shall sit, and rule upon his throne: and he shall be a priest upon his throne.* (Zach 6:12-13)

If a Church is not built eastwards, still the spiritual intention of those who pray counts more than geography. Yet if the priest *chooses* to face in the wrong direction, to face the people instead of God, what does that say of his spirit? He is disorientated.

When we all face the Cross, priest and people together, we see much further. For a restoration of the Mass of Ages and for the final triumph, surely Catholics must recall the Jewish heritage of our faith, to value our ancient roots, and never allow anyone to tear these out of our hearts.

A sure way to be convinced that the saving Lamb of God is eternally powerful is to recognise Jesus prefigured on an epic scale in the sacrifices of Solomon's Temple, and featured so centrally for Israel's deliverance at the Exodus, and so perfectly pleasing to God in the offering of Abel. The Lamb is a root of the Mass which goes back from the Crucifixion to Creation.

When failing clerics remove crucifixes from churches, what better way to be assured of its ubiquity than reading the OT? The countless mentions of trees or wood, as well as their presence in nature, show the universality of the Cross. It is a living root of the Mass which goes back from the Crucifixion to Creation.

When Catholics prefer tables to altars, how are they worshipping the ever-living God, Who delighted in His favourites, like Noah and Abraham and Moses, building altar after altar after altar? Tables have no foundation at Creation.

When priests or bishops offer black Masses, we know the devil has not won but that these clerics are lost. The Menorah was plundered in AD 70 but its light has never gone out — for even two candles with a crucifix suffice to remind us that light, an essential element of worship which the satanic darkness cannot overcome, traces back to God's very first utterance of Creation.

Can egalitarians or communists or perverted promoters of inclusivity prevent us from ascending the mountain? Do they think that by ripping out communion rails and removing the steps going up to the altar we will not know we are called to rise up to God? They say we do not need barriers. They say we are already there. But they lie. The mountain, the spiritual ascent, is a truth of the Mass which goes back from the Crucifixion to Creation.

Do those who separate tabernacles from altars, and remove them from the sanctuary, think they can expunge the tabernacle of Moses from the OT? They cannot. And the whole of it is Christ. The whole Temple is Christ. Every part is Christ and the entirety is Christ! No wonder rabbis teach the tabernacle is the first idea for creation, given by God in its time so the whole could reach completion. It had to be built to advance the very goal of creation: God dwelling with man. For it was named the *"Tent of Meeting"*, where God met with Moses. But that tent was taken down. The Temple was destroyed. Has creation failed? By no means. In the Son it finds its purpose. Literally in Him is the union of God and man. The Temple is built exactly as God wills in the Risen Christ, never to be taken down. The Mass multiplies man's encounters with God and cements us into this New Temple. Christ's Temple Body is being built up with souls made as living stones through reverent Communions and proper preparation for death.

The Temple was magnificent to behold, but Jesus is greater: *"But I say to you, that something greater than the temple is here"* (Mt 12:6). God's plans are eternal. The material world is a hint for us, a launchpad. God allows us to offer material goods and in return God bestows everlasting goods: "Receive moreover their eucharistic gifts and give back to them heavenly things for earthly, eternal for temporal".[230]

---

[230] Ancient Alexandrine rite, cited by Fortescue, *The Mass*, p.33. See also Origen, *Homily XXXIX on St Luke*, end: "Let us stand and pray God that we may be worthy to offer Him gifts which He will give back to us, returning heavenly for earthly", an idea echoed in the Roman rite's *Quod ore sumpsimus.*

We have one perfect agent, Jesus Christ. His strength, fortitude of the Omnipotent, is the efficient cause of our redemption, assimilating us as members of His Body. None can stop this for none can stop Him. His Most Precious Blood fills the cosmos, ordering it, sweetening it, vivifying it, healing it, cleansing it, making it holy like Him. The Holy of Holies is His Heart.

Jesus calls men to be priests after His own Heart. But to depart from Holy Orders, as the Synod on Synodality seeks, is to depart from God. How long will priests hold back from vesting themselves properly? Can they read the OT and imagine they should wear less than Aaron? Shall a priest say he does not need amice and chasuble and maniple because he wears these spiritually? Then he lives for himself not for others. But let the priest put on Christ in all visible glory: let him vest fully. As God vested Adam, the clothes He orders for sacrifice are a life-giving root of the Mass which go back to Eden.

The Traditional Mass — the rite, not the men involved — is impregnable against the hydra of corruption. The fight for the soul of the Church, the life of the world, continues. The Mass is at the centre of it:

> *The sanctuary shall be for the priests of the sons of Sadoc, who kept my ceremonies, and went not astray when the children of Israel went astray, as the Levites also went astray.* (Ezek 48:11)

Should God's order be overturned by man, the Creator outfoxed by His creatures? Can the immutable pattern of reality be redrawn by modernist liturgists? The place that was the centre of reality — since the taking of Adam from the garden soil right through to the Resurrection of Jesus from the garden tomb — was constantly guarded by God in order to fulfil its purpose. The continuity of events in the place prove that the offering of Jesus on Calvary was God's fixed plan from always. With Holy Mass Our Lord made this place universal. The place is now everywhere. The continuity of meaning cannot be broken. The Mass is the place God brings us to life, vivifies us, like Eden for

Adam, like Jerusalem for Jesus. It is all the same place. Therefore we sing in almost every Preface of this universalisation: *"semper et ubique* — to Thee *at all times and in all places* give thanks"*.

The identity of the place — *HaMakom* — is so important to orthodox Jews that although there is no project more important to them than the rebuilding of the Temple, never in 2,000 years have they sought to do it anywhere but where the original Temple stood: not just Jerusalem, not just Temple Mount, but on the Foundation Stone. What does this mean for Catholics? We are not tied to a single space, not to Calvary or Jerusalem or Rome, for Jesus has translated the Covenant, universalised the space, made eternal what was temporal, made spiritual what was material. Where the Jews had geographical continuity from Eden to the Temple, from Paradise to Golgotha, Christians require a spiritual continuity. We record pan-generational continuity from the current pope back to St Peter, and from his Lord Jesus back to Adam. What is at the heart of this continuity for the Church? Is there any more integral answer than transubstantiation within an apostolic liturgy? This is personal, this is eternal, this is universal, this is heavenly, this has conquered throughout history and gone global, supra-personal, feeding all the saints. Taking the traditional Latin Mass as the most visible and widespread of these apostolic rites, it exists to communicate God's union with man through the greatest wonder on earth, prepared for since the foundation of the world: the changing of bread and wine into the Body and Blood of Jesus Christ — and a related change in those who worthily receive.

As the bread and wine are changed completely, but still recognisable as what existed before, so in the Mass the sacrifice is one with Heaven yet recognisably in continuity with that which went before. In the traditional Mass we can see and hear the Old Covenant, but we consume the New. That which was once present has been elevated beyond all imagination to the universal, eternal, spiritual: to God Himself.

All this occurs through Jesus Christ because His Humanity (the particular, His Body, His Blood, His Soul) is hypostatically united with His Divinity, God. Therefore anyone who really joins themself to Jesus the Man (cleansed by His Blood, receiving His Body, imitating His Soul) is thereby vivified by His Spirit, united with God. And there is literally no other Way to God, including by natural law, except through Jesus. In Him Divinity and humanity meet. The Holy Eucharist is the fullest way on earth to enter into this union, when Jesus is received with the three theological virtues: faith in His Real Presence, hope in His salvation, and love for God.

The reason for the irradicable continuity of the traditional liturgy is that it is and has always been connected with the Heavenly reality. Jesus unites something earthly, limited, temporal, local and material with the heavenly, infinite, eternal, universal and spiritual. Holy Mass makes a slow change in society which ends up as a translation akin to transubstantiation, like changing bread for God. So the priest sings in the Preface:

> *Cæli cælorumque Virtutes...* Which the heavens and the hosts of heaven together with the blessed Seraphim joyfully do magnify. And *do Thou command that it be permitted us to join with them* in confessing Thee...

By God's command, in the Mass we are united with the powers of Heaven. Singing the triple *Sanctus*, adoring the Holy Trinity, we participate in this ultimate reality. The earthly society of the Church introduces us to the celestial city: now in spirit, then in substance.

Can Christians dismiss the OT? Or how shall we relate the Old to the New? Are they different religions or one? St Paul supplies the answer that the relation is a translation. Jesus Christ translates the Old into the New.[231] The better we understand this, the more we may love both, each in its proper way:

---

[231] St Thomas, *S.Th.* III Q.22 a.1 ad.2 "Since, therefore, the priesthood of the Old Law was a figure of the priesthood of Christ, He did not wish to be born of the stock of the figurative priests, that it might be made clear that His priesthood is not quite the same as theirs, but differs therefrom as truth from figure."

If then perfection was by the Levitical priesthood (for under it the people received the law), what further need was there that another priest should rise according to the order of Melchisedech: and not be called according to the order of Aaron? For the priesthood being translated, it is necessary that a translation also be made of the law... (Heb 7:11-12)

The meaning of *"the law"*, the pattern of Heaven implicit in Eden, tabernacle and Temple, translated and made explicit by the Crucifixion, is divine charity, Self-sacrifice. It is immutable.

Jesus put it into a language we understand by actually doing it before our eyes. God, came among us: God with man not only spiritually but bodily too. He came to lead us, to lead us through death which had trapped us. He did that: He died for us, killed by our sins, and He defeated death and also defeated the cause of death, which is our sins. And He rose again and ascended into Heaven. By His Self-sacrifice God opened Heaven for man so that following God with man, Emmanuel, now man is with God.

In every translation there is a change of material but a continuity of meaning. When Jesus was 'lost' for three days, it was at the time of His transition from Boy to Man. This was a prefiguration in His own Life of that greater transition, when Jesus was "lost" for three days in the tomb, and there made the move from Old Testament to New, to maturity (the Covenant fit now to multiply from one to all peoples). A priest who attempts to offer Mass without bread cannot do it. So a priest who tries to understand the New Covenant without the Old cannot do it. A hierarchy which tries to invent a form of worship which does not encapsulate the Old will fail: our daily Mass must come to us via Trent, Pope St Gregory, the Last Supper, the Temple, the tabernacle, the *Akeidah* and Eden. It is Calvary which connects us to all these. Materials change, but the meaning, implicit or explicit, stays the same — God's Self-sacrifice.

To understand this about God is to enter eternity with our mind. To imitate this about God in our life is the way to enter Heaven also with our body. Who we are in Heaven, our eternal identity given by God, is not less than all the acts of charity we ever committed. These form us. They are our form. Yet they are a gift, for all such acts were done by grace, done in us, with our cooperation, by God.

What is our cooperation? To conform to Christ as much as we are called by carrying our cross and adoring at Mass. We do not have the same roles. Without mothers there can be no virgins. Without fathers there can be no bishops. Without a lower step there can be no higher. Without an outer court there can be no inner. Gold is good, but silver and brass in proximity set it off more gloriously still. Not every place is God's altar, but all places lead to it or from it. Not every day is Good Friday, but all days anticipate or recall it. Not every soul is called to martyrdom but all are called to carry their crosses. And all are called to Holy Mass. The Cross and the liturgy make us like Christ, for invariably they involve love of God and neighbour. This way we enter the Temple, the Holy Place, the Tent of Meeting, we ascend Mount Moriah, we embark on the Ark, we gain Paradise, we enter Heaven, we become like God: self-sacrificial.

When you go up to the altar of God, spiritually, you are going up Calvary to the Cross. The Crucifixion was God's *Akeidah* for our salvation. You are going to take the fruit from the tree. If you are in a state of grace this is no disobedience, for God has invited you: "Take and eat. This is My Body." To be in a state of grace you needs must clear the sins from your soul, that is the thorns from the garden, return paradise to its pristine condition. You cannot? Christ can. He is the Gardener of your soul. Adam and Eve brought you into this world. Jesus, assisted by Mary, Co-Redemptrix, bring you into the next.

The eternal paradise, then, is not about eating fruits from biological trees. Our substance there is God Himself; Him we take in, constantly, for our boundless banqueting is upon Him. God's substance is spiritual. Therefore our feasting is spiritual, in knowledge. Instead of eating fruits we assimilate truth. To know something true about creation or history or a saint is what fills us, delights us, satisfies us, perfects us, makes us be like God and love like God — for they are all reflections of Him. The facts we will know in Heaven are acts of charity, the personal summations of which are the names and identities of the saints and angels all around us. Seeing these as they are, we cannot fail to love them.

And what is the supreme fact, the supreme act of charity? Christ laying down His life for us. To know Jesus Christ crucified is to have apprehended the eternal pattern into which all the saved fit together. Beginning with Mary, they imitated Him. Therefore the *"Book of Life"* is the Lamb's book (Apoc 5:3-8). He Who was before the beginning understands what will come in the end. Or *"Where were you, when I set the foundations of the earth? Tell me, if you have understanding"* (Job 38:4).

In the beginning, Adam offered his sacrifices at the Foundation Stone. Following Jesus is our homecoming. There is nothing better than to know and imitate His love. Calvary is not merely the way to Paradise, it is Paradise.

EPILOGUE: ENTERING ETERNITY

Eternity is a vision, a contemplation. Eternal life is a knowledge of God which cannot be lost, an everlasting union. In eternity everything is happening all at once. Everything that is love. To know the highest love, is to understand the form of everything else. What is this highest love? We may begin with the lamb.

God created lambs to figure His silent Self-sacrifice. The significance of silence is His love of sinners. From the beginning before sin there was Self-gift of God in all the good things of Eden with the pledge of His Life in the fruit of the tree. Evidently, God loved us. After sin, man fell into a debt he had no way of paying. Now we owed God an exceptional sacrifice. But what was sufficient? In translating the Law, Jesus revealed the nature of the sacrifice needed: God Himself, His Son, the Lamb.

The point of the Lamb is silence. Why? It shows the extent of love, for it is normal to be orientated to the other when you hope to have something from them. But to be orientated to the other when they give you nothing, that is a more impressive love. Then to be orientated to the other, to will their good, to spend yourself for them, when they are hurting you, persecuting you, lying about you, nailing you to a cross, now that is love! Jesus' silence meant He came not to condemn but to save, to give us a chance to repent. Silence says it all. Words are only a preamble. And this we should grasp about God, that He is still interested in our eternal salvation, our happiness and life even when we are sinners. This is divine love: to love one's enemy. It demonstrates that His love is total. Those who reject this love go to hell, because to reject such perfection is to have a hellish soul anyway; but God does not will the death of the sinner, not even when we crucify Him. God's desire to be with man forever is the strongest force in the universe. The Lamb is Emmanuel.

The Cross means the connecting of heaven and earth. It means mankind forgiven and embraced. It is the sign of God with man. Emmanuel.

The Altar means sacrifice and secondarily it has the form of a table, indicating that from sacrifice comes life (a meal) and, astonishingly, God always intended to nourish us with Himself, unite us with Him. Man with Emmanuel with God.

These Eternal Elements — the Lamb, the Cross, the Altar — appeared at the beginning so we can apprehend God's deepest intention for us: the silent victim more concerned for His persecutors than for Himself (the Lamb); Who dies to join Heaven and earth (the Cross); offering a sacrifice that is also a meal (the Altar); this God Himself will do, for only God can lay up truth from eternity. He wants us to understand it because to know it is to become like Him. God's first creature was light — the condition for sight and for life; understanding and growth; knowledge and eternity (the Light). It is simple. God retells it in endless ways.

How is it entering eternity to see this? Because to understand silent self-sacrifice is to know the highest love. This is the reality of Heaven and it is the single theme of human history which matters. In Heaven one sees all the saints in God. One sees everything they ever did. That is to say, everything good. That is to say, every act of charity. That is to say, one sees the extent of their charity, the result of it, how each person has conformed themselves to Christ. In this way one sees in a moment the entirety of human history — all of it that matters. The saints are 'new things', realising the potential life of Christ, telling of it forever, their everlasting love shining like gold, showing forth the power of the King.

Now it is a great thing to know all the acts of charity ever committed (or even here on earth to catch a glimpse of it by realising some examples). This is indeed a knowledge of God, for it is knowledge of the love He has poured into the world, for our acts of charity are all done by grace, all by His aid and direction, all a holy concurrence with Him. But our knowledge of God takes off when we see or consider the scale of all His saints. This boundless crowd has God for their Maker — Who can create such a wonder? The Creator is always greater than His creatures. To know the saints is to know God as their Master, Who taught them everything true. It is to know God as their Shepherd, Who guided them into everything good. It is to know God as their Saviour, infinitely merciful, Who rescued them from the jaws of death, from sin. Not one of the elect was lost. Not one. Think how great is God Who guaranteed that from the outset.

To think God did this for billions of souls, for all generations, across all lands — our minds go off the scale here. This will amaze us in Heaven, to see it at once. We can begin to think of it now. It is a great thing to know saints, to know SS Peter and Paul, or St Joseph, or St John the Baptist. In each we know something new about Christ, an example of self-sacrifice. Yet the whole Body of all the saints is something infinitely greater than the sum of the parts. The proper equation is not simple summation but factorial (!), a multiplication: each additional 'part' increases the wonder of every other 'part'. Like a human body: the cells and organs are excellent, but the whole is on another level, a basis for a living spirit. Our closest idea of the whole is to behold the Blessed Virgin Mary, God's greatest creation.

The best place to do all this is Holy Mass. If going up to the altar of God we love Abel, Abraham and Melchisedech, then we have understood the Old Testament. For these men show us the love of the Holy Trinity, and show us that Jesus' sacrifice on Calvary — which they each anticipated — encompasses all generations. At Mass we love the same reality that all the saints who ever breathed did love: the Self-sacrifice of God. We know they loved it because each one of them, according to their measure, imitated it. The thought of Abel alone should be enough to open our mind to eternity. This side of Heaven, it is Holy Mass that most perfectly joins us to him.

At the altar of God we know we are at that *place* which from the beginning signalled that something stupendous was coming. Whether we think of the Foundation Stone as the seed of creation, or the Garden of Eden as the seed of Heaven, or of Adam as the seed of mankind, or Jesus Christ as the seed of the saved, the altar of God is the *place* to appreciate all these coming together. It is the *place* of Abel's sacrifice and self-sacrifice, it is the place of Abraham's and Isaac's self-sacrifice, the place of Isaac's union with his beloved Rebekah, signifying Christ with His Bride, God with man, the place of new life, a new creation, of resurrection. It is the place of an encounter with God, of a dream connecting Heaven and earth, a place for a house of worship. The Temple is the Body of Christ, Jerusalem the sign of the heavenly Jerusalem. It is the place of the Cross, the Altar of the Lamb, Who is the Light of the world. Holy Mass is the place of the Crucifixion.

Obviously reaching Heaven is an ascent. We must work in order to contemplate. It is as difficult, and as simple, as living justly. The Spirit asks: *"Lord, who shall dwell in thy tabernacle? who shall rest in thy holy hill?"* (Ps 14:1). This 'dwelling' is for eternal life, this 'resting' is the complete ontological satiety of Heaven. The same Psalm quickly concludes that he who lives justly *"shall not be moved for ever"* (Ps 14:5), that is he shall have been assimilated to the immutable pattern.

The complexity is presented to us by the tabernacle: an arrangement of beauty, a story of many parts, an intricate harmony. Yet its purpose is simple: here God meets man, man worships God. This is the point of creation, the purpose of the universe, shown by the tabernacle, for Heaven *is* God with man. To lead us He set His tabernacle amongst us — not stopping at a Tent in the desert, but taking on flesh in the Virgin Mary to dwell among us. Jesus Christ is Emmanuel — literally God with man, united hypostatically; and then with the Church, with everyone who will be saved. God with man, man with God. All the saints live in Him. They live in Him to the extent that they imitate His love, that they offer silent self-sacrifice.

Silence does not mean they cannot mention their suffering but that it is not made into a complaint, it is a price worth paying, their concern is more for God and others who gain by their sacrifice, than for themself (1 Cor 4:9-16; 2 Cor 11:23-30). This is the immutable pattern. This is the charity that builds civilisation. This is why to know Calvary is to know all human history and finally the City of God.

And it is to know the Blessed Trinity, for Their life, translated to earth, is silent Self-sacrifice. The Son on Calvary reveals the nature of the Father, His total love. In eternity, does not the Father give all He is to the Son? And the Son refuses nothing. They are alike. The proof of Their perfect congruity is the Holy Ghost, Whose existential passivity is also Self-sacrificial. Hence to know Calvary is to know the highest reality, the Trinity.

Jesus on Calvary joins Heaven and Earth. Our one Mediator unites the Blessed Trinity with all human history that matters. He is the One Perfect Agent of the Mass. To know what He is doing in Holy Mass, to know Christ's action, is to begin to enter eternity through Him Who contains all.

What is His action in the Mass? By His Self-sacrifice, Jesus feeds us through His ministers with His Body and Blood, thereby making us like Himself, making us like unto God. This transformation of our souls is too great for us to see, but by faith we are called to believe nothing less. It is invisible as is transubstantiation. God enlivens our substance with His. How stupendous this fruit of the tree, this work of the Cross, done at this place — the altar of God in Holy Mass — which is the place of the sacrifice of the Lamb of God.

As a hint that eternity can be tasted in time, that Heaven itself can be fleetingly felt even on earth, that Adam and Eve once knew something of the final Paradise from the first Paradise, that the end is written into the beginning, all the chief ideas explored in this epilogue can be found in the preamble prayers before Mass, that is before the priest prays the *Introitus*. The first thirteen chapters of this book (on the Lamb, the Cross, the Altar, the Light, the Place, the Mountain, the Tabernacle, the Blessed Trinity, the Body, the Blood, the Priesthood, the Vestments and Transubstantiation) are each headed with a few suitable words chosen from the Prayers at the Foot of the Altar or from the sacristy before this. We cannot recall all these ideas before every Mass, but we can recall some as a preparation, enough so that we taste eternity during the ceremonies.

The traditional Mass is endlessly rich, wonderfully woven, compactly built. The old Missal — a Christocentric, saint-filled Paradise — is the earthly figure of the Book of Life. Imitating Heaven, all the parts communicate with all the other parts.

Eternity is seeing the highest truths immediately, a spiritual vision, a contemplation. Eternal life is a knowledge of God which cannot be lost, union with Him, the beatific vision. Heaven is banqueting with God among the Communion of Saints. Already on earth, we can enter this eternity — tentatively, imperfectly — by understanding the highest truths, by loving Jesus Christ, by worshipping with His saints.

Thy name, O Lord, is for ever:
thy memorial, O Lord, unto all generations.

— Ps 134:13

ABOUT THE AUTHOR

Born in 1973, James Mawdsley grew up in Lancashire, England. He was ordained a Catholic priest in 2016.

In 2020 Fr Mawdsley was removed from his assignment for offering Masses open to the faithful during lockdowns and for giving Holy Communion on the tongue. In 2021 he was removed from his next apostolate for refusing to turn souls away from the Easter liturgies. After this he was not permitted to say public Masses because he refused to wear a mask while distributing Holy Communion. Toward the end of 2021, Fr Mawdsley learned that his expected reassignment would not happen because the local bishop was eager to implement *Traditionis custodes*.

The precondition to exercise public ministry had become, for Fr Mawdsley, compliance with illegal and irrational instructions which harm the common good and hinder the salvation of souls. Having weighed the option of simply praying and waiting for the situation to improve, after a total of fourteen months with scarcely any public ministry, Fr Mawdsley left his assignment without permission. For this he knowingly incurred a canonical suspension. So long as the Roman Curia submits to worldly forces intent on destroying the worship of God, the best obedience Fr Mawdsley believes he can offer the hierarchy is to accept their penalties but not to follow their man-made agenda.

Fr Mawdsley began publishing the New Old book series to address what he perceives to be the major problem in Church and state at present: both realms are ruled by the faithless.

THE NEW OLD SERIES

- *Adam's Deep Sleep: The Passion of Jesus Christ Prefigured in the Old Testament* (2022)

- *Crushing satan's head: The Virgin Mary's Victory over the Antichrist Foretold in the Old Testament* (2022)

- *Crucifixion to Creation: Roots of the Traditional Mass Traced Back to Paradise* (2023)

- *If You Believed Moses* (Vol 1)*: The Conversion of the Jews Promised in the Old Testament* (2023)

- *If You Believed Moses* (Vol 2)*: The Conversion of the Jews as the Close of History* (2023)

Printed in Great Britain
by Amazon